Building a Legislative-Centered Public Administration

Building a Legislative-Centered Public Administration

Congress and the Administrative State, 1946–1999

DAVID H. ROSENBLOOM

THE UNIVERSITY OF ALABAMA PRESS
Tuscaloosa and London

1 2 3 4 5 6 7 8 9   08 07 06 05 04 03 02 01 00

Typeface: Bembo

∞
The paper on which this book is printed meets the minimum requirements of
American National Standard for Information Science–Permanence of Paper for
Printed Library Materials, ANSI Z39.48–1984.

Library of Congress Cataloging-in-Publication Data

Rosenbloom, David H.
   Building a legislative-centered public administration : Congress and
the administrative state, 1946–1999 / David H. Rosenbloom.
      p. cm.
Includes bibliographical references and index.
   ISBN 0-8173-1048-7 (hc : acid-free)
1. Administrative agencies—United States. 2. Administrative
agencies—Law and legislation—United States. 3. United States.
Congress. 4. Administrative law—United States. 5. United
States—Politics and government—20th century. I. Title.
   JF1601 .R58 2000
   328.73'07456—dc21
                        00-008739

British Library Cataloguing-in-Publication Data available

To Professor Robert Boynton, whose knowledge of
public administration is second to none

Contents

Preface

What is the appropriate role in large-scale public administration for a national legislature in a separation-of-powers system? That question became central to the United States in the 1930s as the New Deal rapidly transformed the size and scope of federal administration. There is no easy answer. The Constitution's framers could not have anticipated the modern administrative state, and they provided no blueprint for integrating it into the government they charted. Nor could more than scant guidance be gleaned from abroad: the American experience with the constitutional separation of powers has been unique. No nation ever faced the question quite like America. The weight of public administrative expertise advised that in the interests of unity of command, efficiency, economy, and organizational effectiveness, the congressional role should essentially be limited to authorizing, funding, and periodically reviewing administrative operations.

Congress in 1946 provided a very different answer, and one that has profoundly affected American public administrative thought, practice, and reform ever since. It self-consciously framed a comprehensive role for itself in federal administration. The purpose of this book is to explain how and why Congress adopted that role, its underlying coherence, its durability as a platform for seemingly ever-increasing congressional involvement in federal administration, and its continuing significance for public administration as a field of study.

In 1946, Congress reluctantly accepted the likelihood that the growing complexity of public policy would require it to delegate its legislative authority more broadly to the agencies as time went on. But it was unwilling to abdicate that authority, as many of its members thought it had done throughout the New Deal and World War II. Instead, it decided to treat the agencies as extensions of Congress for the performance of legislative functions, such as rulemaking. It established a statutory framework for comprehensively regulating their procedures. It also reorganized itself partly in order to supervise the agencies on a continuing basis. These steps, taken primarily in the Administrative Procedure and Legislative Reorganization Acts of 1946, subsequently provided the basis for further expansion of the congressional role in federal administration through future legislation.

Congress also adopted several measures to enable it to deal more efficiently, effectively, and rationally with the agencies when providing two historic legislative functions: constituency service and the allocation of public works projects. By 1946 both had become major—but very time-consuming—activities. Congress shed some of the load to the agencies through the Federal Tort Claims Act and the General Bridge Act, both of which were separate titles of the Legislative Reorganization Act. It sought to make public works policy more systematic and economically productive via the Employment Act of 1946. It also began to increase significantly the number of personal staff assigned to the members and to rely far more heavily on them to intercede routinely in administration to champion the interests of their constituents and districts.

These developments were deliberate, and they fit together coherently. They grew out of Congress's collective sense that the rise of the federal administrative state had upset its institutional place in the constitutional scheme and, accordingly, that it needed to reform and reposition itself. Each measure enjoyed strong bipartisan support. There was no single comprehensive plan or set of leaders or policy entrepreneurs, but there was an extended conversation about the roles Congress, its committees, and its members could appropriately play in federal administration. Debate often went to the core concerns of American democratic-constitutionalism. Much was discussed and written into legislation on the floor of each house. It was through the development of a common institutional understanding, as well as specific legislation, that Congress reconceptualized its position vis-à-vis federal administration in 1946.

The 1946 congressional framework views the legislature and the agencies as largely fused rather than separated. The agencies serve as extensions of Congress, which establishes, funds, and empowers them. Congress has a legitimate constitutional role in regulating their procedures as well as in supervising and steering them. One can refer to "the executive branch," but administration is not solely the domain of the president and his appointees. The framework and its subsequent development are about Congress, its constitutional roles, legislative functions, the agencies, and federal administration. They are not about a protracted separation-of-powers contest. As this book will show, traditional three-branch thinking seriously misreads the Constitution, obscures congressional motive, and cannot account for administrative reforms.

With the type of congressional involvement in federal administration initiated in 1946 comes the imposition of legislative values on administrative practice. The orthodox managerial values of efficiency, economy, and internal organizational effectiveness retain importance, but they are augmented and sometimes subordinated to representativeness, participation, openness, responsiveness, procedural safeguards, and public accountability. As Congress further developed the 1946 framework, ideas voiced in conjunction with its creation found their way into such major statutes as the Freedom of Information Act (1966), the Federal Advisory Committee Act (1972), the Privacy Act (1974), the Congressional Budget and Impoundment Control Act (1974), the Government in the Sunshine Act (1976), the Inspector General Act (1978), the Regulatory Flexibility Act (1980), the Paperwork Reduction Acts (1980, 1995), the Negotiated Rulemaking Act (1990), the Chief Financial Officers Act (1990), the Administrative Dispute Resolution Acts (1990, 1996), the Government Performance and Results Act (1993), and the Small Business Regulatory Enforcement Fairness Act (1996).

The 1946 framework and its subsequent development are coherent and comprehensive. However, their underlying logic has been buried in congressional debates, legislation, and decisions that took place over a half-century in a number of separate policy arenas, including administrative procedure, congressional organization and oversight, constituency service, and public works. This book uses a theoretical construct, called "legislative-centered public administration," to reconstitute that logic. It is derived from Congress's prolonged and continuing conversation about its place in the federal administrative state. Legislative-centered public administration is the equivalent of a judicial doctrine that encapsulates the reasoning behind a series of related court decisions. Such doctrines place order on what otherwise may appear disconnected or chaotic, and often speak to lasting institutional interests, value premises, and decision-making criteria. Chapters 1 through 4 develop various aspects of legislative-centered public administration. Chapter 5 pulls them together and evaluates the overall importance of legislative-centered perspectives for administrative theory, practice, and reform.

In many respects, the question of how Congress fits into the administrative state remains in the forefront of federal administrative concerns. Vice President Al Gore's effort to reinvent federal administration asks for a much smaller congressional role (as is noted in Chapter 5). In

Gore's view, Congress engages in "micromanagement," breeds highly encumbering red tape, and impedes performance. He may be correct. But he may also be asking the wrong questions.

Critics of Congress clearly go astray when they contend that congressional regulation, supervision, and participation in federal administration constitutes a violation of the separation of powers. With few exceptions, such as the legislative veto, even deep congressional intrusion into federal administration is currently constitutional. Moreover, as this book demonstrates, it is not accidental. It is intended to force democratic-constitutional values into administrative practice.

In sum, over the past half-century Congress created a legislative-centered public administration. This book elucidates and analyzes this development, making it accessible. Although this book is written primarily for scholars and reflective practitioners of public administration, students of Congress and bureaucratic politics will also find it of considerable interest. It is a necessary book because inadequate understanding of legislative-centered public administration's values, coherence, and claims to legitimacy promotes an excessively narrow conception of public management, a misunderstanding of practice, faulty prescription, and the frustration or failure of administrative reforms. Congress is clearly part of the picture; this book comprehensively explains the institutional interests, values, and logic behind its contemporary role in federal administration.

Acknowledgments

This project began in the early 1990s and has benefited from much assistance along the way. I was privileged to present the core ideas at the Boyne Lecture Series of the University of Alabama at Maxwell Air Force Base in September 1998. The faculty, staff, and students I met there extended warm hospitality, great interest in the study, and a wide range of helpful insights and suggestions. In particular, I want to thank Professor William Stewart for inviting me to lecture, for his enthusiasm for the book, and for his solid recommendations regarding its direction and content.

American University has been an ideal environment for an undertaking of this kind. My colleagues in the School of Public Affairs know their public administration and take it seriously. I would especially like to thank Professors Anita Alpern, Robert Boynton, Robert Cleary, Cornelius Kerwin, Bernard Ross, and James Thurber for their careful reading of the manuscript, thoughtful suggestions, and encouragement. I am grateful as well to Professors Thomas Sargentich and Robert Vaughn in the university's Washington College of Law for their interest in the project and readiness to share their vast knowledge of federal administrative law. I also enjoyed a great deal of help from several M.P.A. and Ph.D. students: Beth Cooper, Allan Porowski, Dawn Roberts, and Henry Hogue all provided substantial assistance with the research. Henry also brought his fine editorial skills to bear on preparation of the final manuscript.

Additional thanks go to Professor John Rohr and to my wife, Deborah. John read the manuscript with his usual attention to grand principle and minute detail. We were graduate classmates at the University of Chicago in the 1960s. The reasons why his notes are better than mine have nothing to do with stenographic skills! Deborah, a J.D.-M.P.A. with whom I wrote four editions of *Public Administration: Understanding Management, Politics, and Law in the Public Sector,* cast her critical eye on the text and made a number of substantive and editorial improvements. Other helpful readers included Julie Dolan, Mel Dubnick, Phil Joyce, Robert Kravchuk, and Larry Terry. Working with the University of Alabama Press has been excellent, and just the prospect of being considered among its many distinguished titles in public administration is gratifying. Finally, the "kids"—Lila, Josh, Sarah, and Leah—put up with the usual amount of inattentiveness that writing a book causes. Naturally, I am solely responsible for whatever shortcomings the analysis and text may still have.

Abbreviations and Acronyms

ADR   Alternative Dispute Resolution
ADRA   Administrative Dispute Resolution Act
APA   Administrative Procedure Act
CBO   Congressional Budget Office
CFO   Chief Financial Officer
CRS   Congressional Research Service
DBCRC   Defense Base Closure and Realignment Commission
FACA   Federal Advisory Committee Act
FOIA   Freedom of Information Act
FTCA   Federal Tort Claims Act
GAO   General Accounting Office
GPRA   Government Performance and Results Act
IG   Inspector General
LRA   Legislative Reorganization Act of 1946
NPR   National Performance Review
NPRM   Notice of Proposed Rulemaking
NRMA   Negotiated Rulemaking Act
OIRA   Office of Information and Regulatory Affairs
OMB   Office of Management and Budget
PAYGO   Pay-as-you-go
PCAM   President's Committee on Administrative Management
Reg-Flex   Regulatory Flexibility
Reg-Neg   Regulation by Negotiation
RFA   Regulatory Flexibility Act
SBREFA   Small Business Regulatory Enforcement Fairness Act

*Building a Legislative-Centered
Public Administration*

I | The Problem
Repositioning Congress in the Modern Administrative State

The constantly growing body of executive or administrative law has become both a necessity to the operation of modern government and a threat to the constitutional function of Congress as the legislative, policy-making branch of the government.   —Robert La Follette, Jr. (1943, 93)

Introduction

By 1946, Congress's traditional place in the constitutional separation of powers had been thoroughly upset by the vast growth in the size and power of the federal bureaucracy during the New Deal and World War II. Congress had become a delegator, vesting much of its legislative authority in administrative agencies, and a great deal of the initiative for policy making and budgeting had passed to the executive branch. The legislature, the framers' "First Branch," was becoming more reactive than proactive. But even its capacity to react was sorely challenged by the haphazard quality of administrative processes and illogical state of agency design, as well as by the limitations of Congress's own organizational arrangements. A common theme among its members was that Congress had lost its mission and was consequently atrophying and becoming irrelevant.

The question in 1946—openly asked and discussed—was how Congress could reposition itself in the constitutional framework to protect its coequality, fulfill its legislative and representational roles, and promote institutional revitalization. For example, Senator William Fulbright (D-AR) saw the "basic problem" as "one of combining a strong executive with the maintenance of legislative supremacy" (U.S. Congress 1945b, 20), while Senator Robert La Follette, Jr. (Progressive-WI) shared a broad concern that Congress might "lose its constitutional place in the Federal scheme" (La Follette 1946, 11). Any lasting response would also have to speak to the members' own interests in power, legislative careers, and public service. The issues were debated extensively, if somewhat disjointedly, on the floor of the House and Senate and in committee hearings as Congress enacted four landmark statutes: the Administrative Procedure Act (APA) (June 11, 1946); the Legislative Reorganization Act (LRA) of 1946 (August 2), which included the Federal Tort Claims Act (FTCA) among its titles; and the Employment Act (February 20, 1946).[1] The discussion of Congress's appropriate roles and functions in federal administration was self-conscious, and the linkages among the key measures were explicitly considered. Debate often reached to the center of constitutional concerns.

The outcome was a new legislative understanding of Congress's constitutional relationship to federal administration. Agencies were reconceptualized as extensions of the legislature and, to some extent, its processes. They were appropriately subject to its continuous legislative "watchfulness," or as some members would have it, supervision and direction. Additionally, the relationship between agencies and the traditional elements of Congress's district-oriented service—casework and public works projects—was adjusted. Agencies would carry more of the burden of compensating for their torts, and the legislature would have more time to help constituents with red tape and other administrative problems. Congress would strengthen its control of the dispensation of public works, which ideally would be systematized and legitimized as a means of maintaining full employment.

The administrative ramifications of the congressional repositioning of 1946 have been profound, though largely misunderstood. At the time, expert public administration embraced three values above all else: efficiency, economy, and organizational effectiveness. To secure these values it sought to exclude politics—both partisan and policy-oriented—from administration.[2] For the same reason, public administration was defined as a field of management rather than of law. It was also executive-centered, prescribing the "unity of command" and advising that legislative involvement in administration necessarily promoted inefficiency.

Congress's collective view in 1946 was considerably different. It certainly favored efficiency, economy, and effectiveness, but did not think achieving these values depended on separating politics from administration or limiting Congress's interaction with agencies. To the contrary, the congressional understanding of 1946 does not embrace a politics-administration dichotomy. Rather, it considers agencies almost seamless extensions of the legislature for supplementary legislation through rule-making and order making (adjudication). Moreover, because the agencies exercise delegated legislative authority, their processes should embrace the legislative values of representation, participation, and open information. With its emphasis on politically neutral technical expertise, traditional public administration was actually hostile to these values (Waldo 1948, 1984).

Congress and public administration were also at odds over constituency service. From the legislative point of view, casework and obtaining federal funding for local public works are legitimate, core representational functions. They are an integral feature of legislative "home style," which is highly valued by the members (Fenno 1978; Fiorina and Rohde 1989). Even "pork-barreling" is widely accepted and supported by congressional norms (Fitzgerald and Lipson 1984, xix). But from a public management perspective, the members' district orientation can constitute interference with the cost-effective implementation of general rules in the public interest. In short, from a public administrative perspective, the new congressional framework was seriously misguided and apt to foster particularism and "micromanagement."

Politically, the 1946 repositioning proved advantageous for members of Congress. Incumbency became a defining element of Congress as an institution. Between 1946 and the 1970s roughly 90 percent of all the members of Congress ran for reelection, and 90 percent of those running were successful (Fiorina 1977, 5). Service in Congress increasingly resembled a career (Hibbing 1991). According to Morris Fiorina (1977, 1989), a leading political scientist, the historically high levels of incumbency were largely the result of more efficient and extensive casework by the members' offices, better congressional leverage over administrative pork, and, perhaps, the legislators' ability to duck some divisive political issues by delegating them to the agencies (which could later be criticized in order to score points with segments of the electorate who were aggrieved or bothered by the administrators' actions).

The "1946" framework has been highly durable. It was a "founding" upon which much has been built. For instance, the APA, which remains the generic law regulating federal administrative process, has been amended or augmented by such major statutes as the Freedom of Information Act (1966), the Federal Advisory Committee Act (1972), the Privacy Act (1974), the Government in the Sunshine Act (1976), the Paperwork Reduction Acts (1980, 1995), the Negotiated Rulemaking Act (1990), the Administrative Dispute Resolution Acts (1990, 1996), and the Small Business Regulatory Enforcement Fairness Act (1996), among others.[3] The committee and subcommittee structure and roles created by the Legislative Reorganization Act provided a platform for greater congressional oversight of administration, increases in staff, and additional legislation such as the Inspector General Act (1978) and the Government Performance and Results Act (1993).[4] Although the Employment Act is no longer the main tool for federal regulation of business cycles, public works are still a major congressional interest and pork remains a staple of federal expenditures.

The purpose of this book is to explain how and why Congress repositioned itself with respect to federal administration in 1946 and to analyze the impact of that action on public administrative thought, practice, and reform. Its underlying premise is that one can establish a theoretical construct, based on congressional debates, legislation, and activities, that offers a comprehensive and coherent vision of Congress's appropriate roles in federal administration. Such a construct, called "legislative-centered public administration" here, is partly developed throughout the text and fully explicated in Chapter 5. Failure to understand it and its claims to legitimacy renders administrative thought seriously incomplete, as well as prone to faulty diagnosis and prescription. Reformers from Louis Brownlow in the 1930s to Vice President Al Gore in the 1990s have tended to wish Congress away and design reforms as though the legislature's views and institutional interests regarding administration are identical to or wholly compatible with those of the executive branch. But the 1946 framework is grounded in the interests of Congress in exercising its constitutional authority, in its members' interest in long legislative service, and in a coherent vision of the values federal administration should embody. Overall, the 1946 design shows few signs of faltering, and, in fact, is being strengthened in important respects.

The analysis primarily draws on the legislative histories of the APA, the LRA, and the Employment Act. Legislative intent can be elusive. The *Congressional Record* for 1946 contains about sixteen thousand pages, of which perhaps a thousand or more relate directly to these statutes. Many views were expressed, but overall the supporters of each statute were able collectively to make a coherent public case for enactment that centers on the appropriate role for Congress in the administrative state. This book reconstructs their public explanations of their thinking, objectives, and expectations. It does not deny that members of Congress are also motivated by concerns they do not express publicly. The same was true of the Constitution's framers and the authors of the *Federalist Papers* (Beard 1913). However, the public explanations and rationales for governmental process and design may develop an independent force. The constitutional "founding" was a deliberative event that certainly went well beyond the document's text (Storing 1981). On a lesser scale, the legislative discussions of 1946 set forth Congress's institutional vision of its appropriate roles regarding federal administration. They have had lasting importance in establishing intellectual, legal, and political parameters for congressional interaction with agencies and administrative processes. In order to convey these public understandings, the analysis relies heavily on the words of members of Congress, the testimony given during congressional hearings, and contemporaneous commentary and analyses. In large part, the words quoted throughout the text are the data.

Chapters 2 and 3 develop the themes of agencies as extensions of Congress and the legislature as supervisor of agencies. Chapter 4 explains how Congress transferred particularly unproductive forms of constituency service to the agencies, began to improve staffing arrangements to handle casework more efficiently, and tried to strengthen its role in the selection and timing of public works projects—all with an eye toward incumbency. Chapter 5 concludes the study with an assessment of the importance of the developments of 1946 for American administrative thought, practice, and reform. Each of the core chapters shows how the 1946 blueprint has been augmented and strengthened by additional statutes and/or developments that are based on essentially the same understandings of Congress's roles vis-à-vis federal administration as were developed then. The analysis begins with a discussion of the background problem Congress faced in 1946: how to respond to the emergence of a sprawling, poorly regulated, and powerful administrative component.

Administrative Growth, 1933–1945

The New Deal and World War II fundamentally changed the structure and politics of American national government. They enlarged the size and power of federal administration beyond anything previously imaginable. President Franklin D. Roosevelt sometimes complained about administration, but he believed in it. Facing the worst economic depression in the nation's history, he called on the federal government to create jobs through public works and to promote recovery by regulating production, prices, and working conditions. He often favored empowering new agencies rather than relying on existing ones. As he once remarked to his secretary of labor, Frances Perkins, "We have new and complex problems. . . . Why not establish a new agency to take over the new duty rather than saddle it on an old institution? . . . If it is not permanent, we don't get bad precedents" (Polenberg 1966, 9).

In keeping with this philosophy, by the end of 1934 some sixty new agencies had been created (Van Riper 1958, 320). Some, including the Commodity Credit Corporation, the Federal Deposit Insurance Corporation, the Federal Communications Commission, and the Security and Exchange Commission, proved long-lived. Additional major New Deal agencies included the Social Security Administration, the National Labor Relations Board, and the Civil Aeronautics Board. By 1937 there were approximately one hundred separate agencies or units reporting directly to the president (U.S. President's Committee on Administrative Management [PCAM] 1937, 3). The war, of course, led to the creation of a multiplicity of new units, many presumptively temporary, for defense, mobilization of resources, and management of the economy.

The New Deal also relied on government for direct employment. The main purpose of the Works Progress Administration was to provide jobs as an alternative to welfare or other relief. But even within the regular administrative structure, employment grew rapidly. In 1931 there were approximately 610,000 civilian federal employees, up from 560,000 a decade earlier (U.S. Bureau of the Census and Social Science Research Council 1965, 10). By 1939 the number had increased to some 900,000 (Van Riper 1958, 372). After that, as the threat of war became greater, federal employment virtually exploded. Throughout 1940 and 1941 the federal service was growing, on average, by over 35,000 employees per month. By December 1941 it included about 1,800,000 employees (Van Riper 1958, 373). Executive-branch employment peaked in July 1945 at more than 3,800,000 civilian employees—a figure that does not include an additional 330,000 "without compensation" and dollar-a-year personnel (Van Riper 1958, 373). The total was roughly equal to the entire population of the United States in 1787 when the framers wrote the Constitution.

The New Deal and World War II also produced a huge budgetary deficit. Throughout the 1920s the government ran surpluses, but as the depression and governmental efforts to combat it took their toll there were deficits every year from 1931 through 1941, reaching a total of more than $32 billion. Once the nation fully engaged the war, the deficit soared to $54 billion in 1943 alone (U.S. Office of Management and Budget 1985, 79). The long string of deficit budgets was broken in 1947 with a small surplus, though deficits soon resumed.

These changes in the number of agencies, employees, costs, and scope of deficit spending signaled a qualitative shift of political power from elected officials and judges to agencies and administrators. This shift is the essence of the modern American administrative state (Rosenbloom 1998), and its importance for constitutional structure, governing, and politics is profound. It was no exaggeration when Supreme Court Justice Robert Jackson noted in 1952 that administrative agencies "have become a veritable fourth branch of the Government, which has deranged our three-branch legal theories much as the concept of a fourth dimension unsettles our three-dimensional thinking" (*Federal Trade Commission v. Ruberoid* 1952, 487). If the United States had an administrative state prior to the 1930s, the New Deal and World War II certainly expanded it greatly.

By the end of the 1930s, Congress considered federal administration to be very powerful, somewhat menacing, and inadequately controlled. This view was pronounced in the effort to enact the Walter-Logan Act of 1940 (a precursor of the APA), which was successfully vetoed by President Roosevelt. Congressman Earl Michener (R-MI) feared "bureaucrats gone mad with power" who "usurp power belonging to the Congress" and promote "a dangerous centralization of governmental power in the administrative branch." He complained that "when we allow Government bureaus to make rules that are tantamount to laws, and then permit no appeal from them, we are rapidly approaching the totalitarian state" (U.S. Congress 1940, 4534). Congressman E. E. Cox (D-GA) charged that "this mixing of powers—legislative, judicial, and executive—which is being practiced on the part of these administrative agencies, constituting a fourth department of government, will certainly bring us to ruin sooner or later unless they are checked by the Congress" (U.S. Congress 1940, 4533).

Similarly, in 1946, during debate on the APA, Congressman Francis Walter explained that "for a generation Americans have been brought face to face with new forms or methods of government, which we have come to call administrative law. It is administrative because it involves the exercise of legislative and judicial powers of government by officers who are neither legislators nor judges. It is law because what they do is binding upon the citizen exactly as statutes or judgments are binding" (U.S. Congress 1946a, 349). Walter's concern was shared by Congressman John Robsion (R-KY), a strong supporter of the APA and critic of administrative power, who noted that the agencies "have assumed the function of making laws" (U.S. Congress 1946a, 383).

Some members were particularly opposed to the discretionary nature of administrative power. Robsion protested that the administrators "change the rules of the game from day to day and without any notice to the American people" (U.S. Congress 1946c, 5659). Perhaps none outdid Congressman John Jennings (R-TN) for imagery: "The Federal Government now touches almost every activity that arises in the lives of millions of people who make up the population of this country. The chief indoor sport of the Federal bureaucrat is to evolve out of his own inner consciousness, like a spider spins his web, countless confusing rules and regulations which may deprive a man of his property, his liberty, and bedevil the very life out of him" (U.S. Congress 1946c, 5662).

Congress recognized that administrative power is largely a product of delegation, but by 1946 there seemed to be no alternative to vesting substantial legislative authority in the agencies. For example, despite his unease with the administrative state, Robsion noted that "it has been necessary for the Congress to pass laws delegating to various agencies their administration" (U.S. Congress 1946a, 383). In Representative Estes Kefauver's (D-TN) view, agency power was inevitable because "Congress cannot, by the very complexity of the situation, make all of the detailed rules and regulations" (U.S. Congress 1946c, 5661). Robert La Follette, a chief sponsor of the Legislative Reorganization Act, noted "a growing tendency for Congress to turn to the Executive for guidance in drawing new legislation—not out of any lazy desire to avoid its responsibility, but rather out of conscientious effort to frame good legislation that will prove workable" (La Follette 1943, 93). There was general agreement with Walter's prediction that "administrative government . . . is obviously here to stay" (U.S. Congress 1946a, 350).

The growth in agencies, number of employees, budgetary deficits, and administrative power had important ramifications for Congress. Congress lacked the capacity to exercise comprehensive and routinely effective oversight of administrative operations. Given the disorganization of the executive branch the challenge would have been substantial under any circumstances, but Congress lacked a comprehensive strategy, the organizational arrangements, and sufficient staff to exercise anything other than scattershot oversight. Its members were fragmented by service on multiple standing committees. These often functioned with only a few members present or barely at all. Overlapping jurisdictions were common. Though committee chairs apparently enjoyed their perquisites, the entire system seemed to lack any compelling rationale.

During the 1946 repositioning, several members of Congress openly wondered whether the legislature was hopelessly behind the times. Con-

gressman A. S. Mike Monroney (D-OK), a sponsor of the reorganization, explained the need for thoroughgoing change:

> Today we are confronted and confounded by the problems of a
> $35,000,000,000 government trying to do the job with tools
> so absolutely obsolete and antiquated that 435 saints could not pos-
> sibly do with our present equipment and organization. . . .
> . . . [W]e are sitting before this country today serving as the
> board of directors of the world's largest enterprise. It is a hundred
> times larger than General Motors, Ford Motor Co., A. T. & T., the
> Pennsylvania Railroad System, and General Electric all rolled into
> one. Yet we are trying to do this work sitting on an old-fashioned
> high bookkeeper's stool with a slant-top desk, a Civil War ledger,
> and a quill pen. Unless we get new techniques, the tools, the or-
> ganization, we simply cannot handle the work load that the coun-
> try expects us to carry. . . .
> We cannot be coequal; we cannot do this fundamental task of
> supervision that the framers of the Constitution had in mind
> unless the Congress is virile, strong enough and well equipped
> enough to handle this magnitude of work that is dumped on us.
> Five hundred and thirty-one men that compose the member-
> ship of the House and Senate are going to have a pretty hard
> time in handling, in supervising, in surveying the work of over
> 3,000,000 men scattered throughout the executive department. It
> is like trying to move a battleship with a Jeep or a model T Ford.
> (U.S. Congress 1946c, 10039)

Congressman Michener may have captured the congressional organizational idiom best: "The present committee system is a glaring example
of the horse-and-buggy days brought up to date, but still using the horse
and buggy" (U.S. Congress 1946c, 10016).

The number of administrative appointees also presented Congress
with some thorny challenges. Under the Constitution, Congress has
authority for federal personnel arrangements. The system it outlined in
the Civil Service Act of 1883, which was much modified and augmented subsequently, became notoriously cumbersome and seemed in-
capable of staffing the New Deal. Consequently, as Van Riper (1958, 320)
reported, "By the end of 1934 Congress had exempted from merit system regulations the personnel of almost sixty new agencies, totaling approximately 100,000 offices, and had placed only five agencies under the

jurisdiction of the Civil Service Commission." Overall, about 80 percent of the 250,000 federal employees hired during Roosevelt's first term were exempt from the civil service system (Polenberg 1966, 22). The proportion of executive-branch employees covered by the merit system dropped from 80.1 percent in 1932 to 60.5 percent in 1936 (U.S. Commission on Organization of the Executive Branch of the Government 1955, 97–98).

Although such large-scale exemption may have been a necessity and/or appropriate policy response to the economic crisis, it was not necessarily good for Congress. To a large extent, patronage appointments were made on the basis of intellectual ability and pro–New Deal sensibilities rather than traditional partisan concerns (Van Riper 1958, 324–328). This meant that appointees would favor administrative and executive power. Political appointment gave them some claim to independence from Congress and helped to legitimate their policy making. Another problem for Congress was that within the legal framework of the time, exempted employees essentially served at the will of the president and the political executives. They could be used for partisan and even factional purposes.

To many members of Congress, that appeared to be exactly what happened in the 1938 midterm elections when Roosevelt worked to defeat anti–New Deal incumbent *Democrats*. The president "went over the whole political field as he prepared to distribute patronage rewards for 'going along' and punishments for not 'going along' to twenty-seven Senators and some three hundred Representatives" (Farley 1948, 121–122; cited in Van Riper 1958, 340). The "purge" was unsuccessful and a major political defeat for the president (Burns 1956, chap. 18; Karl 1963, 247). Congress nevertheless responded in 1939 by passing the Hatch Act, which prohibited almost all federal executive-branch employees from taking an active part in partisan political management or campaigns (Van Riper 1958, 339–343).[5] The act served Congress's immediate objective of eliminating the potential for a presidentially dominated national political machine. However, it did little to prevent the continual strengthening of the presidency through political appointments to an enlarged executive branch with ample discretionary authority. A framework for regulating the latter comprehensively would have to wait until 1946.

Budgetary deficits were another problem for Congress. They eroded its traditional claim to the power of the purse (which appeared to be wide open). If Congress's job was to ensure fiscal discipline, by 1946 it had failed completely. The huge debt and the need to control it were constant themes in congressional decision making and contributed substantially to the overall legislative mood favoring greater regulation and supervision of the administrative agencies. Time and time again, a member of Congress would remind his or her colleagues that the debt was daunting. For instance, Representative Robert Rich (R-PA) explained: "Our indebtedness of $268,000,000,000 now certainly is an amount that ought to make every one of you shudder. Each one of you owes $2,000 of that debt, and every man, woman, and child in your district owes the sum of $2,000. A family of five owes $10,000 of that debt of this country, and they have to pay it" (U.S. Congress 1946c, 10060). At the time, congressional salaries stood at $10,000 annually, and $5,000 to $8,000 was considered generous pay for legislative staff (U.S. Congress 1946c, 10082–10085).

However, the debt was viewed as perverse in some respects, since it might be necessary to spend more in order to reduce it. For instance, the Employment Act was dexterously presented, with some effectiveness, as a tool for reducing the debt. As Senator Joseph O'Mahoney (D-WY) explained, "The opponents of the bill criticize it upon the ground that we cannot provide for public works and Federal expenditures without increasing the debt. . . . [T]he answer to that is that we cannot pay the interest on the national debt unless we have full employment" (U.S. Congress 1945a, 9056). Representative Wright Patman (D-TX) made the identical point in the House (U.S. Congress 1945a, 11987).

The same type of reasoning underlay Congress's willingness to increase its staff, budget, and compensation in the Legislative Reorganization Act. Senator La Follette defended its provisions for members' benefits:

> It is easy to say that we are in the unfortunate position of having to pass upon our own compensation and upon our retirement system. But I say . . . that I think the time has come, if representative government in America is to be supported, when we must attract men of the highest abilities, and we must retain, insofar as the people are willing to retain them, the men who have by experience and ability become familiar with the intricate problems of government with which the Congress now has to deal.
>
> I say very frankly that I believe the people will support us if we have the courage to meet this situation and to strengthen the personnel and independence of the Congress. (U.S. Congress 1946c, 6570)

Despite such arguments, throughout 1946 there was always an undercurrent of fear, as observed by Representative Max Schwabe (R-MO), that "if the good people of this country ever awaken to the way they are being plundered by their own spendthrift Government their wrath and righteous indignation will mount to unknown heights" (U.S. Congress 1946c, 10099). It was a time to watch spending carefully.

Administrative Disarray

The rate at which the New Deal and World War II promoted administrative growth frequently overwhelmed the capacity of traditional organizational structures, processes, and systems. From an administrative point of view, some New Deal agencies and programs were poorly conceived. Roosevelt was at ease with overlapping jurisdictions, and they were common. By 1936, however, he thought it was time to take stock, no doubt with a view toward gaining greater control over the executive branch (Karl 1963; Polenberg 1966).

Roosevelt appointed the President's Committee on Administrative Management (generally known as the Brownlow Committee, after its chairman, Louis Brownlow)[6] to diagnose administrative problems and prescribe solutions. To no one's surprise, the committee found organizational disarray of considerable proportions. Overall, it concluded "that the work of the Executive Branch is badly organized; that the managerial agencies are weak and out of date; that the public service does not include its share of men and women of outstanding capacity and character; and that the fiscal and auditing systems are inadequate" (PCAM 1937, 3). Furthermore, the executive branch had "grown up without plan or design like the barns, shacks, silos, tool sheds, and garages of an old farm. To look at it now, no one would ever recognize the structure which the founding fathers erected a century and a half ago to be the Government of the United States" (PCAM 1937, 32).

Particularly troubling was the "headless 'fourth branch' of the Government," that is, the independent agencies, which were "responsible to no one, and impossible of coordination with the general policies and work of the Government as determined by the people through their duly elected representatives" (PCAM 1937, 32). The committee was also highly critical of units organized as boards, such as the Civil Service Commission (CSC): "This form of organization . . . has everywhere been found slow, cumbersome, wasteful, and ineffective in the conduct of administrative duties" (PCAM 1937, 10). Finally, the committee found serious inefficiencies and other administrative problems in several administrative systems, including personnel, auditing, and budgeting, and in overall accountability.

The committee's recommendation that the CSC be reorganized under a single director in the White House was never adopted. However, by 1939 there was independent evidence that the personnel system, facing the twin strains of underfunding and an increasing volume of work, was on the verge of collapse. The CSC reported having to authorize thousands of temporary appointments because it was unable to keep up with the demand for new hires (Van Riper, 1958, 363). It fell seriously behind in grading papers, examining, completing background investigations, classifying positions, handling appeals, and keeping its eligibles' registers up-to-date (Van Riper 1958, 363–364).

By many accounts, the administrative process was anything but user-friendly. In 1941, Assistant Secretary of State Dean Acheson, who chaired the U.S. Attorney General's Committee on Administrative Procedure,[7] ventured that

in many cases— . . . perhaps in the majority of them—the agency is one great obscure organization with which the citizen has to deal. It is absolutely amorphous. He pokes it in one place and it comes out another. No one seems to have specific authority. There is someone called the commission, the authority; a metaphysical omniscient brooding thing which sort of floats around in the air and is not a human being. That is what is baffling. The citizen goes to it. He goes to room 835 and, then he is sent to some other room. Finally somebody says, "I have no power to decide this, but I will recommend it to the commission." Then he says, "How can I talk to the commission?" But he can't talk to the commission. That is the thing that is baffling. (U.S. Congress 1941, 807)

The hurdles of mysterious process were compounded by the absence of systematic information about agencies' regulatory output. According to the American Bar Association's Special Committee on Administrative Law (1934, 228),

Practically every agency to which legislative power has been delegated (or sub delegated) has exercised it, and has published its enactments, sometimes in the form of official printed pamphlets, bound or looseleaf, sometimes in mimeograph form, sometimes in privately owned publications, and sometimes in press releases. Sometimes they exist only in sort of an unwritten law. Rules and regulations, upon compliance with which important privileges and freedom from heavy penalties may depend, are amended and interpreted as formally or informally as they were originally adopted.

The potential for better presidential control and direction was improved by the creation of the Executive Office of the President in 1939 and some reorganizations. But during the war years the desire for more rational, economic administrative arrangements was understandably eclipsed by military and defense needs. Administrative procedure was not standardized or more comprehensively regulated. No overall or general restructuring occurred, and none was called for by outside experts until the first Hoover Commission issued its *Report* in 1949 (U.S. Commission on Organization of the Executive Branch of the Government 1949). By then, rapid demobilization, veterans' programs, the beginning of the Cold War, and the growing Red Scare had created altogether new administrative problems and issues.

The Question in 1946: "Whose Bureaucracy Is This, Anyway?"[8]

Looking at the large, powerful, disorganized, and poorly regulated executive branch in 1946, Congress faced an overall choice. It could follow the advice of the Brownlow Committee and orthodox administrative thought by viewing a stronger president as the best—and perhaps only—means of bringing the executive branch under control, instilling good management, and making agency processes rational and fair. Alternatively, Congress itself could try to exercise a greater degree of control over administration. This course required forging something new. There was a blueprint for presidential control, but none for a larger and more productive role for Congress in administrative matters. To the contrary, leading public administrative thought considered legislative involvement largely antithetical to efficient, economical, and effective public administration. At the very least, mapping out new roles for Congress would require legislative reorganization and some degree of institutional redefinition.

Theoretically, Congress also could have sought to rely on the federal courts to supervise administration more thoroughly. However, the Walter-Logan Act was ultimately defeated partly because it took this tack. There was considerable distrust of the courts and corresponding reluctance to subject a great deal of administrative action to expensive, time-consuming, and potentially obstructionist litigation. In the florid words of one opponent, Congressman John Rankin (D-MS), it "would destroy democracy and set up a judicial fascisti that would paralyze every governmental agency they did not like by interminable and endless litigation" (U.S. Congress 1940, 13947).

Congress also could have done nothing at all, though the public policy necessity of putting the administrative apparatus under better controls was plain. The year 1946 was a troubling one, economically and politically. The debt has already been mentioned. It was also necessary to absorb demobilized veterans into the economy and society. The public was impatient with remaining price and other wartime controls. Organized labor, anxious to reassert its economic influence, engaged in several high-profile strikes and threatened to go out on others. Politically, much of the world was in flux. Efforts by European nations to reestablish or maintain their colonies were meeting organized (and ultimately very successful) opposition. Cooperation between the United States and the Soviet Union was limited, and tensions were rising. With Nazism and Imperial Japan defeated, Communism—foreign and domestic—was perceived as the greatest threat to American democracy. All in all, members of Congress thought the situation was too urgent for inaction, or even substantial contemplative delay.

Perhaps Representative Monroney captured the sense of urgency best:

> Representative democracy is on trial. We must make it work and make it work well. Around the world the lights of democracy have gone out. They burn here alone, bright enough to rekindle the fires of freedom and democracy. If we fail, we fail the world which looks to us for leadership in this perilous hour.
>
> Remember, gentlemen, that in other countries overseas, where dictators have taken over, they took over when the legislative branches of those nations disintegrated and failed. Then, when their representative system proved incapable of properly handling the problems which faced them, the road to total power was easy.
>
> The representative system is the best guardian of the people's liberty in the world. It can only be able to guard liberty where it

is strong enough and well organized enough to carry the load
that present day problems place upon them. (U.S. Congress 1946c,
10041)

So, if action was necessary, what to do?

In a sense, turning the executive branch over to the president would
have been the easiest course. It would have followed the prescriptions of
the nation's leading public administrative thinkers, probably improved
federal management, and perhaps even made agencies as cost-effective
as they can be within the framework of the separation of powers. The
Brownlow Committee made a strong case for presidential domination.

First, in the committee's view, the presidency had virtues that made
consolidating administration under it a highly rational solution to the
problem posed by retrofitting the fourth branch into the Constitution's
three-branch structure.

- The President is indeed the one and only national officer representative of the entire Nation. (PCAM 1937, 1)
- As an instrument for carrying out the judgment and will of the
people of a nation, the American Executive occupies an enviable position among the executives of the states of the world, combining as
it does the elements of popular control and the means for vigorous
action and leadership—uniting stability and flexibility. The American
Executive as an institution stands across the path of those who mistakenly assert that democracy must fail because it can neither decide
promptly nor act vigorously. (PCAM 1937, 2)
- Our Presidency unites at least three important functions. From one
point of view the President is a political leader—leader of a party,
leader of the Congress, leader of a people. From another point of
view he is head of the Nation in the ceremonial sense of the term,
the symbol of our American national solidarity. From still another
point of view the President is the Chief Executive and administrator
within the Federal system and service. (PCAM 1937, 2)

The thrust of the committee's effort was to strengthen the president's
ability to satisfy this last point of view.

The committee's various recommendations were largely guided by its
belief that, "Stated in simple terms . . . canons of efficiency require the
establishment of a responsible and effective chief executive as the center of energy, direction, and administrative management" (PCAM 1937,

3). Among its proposals were sweeping consolidation of administrative units to enhance presidential control and direction, expanding the White House staff, strengthening the "managerial agencies . . . particularly those dealing with the budget, efficiency research, personnel, and planning," and making them "arms of the Chief Executive" (PCAM 1937, 4).

The committee argued for a limited congressional role in federal administration. In its view, Congress could legitimately empower, fund, and hold agencies accountable, but it should not be involved in their decision-making, organizational, or managerial processes. The committee wanted to fence Congress broadly out of the executive branch. For example, with regard to agency spending, it boldly asserted, "We hold that once the Congress has made an appropriation, an appropriation which it is free to withhold, the responsibility for the administration of the expenditures under that appropriation is and should be solely upon the Executive" (PCAM 1937, 49–50). In particular, the committee attacked pre-audits by the comptroller general, who heads the General Accounting Office, which is located in the legislative branch.[9] According to the committee, the comptroller general's functions were administratively and constitutionally misguided:

The removal from the Executive of the final authority to determine the uses of appropriations, conditions of employment, the letting of contracts, and the control over administrative decisions, as well as the prescribing of accounting procedures and the vesting of such authority in an officer independent of direct responsibility to the President for his acts, is clearly in violation of the constitutional principle of the division of authority between the Legislative and Executive Branches of the Government. It is contrary to article II, section 3, of the Constitution, which provides that the President "shall take Care that the Laws be faithfully executed." (PCAM 1937, 22)

Finally, with regard to post-audits, or after-the-fact oversight, the committee questioned Congress's organizational capability to avoid duplicative hearings and requests. It also may have thought such oversight should go through the president: "The Congress has not in either House adequate machinery for the collection and coordination of the information which it requires if it is to hold the President effectively accountable for the conduct of the Executive Branch as a whole" (PCAM 1937, 50).

The committee's theory of presidential responsibility for federal administration was broadly criticized in 1937. The legislative proposal following its *Report* was termed "the dictator bill" (Karl 1963, 24). As John Rohr, a leading constitutional scholar of the administrative state, points out, it rested on a blatant misreading of the Constitution: "At the heart of the [committee's] doctrine is a fundamental error that transforms the president from chief executive officer into sole executive officer" (1986, 139). The committee's answer to critics was just as plain, and politically inefficacious as well: "Those who waiver [sic] at the sight of needed power are false friends of modern democracy. Strong executive leadership is essential to democratic government today. Our choice is not between power and no power, but between responsible but capable popular government and irresponsible autocracy" (PCAM 1937, 53).

Most of the committee's specific recommendations failed to win congressional support. In large part, Congress was uneasy with the committee's call for so substantially strengthening the presidency. For instance, Representative Hamilton Fish (R-NY) denounced its *Report* as "a step to concentrate power in the hands of the President and set up a species of fascism or nazi-ism or an American form of dictatorship" (Polenberg 1966, 50).

The committee's embrace of large-scale administration also raised concern. Senator Harry Byrd (D-VA), who emerged as the chief legislative opponent, criticized the committee's plan for doing away with the comptroller general's pre-audits, its failure to abolish emergency agencies, its lack of promise to return to normal administrative arrangements, and its failure to demonstrate specific savings and economies (Karl 1963, 249–250). Members of Congress also expressed concern with the committee's call for the replacement of the CSC with a single civil service administrator in the White House. To many it looked like "an out-an-out [sic] return to the spoils system" (Karl 1963, 250).

More generally, the committee was unable to offer Congress a satisfactory role in federal administration. It seemed, as Senator Joel Bennett ("Champ") Clark (D-MO) claimed, that "no member of that committee had any real belief in Congress or any real use for the legislative department of government" (Polenberg 1966, 127). In Senator Frederick Hale's (R-ME) view, accepting the committee's recommendations would divest Congress of any ability to regulate agencies: "It is certainly up to a self-respecting Congress to see to it that this last vestige of congressional control is not taken away from us" (Polenberg 1966, 126).

Such critics were really pointing to a larger problem in American public administration and government. How does Congress fit into the modern administrative state? In parliamentary systems the legislature and executive are fused in their direction of public agencies. In the U.S. constitutional system, by contrast, they are separated and designed to check each other, which often frustrates seamless empowerment and control of administration (Riggs 1991, 1994). In the 1930s and 1940s, mainstream American public administration had no satisfactory answer. *(Though the mainstream has changed, in many respects it still has none.)* It was better at telling Congress what *not* to do than what its role ought to be. Speaking in 1947, Brownlow still had not learned the lesson of his defeat a decade earlier:

> The next step which we the people should take to meet the needs of the Presidency is to persuade the Congress not to yield to the constant temptation to interfere with the administration of the Executive Branch by needlessly detailed requirements for procedures in the execution of the laws it enacts. . . . The President is under the Constitutional obligation to "take Care that the Laws be faithfully executed," and if we mean to help the President to discharge this obligation we must be sure that his authority so to do is not usurped either by the Congress as a whole, by the House of Representatives or the Senate, and—most important of all—by particular committees of the Congress. (Brownlow 1949, 116)

Perhaps Leonard White, a leading public administration scholar and New Deal Republican appointee to the CSC (1934–1937), came closer than any other expert in the field to spelling out orthodox public administration's view of the appropriate legislative role regarding administration. In the end, though, it was not much of a role. White claimed that "the function of a legislative body . . . has consequently changed as the character of our economy has evolved" because

> the details of the business of government have escaped the competence of legislative committees and chairmen; the possibility of deciding policy by settling details, once perhaps feasible, has disappeared; and in the future, legislatures perforce must deal with ad-

ministration on the basis of principle and generality if they are to deal with it effectively and in the public interest.

. . . State legislatures and Congress must be prepared to forego the attempt to act in the capacity of a board of directors energetically running the business. They can be most useful to the American people by concentrating their effort on the study and general formulation of broad public policies, on the education of the voters with reference to these policies, on the establishment of an administrative structure to which should be given powers and responsibilities adequate to enable it to operate effectively, and on everlasting watchfulness to see to it that officials remain responsive to public sentiment. (White 1945, 5–6)

Despite such views, a very good case can be made for the proposition that the framers intended administrative arrangements to be under "joint custody" of the president and Congress (Rourke 1993, 687), and maybe that of the courts as well, given the nation's common-law roots (Johnson 1981; Woll 1963). But historically, counterpoints to mainstream public administration's emphasis on executive leadership and control have had little impact. Indeed, prior to the New Deal only three public administration scholars were able to generate much interest in the possibilities of legislative-centered administrative arrangements.

Legislative-Centered Public Administration: Some Outlines

In his book *Congressional Government* (1885), Woodrow Wilson embraced a more parliamentary Congress with institutional arrangements necessary to deal effectively with the inevitable growth of administration. In the 1890s it briefly appeared that Congress might follow such a course by viewing itself "as holding the answer to administrative disorder, rather than being its source" (Rourke 1993, 688). However, after the civil service reformers and Progressives had successfully installed the politics-administration dichotomy around the turn of the century, almost all reform efforts emphasized the need for greater executive leadership (Rosenbloom and O'Leary 1997, chap. 1; Arnold 1986).

In the 1920s and 1930s, Lewis Meriam and W. F. Willoughby stood virtually alone as prominent scholars calling for a greater congressional role in federal administration. Both worked at the Brookings Institution, and their views apparently strengthened Senator Harry Byrd's negative reaction to the proposals of the President's Committee on Administrative Management (Polenberg 1966, 36–41; Karl 1963, 251–254). Meriam's and Willoughby's ideas were also part of the mix of perspectives available to Congress in the 1930s as it grappled with framing an administrative procedure act, and later, in 1946, as it more fully reevaluated its position in the administrative state. They made a plausible constitutional case for legislative supervision, direction, and control of administration.

Meriam (1939, 131) noted that "under our system of divided powers, the executive branch of the national government is not exclusively controlled by the President, by the Congress, or by the courts. All three have a hand in controlling it, each from a different angle and each in a different way." Aside from funding and establishing the number of employees, according to Meriam, "Congress may go as far as it sees fit in prescribing the organization, procedure, and business practices of an administrative agency" (1939, 125).

Willoughby had a much more expansive and complex view of Congress's responsibility for administration. He argued that constitutionally Congress is "the source" and "the possessor of all administrative authority" (1927, 11; 1934, 115, 157). He variously conceptualized the relationship between Congress and the agencies as one of "principal and agent" (1934, 157) or that of a "board of directors" actively supervising "general administration" (1927, 10). Willoughby was adamant that "the administrative function, that is, the function of direction, supervision, and control of the administrative activities of the government, resides in the legislative branch of the government" (1927, 11). He drew a distinction between executive and administrative power, chastising those who conflated the two:

> Due largely to the unfortunate use of the words "executive" and "administrative" as almost interchangeable terms, the chief executives of our governments are very generally regarded by the public as being the custodians of administrative authority. In this the public is wholly in error. . . . [A] clear distinction is made between executive power and administrative power. The executive power, or rather function . . . is that of representing the government as a whole, particularly in its relations to other governments, and of seeing to it that all of its laws are properly complied with by its several parts. The administrative function is that of actually administering the law as declared by the legislative, and interpreted by the judicial, branch of the government. (1934, 115)

In terms of administration, the president was largely "but an agent of the legislature and subject to its direction and control" (1934, 116).

Based on this constitutional understanding, Willoughby outlined a supervisory role for Congress that included "determination of the rules of procedure to be employed" by the agencies (1927, 14). He was concerned that "Congress makes its instructions in far too great detail" (1927, 17), and urged it to give agencies broad discretion in internal managerial matters (1934, 135–154).

Although Congress did not directly adopt either Meriam's or Willoughby's specific prescriptions in 1946, its repositioning was consonant with their thrust. By developing a constitutional logic for greater congressional direction, supervision, and control of federal administration, these prominent scholars made congressional action along such lines in 1946 plausible and lent considerable intellectual support to its administrative desirability.

Conclusion

In 1946 Congress could not ignore the federal administrative state. Action or deliberate inaction was necessary. In many members' minds, the latter would be failure and prove that the legislature had completely lost its way. It might even spell the end of representative government as it was previously known in the United States. But Congress also had good reason to reject the advice of Brownlow, White, and other orthodox public administrative thinkers. They could design a blueprint for executive government, but could specify only a very limited role for legislatures within it. Following their advice would seriously threaten Congress's coequality in the constitutional separation of powers. Meriam and Willoughby favored a broad legislative role in public administration, but neither offered a politically workable template for change. If there was to be a comprehensive redesign of Congress's role in federal administration, it would have to be fashioned not only from constitutional logic but also out of legislative capacity and political and institutional interest. Writing in 1943, La Follette urged Congress "to devise new instrumentalities and methods which will afford a positive, constructive liaison and high-policy relationship with the administrative arm of the national government" (1943, 94). That was the work of the Seventy-ninth Congress in 1946.[10] It is analyzed in the next three chapters.

2 | The Legislative Process by Other Means
Agencies as Extensions of Congress

Remember, there are very precious values of civilization which ultimately, to a large extent, are procedural in their nature.
—Justice Felix Frankfurter (U.S. Congress 1940, 13664)

Agencies as Extensions of the Legislative Process

Congress's effort to redefine its constitutional position vis-à-vis federal administration in 1946 relied heavily on the idea that agencies should operate and be treated as extensions of the legislature. Administrative agencies had always been considered instruments for implementing legislation, and they always had some degree of discretion. Delegation of legislative authority to the agencies was not new, though its scope increased dramatically during the New Deal. The new element was a collective understanding by Congress that because agencies exercise legislative powers to regulate the economy and society, they should be considered its adjuncts. Consequently, Congress should specify their procedures to promote its views of how legislation by other means—that is, administration—should work.

This new congressional approach to agencies and administration was forged during a protracted legislative struggle in the 1930s and 1940s to enact a single statute that comprehensively and generically controlled agencies' rulemaking, adjudication, enforcement, transparency, and subordination to judicial review. The concept that agencies are legislative extensions underlies the Administrative Procedure Act of 1946 (APA) and is embodied in several subsequent statutes of major importance to federal administration. These include the Freedom of Information Act (1966), the Federal Advisory Committee Act (1972), the Privacy Act (1974), the Government in the Sunshine Act (1976), the Regulatory Flexibility Act (1980), the Paperwork Reduction Acts (1980, 1995), the

Negotiated Rulemaking Act (1990), the Government Performance and Results Act (1993), and the Small Business Regulatory Enforcement Fairness Act (1996). Collectively, these laws, which are discussed in this and the following chapter, regulate agencies' procedures for making rules, collecting and releasing information, holding meetings, addressing the needs of small businesses and other entities, and developing strategic plans and performance measures.

The view that agencies are legislative *extensions* differs substantially from the traditional constitutional and public administrative treatment of them as Congress's *agents*. As extensions, agencies are essentially fused to the legislature. They exercise its core constitutional responsibility— legislation. Administration is very largely a *legislative* function, as W. F. Willoughby (1934) maintained (see Chapter 1).[1] The separation of powers does not cordon off or even insulate administrative decision making and process from the legislature. Congress may constitutionally direct administration by specifying its procedures and values.

This chapter analyzes Congress's development of the concept that agencies are legislative extensions. It begins with a consideration of the formal constitutional theory of Congress's relationship to federal agencies. It then examines Congress's acceptance of the need to delegate its legislative authority to agencies. Next, the chapter reconstructs Congress's overall decision regarding how the exercise of delegated authority should be regulated and according to which values its use should be guided. The chapter also shows how key post-1946 legislation has strengthened Congress's treatment of the agencies as extensions. It concludes with a consideration of the implications of these developments for gaining a better understanding of public administration. Insofar as feasible, the text explains congressional decision making in the members' own words.

The Constitution, Congress, and Agencies

The Constitution unequivocally places a great deal of responsibility for federal administration in Congress. Legislation is required to establish, empower, structure, staff, and fund departments and agencies. Article I, section 9, clause 7 provides that "No money shall be drawn from the Treasury, but in Consequence of Appropriations made by Law." Article II, section 2, clause 2 requires that all offices not specifically created by the Constitution "shall be established by Law." It also authorizes Congress to "vest the Appointment of such inferior Officers, as they think proper, in the President alone, the Courts of Law, or in the Heads of Departments."

By contrast, presidential power over federal administration is long on generalities and short on specifics. Article II, section 1 vests "the executive Power" in the president without specifying its content. The president is also authorized to "take Care that the Laws be faithfully executed" (Article II, section 3). Precisely what these provisions permit the president to do through domestic administration, independently of Congress or the courts, has been the subject of major judicial decisions.[2] But the sum total is not great. Specific powers are even more limited. The president "may require the Opinion, in writing, of the principal Officer in each of the executive Departments, upon any Subject relating to the Duties of their respective Offices," and "shall have Power to fill up all Vacancies that may happen during the Recess of the Senate, by granting Commissions which shall expire at the End of their next Session" (Article II, section 2, clauses 1 and 3).

In view of these provisions, it is not surprising that constitutional law broadly endorses the theory that federal agencies are agents of *Congress.* In an early case, *Kendall v. United States* (1838, 610), the Supreme Court set forth a sweeping conclusion that remains good law to this day: "It would be an alarming doctrine, that congress [sic] cannot impose upon any executive officer any duty they may think proper, which is not repugnant to any rights secured and protected by the constitution [sic]; and in such cases, the duty and responsibility grow out of and are subject to the control of the law, and not to the direction of the President."

This arrangement can create serious problems for administrators, who may find themselves caught in the separation of powers. For instance, in *Local 2677, the American Federation of Government Employees [AFGE] v. Phillips* (1973) the head of the Office of Economic Opportunity stopped spending his current appropriation because the president's budget message called for zeroing out the agency in the upcoming fiscal year. He saw his "duty to terminate that agency's functions to effect the least 'waste' of funds" (*Local 2677, AFGE v. Phillips* 1973, 73). But following the bedrock doctrine of *Kendall* a federal district court held that "No budget message of the President can . . . force the Congress to act to preserve legislative programs from extinction prior to the time Congress has declared they shall terminate, either by its action or inaction. . . . An administrator's responsibility to carry out the Congressional objectives of a program does not give him the power to discontinue that program, especially in the face of a Congressional mandate that it shall go on" (*Local 2677, AFGE v. Phillips* 1973, 75, 77–78).

Kendall's doctrine also allows for a great deal of congressional intrusion into administration. In *Morrison v. Olson* (1988) the Supreme Court upheld the constitutionality of the independent counsel provisions in the 1978 Ethics in Government Act. The independent counsel was appointed by a *court* (called the "Special Division") and had "full power and independent authority to exercise all investigative and prosecutorial functions and powers of the Department of Justice, the Attorney General, and any other officer or employee of the Department of Justice" (*Morrison v. Olson* 1988, 662). He or she could be removed "by the personal action of the Attorney General . . . only for good cause, physical disability, mental incapacity, or any other condition that substantially impairs the performance" of his or her duties (*Morrison v. Olson* 1988, 663). The act also provided for congressional oversight of the independent counsel.

As to whether any of these provisions unconstitutionally encroached on the president's executive powers, the majority reasoned that none "sufficiently deprives the President of control over the independent counsel to interfere impermissibly with his constitutional obligation to ensure the faithful execution of the laws" (*Morrison v. Olson* 1988, 693). Justice Antonin Scalia strongly disagreed. In a blistering dissent he warned: "There are now no lines. If the removal of a prosecutor, the virtual embodiment of the power to 'take care that the laws be faithfully executed,' can be restricted, what officer's removal cannot? This is an open invitation for Congress to experiment. . . . As far as I can discern from the Court's opinion, it is now open season upon the President's removal power for all executive officers" (*Morrison v. Olson* 1988, 726–727).

But Scalia was a lone dissenter: the constitutional law permits a great deal of detailed congressional involvement in federal administration. The case law regarding the clear limits is most revealing. In *Myers v. United States* (1926) the Supreme Court held that Article II's grant of executive power encompasses unfettered presidential authority to dismiss executive officers who are appointed with the advice and consent of the Senate. Congress cannot provide such officers tenure at good behavior or place other restrictions on their removal.

However, this limitation, which was modified in *Morrison*,[3] applied only to "executive" officers—and not all officers appointed by the president with Senate approval fit that category. In *Humphrey's Executor v. United States* (1935, 627–628) the Court held that members of the Federal Trade Commission, which exercises quasi-legislative and quasi-judicial functions, occupy "no place in the executive department" and exercise "no part of the executive power vested by the Constitution in the President." The decision gave currency to the term "headless fourth branch" of the government. Its logic effectively places the independent regulatory commissions outside the reach of many controls imposed on other agencies by the presidential executive order or directive (Moreno 1994).

Congress clearly enjoys broad authority to treat agencies as its agents, but there are some constitutional limits on its ability to transform them into extensions. Members of Congress cannot formally administer agencies because "no Person holding any Office under the United States, shall be a Member of either House during his Continuance in Office" (Article I, section 6, clause 2). Additionally, "no Senator or Representative shall, during the Time for which he was elected, be appointed to any civil Office under the Authority of the United States, which shall have been created, or the Emoluments whereof shall have been encreased *[sic]* during such time" (Article I, section 6, clause 2). Nor under separation-of-powers doctrine can Congress or its elected officers directly appoint the heads or other personnel of administrative agencies outside the legislature (*Buckley v. Valeo* 1976).

Such restrictions are not inconsequential. They serve as a real barrier to parliamentarism, in which distinctions among the legislative, executive, and administrative components of government are blurred at best. However, in practice Congress has found ways of mitigating them, such as using "senatorial courtesy" to block and influence appointments.[4] It has also facilitated the movement of its staff from congressional to administrative employment.[5]

In theory, the constitutional "nondelegation" doctrine could have been the greatest impediment to treating agencies as extensions of Congress. As a majority of the Supreme Court stated in *Schechter Poultry Corporation v. United States* (1935, 529–530):

The Congress is not permitted to abdicate or to transfer to others the essential legislative functions with which it is . . . vested. . . . [T]he Constitution has never been regarded as denying to Congress the necessary resources of flexibility and practicality, which will enable it to perform its function in laying down policies and establishing standards, while leaving to selected instrumentalities the making of subordinate rules within prescribed limits and the determination of facts to which the policy as declared by the legislature is to apply. But . . . the constant recognition of the necessity and validity of such provisions, and the wide range of administrative authority which has been developed by means of them, cannot be allowed to obscure the limitations of the authority to delegate, if our constitutional system is to be maintained.

Formally, delegations of legislative authority to administrative agencies are permissible under the separation of powers only when accompanied by an "intelligible principle to which [the agency must] . . . conform" (*J. W. Hampton, Jr. and Co. v. United States* 1928, 409). In practice though, politics overwhelmed constitutional theory. The Supreme Court's holding in *Schechter* and related cases in 1935 and 1936 threatened core New Deal programs and touched off a firestorm of opposition to the Court.[6] There was some currency to the critics' charge that "the Justices of the Supreme Court are nine old men reciting the parables of the law, and have for years offered a more fascinating study in primitive ritualism than anything the Maylasian [sic] tribes had to offer" (*American Bar Association Journal* 1939, 94). President Roosevelt seized what appeared to be a good opportunity to overcome judicial opposition. In 1937 he asked Congress for the authority to appoint an additional justice for each member of the Court who had held his position for at least ten years and had reached the age of seventy, until the number of justices reached fifteen (see Gunther 1975, 167–171).

The "court packing" plan was never enacted, but between 1937 and 1943 Roosevelt was able to remake the Court by elevating Justice Harlan Stone to the chief justiceship and appointing eight associate justices. Aside from Stone, only Justice Owen Roberts remained from the earlier period, and he had become more supportive of New Deal initiatives after the mid-1930s. Roosevelt was careful to appoint justices who would support legislative delegations and be deferential to administrative expertise (Pritchett 1948). (However, he failed to foresee congressional regulation of administrative procedures and vetoed Congress's attempt to do so in the Walter-Logan Act of 1940, as discussed below.)

Largely as part of the political fallout from the 1930s, since 1937 the courts have failed to overturn even egregious instances of standardless delegation (see Jackson 1941, 48–123).[7] This enables Congress to treat agencies as extensions that share its legislative responsibilities and burdens.

Industrial Union Department, AFL-CIO v. American Petroleum Institute (1980) presents an excellent illustration of the type of delegation that has been permissible for the past six decades. The Occupational Safety and Health Act of 1970 provides that the secretary of labor, "in promulgating standards dealing with toxic materials or harmful physical agents . . . shall set the standard which most adequately assures, *to the extent feasible,* on the basis of the best available evidence, that no employee will suffer material impairment of health or functional capacity even if such employee has regular exposure to the hazard dealt with by such standard for the period of his working life" (*Industrial Union Department* 1980, 671). Upon analyzing how Congress adopted this wording, Justice William Rehnquist concluded, "I believe that the legislative history demonstrates that the feasibility requirement . . . is a legislative mirage, appearing to some Members but not to others, and assuming any form desired by the beholder." In his view, the key standard—"to the extent feasible"—was largely or entirely "precatory" (concurring opinion, *Industrial Union Department* 1980, 681, 682).

Rehnquist noted that the nondelegation doctrine "ensures to the extent consistent with orderly governmental administration that important choices of social policy are made by Congress, the branch of our Government most responsive to the popular will," and provides administrators with "an 'intelligible principle' to guide the exercise of the delegated discretion." He called on the Court "not to shy away from our judicial duty to invalidate unconstitutional delegations of legislative authority solely out of concern that we should thereby reinvigorate discredited constitutional doctrines of the pre–New Deal era" (*Industrial Union Department* 1980, 685–686). But no other justice was willing to take this step, despite the fact that the "feasibility" requirement was subject to contradictory readings by the litigants involved as well as by members of Congress and the justices themselves.[8]

If delegations such as the "feasibility" requirement can survive the nondelegation doctrine, then Congress can freely delegate significant policy choices to the agencies. The constitutional obstacles of the 1930s to Congress's use of agencies as extensions for legislation are now a distant memory—and for most of the justices, apparently a bad one at that. As Rehnquist put it, the nondelegation doctrine "fell under a cloud" (*Industrial Union Department* 1980, 675).[9]

Accepting Delegation as Routine

The fact that after 1936 constitutional law has permitted broad, virtually standardless delegations does not require that Congress actually vest great discretionary legislative authority in agencies. Its decision to shift its constitutional functions to include routinely delegating power and to treat the recipients as extensions was deliberate and difficult. It began in the 1930s with congressional consideration of a number of administrative procedure bills and was fully accomplished and accepted with enactment of the APA in 1946.

There is no systematic record of how members of Congress viewed delegation during the 1930s and 1940s. However, a reading of the entire record of legislative debates and committee hearings on administrative procedure bills, along with members' published statements elsewhere, suggests that Congress became more accepting of delegation as time went on. In the 1930s, delegation was largely viewed as a necessary or unnecessary evil.[10] By 1946, when the APA passed with broad bipartisan support in both houses (Brazier 1993, 311–318), it was more apt to be considered a normal governmental process.

Delegation as a Danger

The Walter-Logan Act of 1940 was Congress's first serious effort to regulate agency procedures broadly and comprehensively. Among the act's more controversial provisions was a requirement that agencies issue their first rules pursuant to new grants of statutory authority within one year. Agencies also had to hold public hearings on rules when requested to do so by anyone substantially interested in their application. Rules less than three years old at the time the act took effect would be subject to reconsideration at public hearings. The act applied to all rules— legislative (substantive), interpretive, and procedural.[11] It also regulated agency adjudication and provided for extensive judicial review of administrative actions. The act contained a number of agency exemptions, but no general exception for emergencies. In some respects, the act would have turned agencies into "the wards of the courts" rather than extensions of the legislature (Rohr 1986, 165; see Brazier 1993, 131–201, for a comprehensive legislative history).

Several members of Congress considered Walter-Logan a means of reclaiming control of the legislative function. One common theme was that delegation led to administrative discretion, which was antithetical to the rule of law. At the time, the term "administrative law" was sometimes used to refer to the substantive output of agencies—rules, orders, and formal or informal decisions. Using the term in this sense, Congressman E. E. Cox (D-GA) explained that "administrative law is the substitution of the discretion of bureaucrats for the rules of fixed, definite law"; therefore, it is "personalized government," which is antithetical to "the supremacy of general rules of law." Cox recognized that the complexity of public policy required agencies and administrative discretion, "but not to the extent of delegating to administrative agents the power of substituting their judgment as to the meaning of law for the judgment of the Congress which enacted the law." He contended that the Walter-Logan Act would enable Congress to "recapture" part of its powers (U.S. Congress 1940, 4531).

Cox's view was widely shared. Various members, including Daniel Reed (R-NY), voiced a genuine fear of bureaucratic "despotism" that would be "difficult to dislodge" (U.S. Congress 1940, 4600). The Senate Judiciary Committee's *Report* (No. 442) on the Walter-Logan bill considered it a defense against "totalitarianism" potentially arising through "the entire subordination of both the legislative and judicial branches of the Federal Government to the executive branch wherein are included the administrative agencies and tribunals of that government" (U.S. Congress 1939, 9392).

Another theme was that delegation fundamentally threatened Congress's position in the constitutional separation of powers. For example, Congressman George Dondero (R-MI) charged that the bureaucracy "is becoming greater as a lawmaking institution than the Congress of the United States itself." In his view, "This process, if continued, will have a tendency to undermine the fundamental principles of this Nation and destroy the confidence of the people in the three departments of our Government as provided in the Constitution" (U.S. Congress 1940, 4672). The *Congressional Record* shows that Congressman Hatton Sumners (D-TX), who chaired the House Judiciary Committee during consideration of the APA, was greeted with applause when he urged overriding Roosevelt's veto of the Walter-Logan Act:

It happens that we live under a system of government, under a Constitution whose first provision places the responsibility of legislating upon the Members of the Congress composed of the two Houses. The Constitution provides that they may have the assistance and benefit of the President's suggestions and advice, but whenever that time comes in America when the Members of the legislative branch of the Government abdicate or surrender this fundamental responsibility set forth in the first provision of the Constitution—and I say this with all respect—and yield its judgment to the judgment of the Executive, the people ought to keep them at home and stop their getting any money out of the Federal Treasury. There is no use for them in the functioning machinery of the Government. (U.S. Congress 1940, 13951)[12]

It is difficult to gauge the extent to which other members of Congress may have viewed delegation with approval. Not everyone spoke to the matter. Congressman Adolph Sabath (D-IL) asked, "Is it not a fact that the legislative branch of the Government authorized these departments to adopt rules and regulations?" He opposed the act for "trying to deprive them of that right" (U.S. Congress 1940, 13952). Congressman Robert Ramspeck (D-GA) raised a similar point, but for the most part, opposition to the act focused on concern that the "machinery set up is absolutely absurd," as Congressman Butler Hare (D-SC) put it (U.S. Congress 1940, 4657, 4658). Opponents thought the act's exemptions were irrational and that it would generate endless litigation, promote poor administration, and undermine specific New Deal programs (e.g., see U.S. Congress 1940, 21215).

Overall, the members tended to view the agencies as agents of Congress or entities that were cordoned off in the executive branch. However, the idea that agencies could be considered legislative extensions was also nascent in Congress's discussion of the Walter-Logan Act. Some members were beginning to look at legislation and administration as related functions. For example, to Representative Albert Austin (R-CT) it appeared that "this Congress from time to time has set up different agencies or bureaus in order to expedite the business of government. They, by the creative body, were vested with certain authorities and a certain latitude of action and decision, but nowhere does it appear that the *part* should become greater than the *whole,* or that these agencies should assume to themselves the legislative function possessed by Congress" (U.S. Congress 1940, 4724; emphasis added). It follows that the whole (Congress) bears substantial responsibility for the performance of the parts (the agencies). Representative John Cochran (D-MO) asked, "Now, who is responsible for the condition [administrative abuses] complained of?" He answered, "The Congress itself. It was the Congress that gave to the administrative officials the power to write rules and regulations. If Congress had not given this power"—or if Congress had given the power with procedural regulations and constraints attached, which was one of the act's purposes—"there could be no abuse" (U.S. Congress 1940, 21505).

Walter-Logan passed the House with strong support, but cleared the Senate by only two votes (see Brazier 1993, 144–180).[13] Roosevelt's veto was sustained by a House vote of 153 votes for override to 127 against, with 8 voting "present" and 141 not voting. James Brazier (1993, 199) attributes the bill's demise to Roosevelt's decision to make it a partisan issue, thereby persuading 95 Democratic supporters to change their stance or refrain from voting.

Delegation as Routine

The legislative debates and hearings on the APA, which was introduced in 1945, reveal a shift in the dominant congressional attitudes toward delegation and administration (see Brazier 1993, 262–352, for a detailed legislative history). Some members continued to decry the "usurpation" of congressional functions and authority. However, on the whole, Congress had come to view the agencies as legitimately engaged in legislating. Its strategy for control had also changed. It relied far less on the courts to review agency decisions and far more on carefully regulating administrative procedures to prevent abuse and to ensure that agency actions were open, participatory, and fair.

The change is fully evident in how the APA was presented to Congress by its chief sponsors. It was introduced as a mature bill, one that was the result of more than a decade of analysis of how to regulate administrative procedures. Congressman Francis Walter (D-PA), its floor manager in the House, claimed that "so much had been done in the prior years that it was perfectly obvious that the problem remaining was one of draftsmanship." He explained: "The people of the country have been of different minds about this new phenomenon ['administrative law' in the sense of substantive rules]. Thirty years ago they were arguing about its validity under the constitutional system of the United States. Twenty-five years ago the argument had shifted to questions of how far the courts should be authorized to control administrative operations. Within the last 10 years the emphasis has swung to problems of administrative organization and administrative procedure" (U.S. Congress 1946c, 5648, 5647).

During the Walter-Logan debates, Walter was more apt to refer to agency rulemaking as "quasi-legislative" (see U.S. Congress 1940, 4535 for an example). In 1946 he presented delegation as inevitable and the exercise of legislative functions by agencies as wholly legitimate, though requiring procedural regulation: "There are the legislative functions of administrative agencies, where they issue general or particular regulations which in form or effect are like the statutes of the Congress. Among these are such regulations as those which state minimum wage requirements or agricultural marketing rules. Congress—if it had the time, the staff, and the organization—might itself prescribe these things. Because Congress does not do so itself and yet desires that these things be done, the legislative power to do them has been conferred upon administrative officers or agencies" (U.S. Congress 1946c, 5648).

Senator Pat McCarran (D-NV), chair of the Senate Judiciary Committee and chief sponsor of the bill in the Senate, also asserted that administration legitimately encompasses a legislative function. Like Willoughby (1934), he viewed administration as constitutionally distinct from the executive branch, though agencies might be housed in it: "We have set up a fourth order in the tripartite plan of Government which was initiated by the founding fathers of our democracy. They set up the executive, the legislative, and the judicial branches; but since that time we have set up a fourth dimension, if I may so term it, which is now popularly known as administrative in nature" (U.S. Congress 1946c, 2190). Administration is not simply an executive matter, since it includes "legislative" and "judicial" functions (U.S. Congress 1946c, 2193). McCarran argued that because of the administrative combination of functions, "the demand for legislation of this type to settle and regulate the field of Federal administrative law and procedure has been widespread and consistent over a period of many years" (U.S. Congress 1946c, 2190).

Congressman John Robsion (R-KY), a strong supporter of regulating administrative procedures, outlined the core argument for the APA. First, the delegation of legislative authority to agencies became unavoidable "as the country has grown and as its activities have become more diversified and complex."[14] Second, Robsion claimed that agencies inevitably issue "orders, directives, and rules exceeding the powers granted to them by the Congress"; that is, they go beyond the bounds of the legislative authority delegated to them and thereby illegitimately assume the "function of making laws." Third, there is no guarantee that enforcement will be fair. As the separation of powers collapses into the agencies, administrators become "the law makers, prosecutors, juries, and judges of their own laws." In Robsion's view, the conclusion was self-evident: congressional regulation of administrative procedures by statute "is very necessary and it is long overdue" (U.S. Congress 1946c, 5659; see also the statement by Congressman Sam Hobbs [D-AL], p. 5659).

Even die-hard opponents of delegation, such as Congressman John Jennings, Jr. (R-TN), indirectly accepted agency rulemaking as inevitable. "It was never contemplated or intended by the founders of this Republic," Jennings complained, "that the power to legislate vested in Congress should be usurped by a bunch of appointive officers here in Washington who were never elected by any constituency and never could be." But he strongly supported the APA because "it puts a legal restraint upon the power of these bureaus to promulgate rules and regulations" by providing for public participation, hearings, and publicity (U.S. Congress 1946c, 5662–5663).

The APA moved through Congress with little controversy, though several somewhat technical amendments were adopted in the House and accepted by the Senate. There was some opposition from agencies.[15] However, President Harry Truman, who was preoccupied with an array of major policy issues and decisions, signed the APA with little hesitation and it became law on June 11, 1946 (Brazier 1993, 318–330). Truman's attorney general, Tom Clark, strongly supported the bill, and the Bureau of the Budget recommended that the president sign it even though it reflected "legalistic rather than administrative thinking" (Brazier 1993, 329). Its underlying premises were no longer controversial.

In the future, Congress would increasingly treat the agencies as extensions. It would delegate and they would "legislate." Congress would regulate administrative procedures to protect core legislative values, including openness and the opportunity to be heard. Fixing the scope and content of such regulations, not whether to have them, became the key issue. The decisions involved were informed by Congress's collective understanding of the problems posed by large-scale public administration.

Diagnosing Administration

Congress's diagnosis of administrative deficiencies was remarkably different from that of the President's Committee on Administrative Management (PCAM) (1937) and mainstream public administration (see Chapter 1). Like the PCAM and orthodoxy, Congress was concerned with efficiency, economy, effectiveness, and coordination. But as discussed above, Congress was more troubled by the usurpation of legislative powers, the combination of legislative, executive, and judicial powers in individual agencies, and a perceived threat to the rule of law. It was also highly critical of the failure of agency action to comport with democratic values such as participation, responsiveness, accountability, fairness, transparency, and freedom from governmental intrusiveness.

Several members of Congress were clearly prepared to sacrifice efficiency for democracy and liberty. Senator William H. King (D-UT) called the view that "individual liberty may be limited in order to obtain 'efficient' government . . . a dangerous doctrine and contrary to the ideals held by the American people" (U.S. Congress 1940, 13671). Congressman Everett Dirksen (R-IL) was also "more concerned about protecting and preserving their rights [the people's] than in the question of momentary and inconsequential delays in governmental action" (U.S. Congress 1940, 4735). McCarran approvingly noted that the Senate Judiciary Committee had "taken the position that the bill [APA] must reasonably protect private parties even at the risk of some incidental or possible inconvenience to, or change in, present administrative operations" (U.S. Congress 1946c, 2150).

The view that agency processes were not democratic is emphasized throughout the legislative debates on Walter-Logan, the APA, and related measures. King succinctly, if forcefully, summarized this problem:

> These appointed legislators [administrators] now strenuously object when it is proposed that they shall hold hearings and listen to those who will be affected by their legislation—a practice which the elected representatives in Congress have followed for 150 years. These public servants raise a great hue and cry when it is suggested that they be subject to the checks and limitations which the Constitution wisely placed upon the actions of the elected representatives of the people. And these so-called judges severely criticize the requirement that they shall hold a hearing and listen to the citizen's evidence before a decision is rendered depriving him of his rights—a method of procedure which the Supreme Court of the United States has repeatedly declared is required not only by the due-process clause of the Constitution, but by any definition of fair dealing and impartiality of decision. (U.S. Congress 1940, 13672)

The problem of inadequate accountability was frequently noted. Unlike the PCAM, however, Congress did not view greater centralization under the presidency as a solution. The PCAM's response to the *Humphrey's* decision was to propose integration of the "headless fourth branch" into the executive branch, where it would be subject to more substantial presidential control. Congress's approach was to subordinate the independent regulatory agencies to the rule of law—law which Congress writes. Congressman Sumners drew applause in the House for his unwillingness to rely on the executive-branch hierarchy for democratic accountability: "Governmental powers are passed on, far removed even from the head. . . . [T]he President of the United States cannot know who those million people are. He cannot know what they are doing with the governmental powers that are trusted to them" (U.S. Congress 1940, 4741–4742).

In Congress's collective view, the agencies were also unresponsive. "They not only pay too little attention to the viewpoint of the public," Representative Walter noted, "but pay less attention to the clearly expressed intention of Congress" (U.S. House of Representatives 1939, 46). Representative Daniel Reed accused the political appointees of having "assumed to rule because of their self-admitted superior excellence and superlative genius" (U.S. Congress 1940, 4600).

A number of members of Congress thought the public was unnecessarily burdened by the lack of uniform procedures among agencies as well as by the difficulty of obtaining information about their operations and rules (see also Chapter 1). For instance, the Senate *Report* (No. 442) accompanying the Walter-Logan bill noted that because of wide variation in agency processes, "individuals and their attorneys are at a disadvantage in the presentation of their administrative appeals" (U.S. Congress 1939, 9394).[16] Senator Walter George (D-GA) believed that "Today the individual citizen remote from the Capital City must forego many rights because he cannot assert them. He cannot have redress for his wrongs—theoretically, yes; actually and practically, no" (U.S. Congress 1939, 7077).

A related critique was that much of the administrative process was unfair. Senator King, a strong supporter of Walter-Logan, noted that many administrative rulings were made "in the form of letters, and nothing in the way of an even informal hearing is required. If the citizen gets a hearing, it is at the grace of the administrator or bureau chief" (U.S. Congress 1940, 13668). Congressman Chauncy Reed (R-IL) agreed that "the rights of individual citizens have been arrogantly disregarded" (U.S. Congress 1940, 4649).

Finally, several members of Congress objected simply to the concentration of power in bureaucracy. Representative Albert Vreeland (R-NJ) succinctly captured this concern, stating that the United States was "fast becoming a government by the government and not by the people" (U.S. Congress 1940, 4648). Senator Henry Ashurst (D-AZ) similarly claimed that "the bureaucrats are drunk with power" and "believe that their ipse dixit should settle all questions" (U.S. Congress 1940, 7176).

Based on these concerns, both Walter-Logan and the APA were frequently presented as a way not only of controlling agencies but also of protecting individuals' rights. In Senator McCarran's view, the APA was best summarized as "a bill of rights for the hundreds of thousands of Americans whose affairs are controlled or regulated in one way or another by agencies of the Federal Government" (U.S. Congress 1946c, 2190). Six years earlier, Congressman Earl Michener (R-MI) had described Walter-Logan in the same fashion (U.S. Congress 1940, 4534).

Prescribing a Cure

Once Congress diagnosed the problems with federal administration, the prescription was fairly evident. Agencies should adhere to legislative values when they make rules, and to judicial values when they adjudicate and enforce. They should also be more open in publicizing information about their organizations, rules, and decisions. The key issues in drafting the APA were how the values should be imposed and in what dosage. In retrospect, the Walter-Logan Act was considered so encumbering that it would have nullified Congress's ability to use the agencies as legislative extensions (Senator Alben Barkley [D-KY], U.S. Congress 1946c, 2196). The APA used a more limited and finely honed approach.

Congress's conception of the agencies as legislative extensions was clearest in its imposition of legislative values on their rulemaking processes. In 1940, Congressman Clarence Hancock (R-NY) made the connection explicit while arguing in favor of the Walter-Logan Act: when agencies "are acting in a quasi-legislative capacity," the law "would compel them to follow the legislative practice of Congress, which from the beginning has held open public hearings on proposed legislation of general public interest" (U.S. Congress 1940, 4591).[17] Representative Walter provided the same rationale for the APA: "Day by day Congress takes account of the interests and desires of the people in framing legislation; and there is no reason why administrative agencies should not do so when they exercise legislative functions which the Congress has delegated to them" (U.S. Congress 1946c, 5756).

Senator Homer Ferguson (R-MI) developed a related premise regarding the treatment of agencies as legislative extensions. Congress can help legitimize their actions: "In my opinion, there will be fewer complaints because of the activities of governmental agencies if they will attempt to live within the rules and regulations laid down by Congress. After all, the Congress is the policy-making body of the United States" (U.S. Congress 1946c, 2205).

The APA is far more limited and flexible than the Walter-Logan Act in its approach to rulemaking. It exempts military and foreign affairs functions, as well as matters concerning agency management, personnel, public property, loans, grants, benefits, or contracts (Section 4). All nonexempt rules must be published in the *Federal Register,* but only legislative rules are subject to specific procedural requirements. Two processes are authorized, though either can be augmented as long as its minimum requisites are met.

The first process, informal rulemaking (also called "notice and comment"), requires that agencies publish a notice of proposed rulemaking (NPRM) in the *Federal Register,* along with information about the time, place, and nature of the proceedings, contact person, relevant legal authority, and terms, substance, or subjects of the rule. Interested parties may submit comments for agency consideration. No hearing, specific presiding officer, or burden of proof is required. The agency must maintain a record, but it does not have to justify a rule in terms of the record as a whole. The final rule must be published in the *Federal Register* along with an explanation. Affected parties must be allowed at least thirty days for conformance. Agencies can avoid such rulemaking for "good cause" when it would be "impracticable, unnecessary, or contrary to the public interest" (Section 4[a]).[18]

A second process, formal rulemaking (also known as "rulemaking on the record"), is considerably more elaborate. However, it need not be used unless required by a separate statute. Hearings, which are central to lawmaking, are mandatory for formal rulemaking. A panel or specific officer, who can be a hearing examiner (or now an "administrative law judge"), must preside. An *ex parte* rule allows decision makers to have one-sided contacts with agency staff, but not outside parties. The agency is required to maintain a complete transcript. The presiding officer issues a formal initial or recommended decision, though the agency does not have to follow it. The proponent of the rule has the burden of proof, and the final decision must be supported by substantial evidence on the record as a whole. As with informal rulemaking, the final rule is published in the *Federal Register* (see Gellhorn and Levin 1997, chap. 9).

Other provisions in the APA deal with public information, adjudicatory hearings, enforcement, and judicial review.[19] The act remains the core statute for generic regulation of federal agencies' procedures. However, over the years its initial simplicity has been transformed into considerable complexity by amendments, related statutes, executive orders, and judicial interpretation (see Kerwin 1999).

Uniformity

By 1946 it was clear that sooner or later Congress would impose regulations on agency procedures, especially for rulemaking, public information, and demarcating the scope of judicial review. But it was not a foregone conclusion that it would write a "one size fits all" prescription. Since the agencies were diverse, why not treat each one individually? The answer was largely based on a practical assessment of legislative capacity.

In opposing Walter-Logan, Congressman Emanuel Celler (D-NY) strongly argued for diversity: "Most agencies are dissimilar in make-up and in functions. You can no more treat them all alike, as the bill does, than you can treat a pigmy like a giant" (U.S. Congress 1940, 4545). In 1940 this concern was handled by exempting entire agencies, such as the Federal Reserve Board, the Federal Deposit Insurance Corporation, and the Interstate Commerce Commission (ICC). However, the exemptions were driven more by politics than by rationality. Attorney General Robert Jackson recommended that the act be vetoed in part because "the principles that governed what should be included and what excepted are not discernible" (U.S. Congress 1940, 21503). "Those bureaus that yelled most loudly got their answer in exemptions," Celler claimed, "and those bureaus that did not yell too loudly did not" (U.S. Congress 1940, 4547). The exemptions also undercut the bill's objective of reducing the "indescribable confusion" caused by a lack of uniform procedures (see U.S. Congress 1939, 9394).

Some agencies, such as the ICC, tried to win exemptions from the APA as well (U.S. Senate 1946, 97), but McCarran and the Senate Judiciary Committee were convinced that specific tailoring was a losing strategy. McCarran explained:

It is sometimes said that . . . the substantive and procedural law applicable to an administrative agency should be prescribed piecemeal, for that agency alone. . . . Diversity merely feeds confusion, which is a great vice in any form of government and operates to defeat the very purposes of good government. Moreover, when administrative agencies are created or when additional powers are given to them, it is because there is some immediate and important public issue to be settled. The question is whether to regulate or not to regulate, and if so to what extent, rather than *how* to regulate. It is utterly impractical to expect Congress, at such a time, to enact a complete procedural law for one agency or one function. Under such circumstances, it is not surprising that procedural provisions respecting particular administrative agencies are often fragmentary, usually hastily improvised, and sometimes unwisely imitative. (McCarran 1946, 829)

In practice, specific tailoring would generally be the work of congressional committees, but at the time the committee system was in disarray and inadequately staffed. Some committees clearly lacked the capacity to write meaningful procedural regulations for agencies (see Chapter 3). Undoubtedly, many agencies would have been able to determine their own procedures, which was precisely an ill that Walter-Logan and the APA sought to cure. Today, by contrast, the committees and subcommittees are strong enough to treat the agencies individually in some contexts, as is explained in the next chapter.

Building on the APA: Extending Control Over the Extensions

Congress's systematic treatment of federal administration as an extension of the legislative process began in earnest with the APA. The act was always perceived by its sponsors as establishing a platform for applying additional procedural controls in the future. In McCarran's words, "This bill enters a new legislative field. . . . In the nature of things, we must anticipate that experience will indicate certain points at which the law should be strengthened or amended" (U.S. Congress 1946c, 2201; see also Robsion's statement, p. 5764). Some supporters of the APA considered it a basic, framing statute—much like the Judiciary Act of 1789 (*American Bar Association Journal* 1946, 377). Over the years, it has lived up to some of these expectations by providing a durable basis for extending legislative control over administrative processes.

In terms of treating the agencies as legislative extensions, the main areas for supplementary congressional regulation of administrative procedures have concerned participation in rulemaking, transparency, and administrative intrusiveness. (Congress also developed a mechanism for directly participating in agency strategic planning under the Government Performance and Results Act of 1993, which is discussed in the following chapter.) Reading the legislative histories of the key statutes amending or augmenting the APA is often like fast-forwarding or revisiting much of the debate over the Walter-Logan Act and the APA. In most cases, at least one agency opposed further legislative controls on the basis that "one size fits all" requirements are inevitably clumsy, impede administrative efficiency, and undercut effectiveness (e.g., U.S. Senate 1974, 65).[20] Congress frequently responded with a key tenet of the legislative-centered public administration it developed in 1946: because agencies are engaged in legislation, procedural controls are appropriate for promoting legislative values, democracy, and administrative legitimacy. Today the 1946 platform holds an elaborate structure of congressionally mandated federal administrative procedures.

Participation in Rulemaking

One of the APA's objectives was to open rulemaking to public participation, especially by those whose interests might be adversely affected by an agency's actions. Congress viewed hearing from such parties as a normal part of the legislative process, and therefore applicable to rulemaking. Since 1946 it has enacted three key statutes to advance participation along these lines: the Federal Advisory Committee Act (1972) (FACA), the Negotiated Rulemaking Act (1990) (NRMA), and the Small Business Regulatory Enforcement Fairness Act (1996) (SBREFA). FACA and SBREFA expand the range of interests that are likely to be involved in rulemaking. SBREFA incorporates Congress itself into the final stages of agency rulemaking. NRMA can be used to broaden participation as well, but its thrust is to deepen it by enabling agencies and interested parties to negotiate rules.

Advisory Committees

FACA is a congressional effort to gain greater control over the creation and operation of advisory committees. The committees are governmentally established and funded. Their purpose is to advise agencies on rulemaking and policy issues regarding specific sectors of the economy and society. Unlike interest groups generally, they have quasi-governmental status and are sometimes considered a "fifth branch" of government (U.S. Senate 1978, 217, 293, 299–300). They provide their members with access to power and influence. The main legislative concerns behind FACA were uneven representation, poor accountability, and inadequate transparency.

Prior to FACA there was no general requirement that the membership on the advisory committees represent a variety of perspectives or interests. Nor were the committees required to operate openly. Their total number was unknown, though believed to be anywhere from 1,800 to 5,400 (U.S. Senate 1978, 46, 281). The potential for conflicts of interest was substantial because committees are often narrowly focused on regulations dealing with specific crops, food products, types of livestock, technologies, or limited geographical areas. Congress was also concerned that the committees were being used by the agencies as "a convenient and effective source of support for established programs or policies or those contemplated by the Government administrators" and even "for the accomplishment of objectives which the departments legally may not directly pursue" (U.S. Senate 1978, 48 [quoting House *Report* 576, 1957]).

FACA seeks to force legislative values into the establishment and operations of advisory committees. Just as congressional committees would ideally hear from a variety of interests when drafting legislation, the act "require[s] the membership of the advisory committee to be fairly balanced in terms of the points of view represented and the functions to be performed" (Section 5). It specifies that the committees "will not be inappropriately influenced by the appointing authority or by any special interest" (Section 5). It also promotes transparency through a number of notice, open meetings, and reporting requirements.

FACA further builds on the concept of agencies as legislative extensions by charging the congressional standing committees with a good deal of responsibility for managing the advisory committee system. The committees are required to "make a continuing review of the activities" of each advisory committee under their jurisdiction, "to determine whether such advisory committee should be abolished or merged with any other advisory committee," and to recommend whether an advisory committee's "responsibilities . . . should be revised" (Section 5).

FACA also mandates that the president make an annual report to Congress on advisory committees. It requires the Office of Management and Budget (OMB) to establish a "Committee Management Secretariat," to review the status of advisory committees, and to issue guidelines for improving their operations. Consistent with OMB direction, the act requires agency heads to issue "uniform administrative guidelines and management controls" for their advisory committees (Section 8).

Like so much federal administrative law, FACA enjoyed strong bipartisan support in Congress (U.S. Senate 1978, 14–19) but met opposition from the president and his appointees. From the executive perspective, legislation was unnecessary because its reforms could be achieved internally without it. In a dramatic effort to make this point, President Richard Nixon sought to head off congressional action by issuing an executive order regulating the advisory committees, but to no avail (Executive Order 11671 [1972]; see U.S. Senate 1978, 19).[21]

Negotiated Rulemaking

The Negotiated Rulemaking Act (1990) supplements the APA's provisions for informal rulemaking. It authorizes rulemaking by negotiation among interested parties, including the agency, through face-to-face exchanges of information and perspectives. Such rulemaking, also known as regulatory negotiation ("Reg-Neg"), is appropriate when only a limited number of identifiable interests will be significantly affected by a rule (Section 583; U.S. Senate 1989, 6). The general procedure is for agencies to establish rulemaking committees after notice and comment in the *Federal Register*. Interested individuals may apply for a seat on a committee, which is typically limited to twenty-five members drawn from the agency, citizen groups, regulated entities, trade unions, and associations. Selection is guided by the principle that the committee must adequately represent the affected interests (Section 583). Pursuant to FACA, meetings are open to the public (Coglianese 1997, 1257). A facilitator, mediator, or similar functionary can be used to orchestrate the proceedings and seek a consensus. The agency ultimately remains in control of the outcome because, as President George Bush emphasized upon signing the act, "Under the Appointments Clause of the Constitution . . . governmental authority may be exercised only by officers of the United States" (Bush 1990, 1945). However, agencies are treated as any other participant in the negotiations. A negotiated rule will be subject to public comment after publication in the *Federal Register* and to judicial review with no special deference (Section 590).

The idea that rules can beneficially be negotiated developed among administrative law scholars and members of Congress in the 1980s (see Coglianese 1997). Eventually Congress embraced the belief, as explained in the Senate *Report* on NRMA, that Reg-Neg can improve on "the poor quality of rules produced, the burdensome nature of the rulemaking process, the length of time it takes to promulgate rules, and the frequency of litigation that follows" (U.S. Senate 1989, 2). Congress permanently reauthorized NRMA in the Administrative Dispute Resolution Act of 1996, which encourages Reg-Neg and seeks to expedite the formation of rulemaking committees. Occasionally, Congress has mandated Reg-Neg in specific statutes (see Coglianese 1997, 1256).

Negotiated rulemaking adds to Congress's treatment of agencies as legislative extensions by statutorily fashioning a rulemaking technique that enhances participation. Informal rulemaking under the APA does not guarantee agency responsiveness to the views and recommendations received. Formal rulemaking, by contrast, requires responsiveness, but it can be very elaborate, expensive, and time-consuming. It may also generate high litigation rates, though this is uncertain (see Coglianese 1997, 1264–1265, 1332–1336). NRMA authorizes and structures something in between. Reg-Neg conforms to the ideal of an open-minded legislative committee seeking to find a solution to an admitted "real world" problem by obtaining testimony from a wide spectrum of knowledgeable, concerned individuals (U.S. Senate 1989, 4–5). Although it may be difficult to imagine Congress negotiating a statute with outside parties, NRMA is a congressional effort to promote consensus in the exercise of the authority it delegates (see Coglianese 1997 for an assessment).

The Small Business Regulatory Enforcement Fairness Act (1996)

SBREFA is a multifaceted statute. Its substantive policy purpose is to reduce administrative intrusiveness by strengthening the Regulatory Flexibility Act of 1980 (RFA). RFA required that in informal rulemaking, agencies prepare regulatory flexibility analyses ("Reg-Flex") to determine the impact of proposed and final rules on small entities, including businesses, not-for-profits, and governments. Among other features, SBREFA seeks to strengthen participation in rulemaking by requiring outreach to individuals who can represent potentially affected small entities and ensuring that their perspectives and recommendations are taken into account in formulating the final rule. Presumably this enhances the level of participation already available to small entities under the notice and comment process, though it is weaker (and less costly) than forming advisory committees to represent their interests.

SBREFA also provides for formal congressional review and disapproval of agency rules. It strongly builds on the APA's treatment of agencies as extensions of Congress by closing a loop in the administrative exercise of delegated legislative authority. At the federal level, the idea that Congress should exercise such review gained serious attention in the early 1940s, if not before. However, in its 1941 *Report,* the Attorney General's Committee on Administrative Procedure opposed any such review as impracticable:

> Legislative review of administrative regulations . . . has not been effective where tried. The whole membership of Congress could not be expected to examine the considerable volume of material that would be before them. Even a joint committee entrusted with the task could not supply an informed check upon the diverse and technical regulations it would be charged with watching. The reporting of individual rules to Congress as they are promulgated would add little or nothing to the opportunity for congressional action, if it is desired, that would be afforded by the publication of regulations in the Federal Register when supplemented by deferred effectiveness. (U.S. Senate 1970, 701)[22]

Partly in consequence, legislative review was given only cursory attention in drafting the APA, which does not provide for it.

Nevertheless, there is also an inherent logic to such review. In 1947, Representative Estes Kefauver (D-TN) and his coauthor, Jack Levin, made the following suggestion:

> Since it is necessary for the legislative branch to delegate such authority in the interest of achieving the goal for which the law was passed, there should be some kind of review to ensure that administrative regulations conform to the intent of Congress. The rules of agencies should be tentative until the appropriate congressional committee has examined them. As soon as an agency has drafted regulations to effectuate a law of Congress, they should be presented to the proper House and Senate committees by the Capitol liaison officer of that agency, who would explain them and answer questions. Thereupon, these proposed regulations would be placed on the committee's docket and dated as to time of filing. If a ma-

jority of the full committee by formal vote did not object thereto within fifteen days from such filing, the rules and regulations would become effective. When Congress is in recess, review by mail should be arranged. (Kefauver and Levin 1947, 151)

Additionally, Michigan adopted legislative review in 1944, and several states subsequently followed its lead.[23]

Under SBREFA, all covered final or interim rules must be submitted to Congress and the General Accounting Office for review before they can take effect. This requirement includes interpretive and other rules that are exempt from the APA's notice and comment requirements (see Cohen and Strauss 1997, 96–99).

SBREFA provides for two levels of review, depending on whether a rule is "major" or "ordinary." Major rules are those expected to affect the economy annually by at least $100 million or have a substantial impact on costs, prices, employment, competition, productivity, or other key economic concerns. With some exceptions, major rules are subject to a sixty-day review period in Congress during which the legislature can pass a joint resolution of disapproval. The resolution is subject to presidential veto and congressional override. If Congress does not disapprove of the rule, it goes into effect after publication in the *Federal Register.* A number of exceptions based on subject matter, practicality, and the public interest are permitted (see Cohen and Strauss 1997, 98–99, for a discussion).

Ordinary rules are also subject to congressional disapproval, but not to the sixty-day review period. A rule that is disapproved cannot be reissued in identical or similar form unless the agency receives specific statutory authorization to do so.

These provisions of SBREFA strongly manifest the view that agencies are extensions of Congress. The act was a Republican initiative that enjoyed broad bipartisan support.[24] Since 1946, congressional control of the exercise of delegated legislative authority by the agencies has been repeatedly defined as an institutional interest, not a partisan one. Potentially, SBREFA is an especially powerful tool. Congress always had the power to overturn rules by statute, but SBREFA establishes a simpler and expedited process for nullifying agency rules. Joint resolutions of disapproval are referred to committees in each house, based on substantive jurisdiction. The committees' recommendations will probably be fatal either to the rule or to the resolution. In practice, the agency rule writers, who put so much effort into rulemaking, will undoubtedly want to avoid "late hits" by maintaining open communication with the committees and their staffs and listening very carefully to them. In effect, Congress has paved the way for a de facto committee (and therefore subcommittee) voice in agency rulemaking. As is almost always the case, Congress's use of this new tool is likely to vary widely by (sub)committee.[25] Rulemaking begins with congressional delegations; and, now, specific instances will end with congressional disapproval.

Transparency

Running through much of the congressional debate on the Walter-Logan Act and the APA is a concern that democracy is undercut by the failure of agencies to provide the public with adequate information about their operations and decision making. Unless the administrative process was demystified, the electorate would be unable to form intelligent judgments about a major component of the government. However, the APA's provisions for administrative transparency were rudimentary, and in some respects counterproductive. In the 1960s and 1970s, Congress built upon the APA by enacting four major statutes focusing on administrative secrecy and information. One was FACA (1972), which, as previously mentioned, opened the agencies' meetings with advisory committees to public scrutiny. The others were the Freedom of Information Act (1966, substantially amended in 1974), the Privacy Act (1974), and the Government in the Sunshine Act (1976). Each was a legislative initiative that enjoyed broad bipartisan congressional support but, at best, garnered limited executive enthusiasm. Each remains a core feature of federal administrative law.

The main impetus for congressional action regarding administrative transparency came from the Vietnam War "credibility gap" and the Watergate events (see U.S. Senate 1974, 82 et passim; U.S. Congress 1976b, 4, 301, 795 et passim). Underlying each statute is a widespread, enduring belief that information is power and that consequently Congress should regulate agencies' activities regarding it. The Senate *Report* on the freedom of information bill approvingly quotes James Madison's observation that "Knowledge will forever govern ignorance, and a people who mean to be their own governors, must arm themselves with the power knowledge gives. A popular government without popular information or the means of acquiring it, is but a prologue to a farce or a tragedy or perhaps both" (U.S. Senate 1974, 37–38 [*Report* 813, 1965]). The Senate *Report* goes on to note that "although the theory of an informed electorate is vital to the proper operation of a democracy, there is nowhere in our present law a statute which affirmatively provides for that information" (U.S. Senate 1974, 38).

Equally problematic, perhaps, is the potential that misuse of information by administrators could lead to some of the abuses that the APA was intended to prevent. In 1974, Senator Sam Ervin, Jr. (D-NC) prefaced his call for privacy legislation with the claim that "Each time we give up a bit of information about ourselves to the Government, we give up some of our freedom" (U.S. Congress 1976b, 4).

The transparency statutes reinforce the idea that the agencies are extensions of Congress. Senator Everett Dirksen (R-IL), who had been a member of the House of Representatives in 1946, explained with reference to freedom of information in 1964 that "the American Bar Association, the press, and the people of this country favor reforms which the Government departments and agencies seem to generally oppose. These departments and agencies have been invested by us in the Congress with certain functions and duties in the administration of programs we have authorized. . . . I am afraid that that means the burden of devising the proper procedures falls upon us in the Congress *who have established the administrative system*" (U.S. Senate 1974, 106; emphasis added). The Privacy Act comes close to *enacting* this perspective in its declaration that "in order to protect the privacy of individuals identified in information systems maintained by Federal agencies, it is necessary and proper for the Congress to regulate the collection, maintenance, use, and dissemination of information by such agencies" (Section 2).

Freedom of Information

The Freedom of Information Act (1966) (FOIA) reflected considerable conflict between the congressional and administrative perspectives. Congress viewed it as a corrective measure to achieve the purposes of the APA's information provisions. As the official legislative history for FOIA explains, "Soon after the 1946 enactment, it became apparent that, in spite of the clear intent of the Congress to promote disclosure, some of its provisions were vague and that it contained disabling loopholes which made the statute, in effect, a basis for withholding information." It was interpreted "as leaving the departments and agencies in a position to withhold information for any purpose," including national security, confidentiality, or internal management. The APA's original provision that those seeking information should be "properly and directly concerned" was interpreted as a kind of standing requirement under which individuals had to show some special need for documents and other materials (U.S. Senate 1974, 6–7).

FOIA is unmistakably a disclosure statute. It explicitly rejects individual standing requirements. By itself, the act *never* specifically prohibits the release of information. However, materials may be—and frequently are—withheld in accordance with the act's broad exemptions. These include trade secrets, intra- and interagency pre-decisional memos, personnel and medical files, banking records, investigatory and national security information, geological and geophysical data regarding mineral wealth, material specifically exempted by other statutes, and anything that would constitute an unwarranted invasion of privacy. The act provides individuals with the right to challenge agency withholding in federal district court and specifically places the burden of persuasion on the government.

President Lyndon Johnson, whose political standing was beginning to suffer from the credibility gap, signed FOIA even though at one time he thought the "goddam bill will screw the Johnson administration!" (Warren 1982, 180). Apparently, every agency that testified opposed it (U.S. Senate 1974, 65; see also p. 70). Major amendments to facilitate enforcement and judicial review were enacted over President Gerald Ford's veto in 1974 (see Warren 1982, 181; 1988, 206–207). Ford's concern that FOIA would become more costly and time-consuming was probably correct, but nevertheless the act has been judged a success (Vaughn 1994; Warren 1988, 202–208).

Open Meetings

The Government in the Sunshine Act is an open meetings law. It responds to the longstanding congressional concern—expressed during the Walter-Logan and APA debates—that agencies were exercising delegated legislative authority behind closed doors rather than in the open. The act applies to multi-headed federal commissions and boards to which a majority of the members are appointed by the president with the advice and consent of the Senate. Covered agencies are required to give at least one week's advance notice of their meetings, and, in principle, "every portion of every meeting of an agency [covered] shall be open to public observation" (Section 3). By majority vote, meetings or portions thereof may be closed in the public interest or for reasons that generally parallel the FOIA exemptions. However, there is one major difference: a meeting cannot be closed simply to protect pre-decisional discussions from public scrutiny. The vote to close meetings must be made public. Depending on the reason for closure, the agency must keep a transcript, recording, or set of minutes of the meeting. The act requires that this record be available to the public, except for discussion that may be properly withheld (e.g., covered by an exemption). Enforcement is by civil suit in federal district court and by required reporting to Congress.

Although the Sunshine Act appears to allow a good deal of flexibility, several agency representatives claim that it has a "chilling effect" on informal, collegial discussions and leads to "scripted," "perfunctory" meetings (May 1997, 421; Coyle 1995, A12). Where boards or commissions consist of three people, any two of them may be reluctant to discuss official business. The act may also undercut collegiality by making it easier to do business by allowing the chairperson to meet with agency staff and private parties alone, in the absence of other commissioners or board members (see Strauss et al. 1995, 950–951).

The Sunshine Act is premised on the concept that the multi-headed regulatory agencies are very much legislative extensions, or "subordinate arms of the Congress," as Representative John Moss (D-CA) put it in the debate on FACA (U.S. Senate 1978, 305). In an earlier form, the Sunshine Act would have placed similar open meetings requirements on congressional committees. This section was subsequently dropped with the understanding that congressional reforms would be addressed in a separate action. Nevertheless, it is a striking example of how Congress may view the operations of agencies as essentially fused with its own.

Overall, openness in government was considered "neither a partisan nor a philosophical matter. It is just a question of good form for democratic government" (U.S. Congress 1976a, 324; Senator William Roth, Jr., R-DE, speaking in 1975). At the time forty-nine states had some form of open meetings requirement, and the bill eventually had fifty-four co-sponsors in the Senate (U.S. Congress 1976a, 202, 321). Some members viewed "access to the decisionmaking processes within the departments and agencies" as a way of ensuring "that the intent of Congress, as expressed in the legislation we enact, is carried out" (U.S. Congress 1976a, 378; Representative Dante Fascell, D-FL, speaking in 1973). However, the dominant view expressed was that sunshine would promote greater public cooperation, trust, understanding, and confidence in government (U.S. Congress 1976a, 95, 200–201, 322, 348–349). As Senator Ferguson pointed out three decades earlier, Congress could help legitimize the exercise of delegated legislative authority by mandating administrative procedures.

Privacy

The Privacy Act has some disclosure features, but it is primarily concerned with limiting the collection, management, and release of information regarding specific individuals. Its protections against the invasion of personal privacy reflect the APA's broad interest in defending individual rights against administrative encroachment. The act also interacts with FOIA by establishing stronger safeguards against the disclosure of personal information. Additionally, it provides individuals with the right to obtain and attempt to correct information about them held by federal agencies. Enforcement is by administrative sanctions and civil suits for damages for "willful or intentional" violations of individuals' rights under the act (Section 2).

The Privacy Act was a legislative response to a variety of issues. There was a long-standing sense that federal agencies were promoting "Big Brother-ism," as outlined in George Orwell's *1984* (1977 [originally 1949]). The investigatory and information-gathering abuses of the McCarthy era in the 1950s were followed by invasive use of lie detectors and telephone monitoring by federal agencies in the 1960s (U.S. Congress 1976b, 297–298; Rosenbloom 1971, 211–218). The advent and spread of computer record keeping and data banks created a continuing stream of concerns about the loss of individual privacy. The act was also a reaction to the Watergate hearings, which revealed the misuse of federally collected information (U.S. Congress 1976b, 301–302).

Executive opposition to an early form of the Privacy Act had a familiar ring: "The problems of privacy and confidentiality are so varied and complex that they are beyond the legislative capacities of Congress to address in a comprehensive bill imposing similar standards on all agencies" (U.S. Congress 1976b, 772–773). So did the congressional response, as rendered by the Senate Committee on Government Operations: "Such a general legislative formula is made necessary by the haphazard patterns of information swapping among government agencies, the diversity of confidentiality rules and the unevenness of their application within and among agencies" (U.S. Congress 1976b, 167–168).

Two specific criticisms of an earlier bill were ultimately successful. In its final form the Privacy Act covered only the federal government, not sub-national governments and the private sector as initially proposed. It also deleted a provision for enforcement by an independent commission.

Although the Privacy Act was ultimately acceptable to President Ford, administration has not always been smooth. The fit between the act and FOIA can be complicated, as is interpreting such terms as "relevant and necessary," "reasonable," "practicable," and "routine use" (see Warren 1996, 191–193; *U.S. Department of Defense v. Federal Labor Relations Authority* 1994).

It should be noted that there is a tendency to view federal transparency policy as simply a contest between Congress and the executive or as an "isolated body of law" (Vaughn 1994, 481; see also Warren 1996, chap. 4). However, the legislative histories of FOIA, the Privacy Act, the Sunshine Act, and FACA clearly support Robert Vaughn's contention that "federal information provisions are firmly embedded in administrative theory. . . . Conflicts regarding information policy inescapably participate in major debates about theories of administrative legitimacy and decision-making" (1994, 481). That is precisely the way transparency issues were presented and discussed in Congress.

Intrusiveness

In the United States, the charge that government agents are too intrusive goes back at least as far as the Declaration of Independence, which complains that King George III "has erected a Multitude of new Offices, and sent hither Swarms of Officers to harass our People, and eat out their Substance." Considerable concern with administrative intrusiveness was evident during the Walter-Logan and APA debates. Both acts sought to stem it by allowing concerned parties to contest or criticize the burdens that proposed rules might thrust upon them. They also sought to incorporate individual rights and protections into administrative law. Subsequently, Congress built on this aspect of the APA by trying to control intrusiveness directly and generically at its source. The two significant cases are paperwork reduction and regulatory flexibility.

Reducing Paperwork

The Paperwork Reduction Acts of 1980 and 1995 seek to control and reduce the considerable paperwork burden that the federal government

imposes on the rest of the society. To understand the basic rationale behind the 1980 act, one need not go further than Brookings Institution
scholar Herbert Kaufman's report in 1977:

> A "Mom and Pop" store with a gross annual income of less than
> $30,000 had to file tax forms fifty-two times a year. A firm with
> fewer than fifty employees had to prepare seventy-five or eighty
> submissions a year for various agencies. A small securities broker-
> dealer sent thirty-eight submissions to seven different agencies in
> one year. A plant employing seventy-five people had two of them
> working half time solely to draw up compulsory plans and reports;
> a company with a hundred employees made seventy filings or pay-
> ments each year to the Internal Revenue Service alone; a small
> radio station assigned two employees full time for four months to
> supply all the information specified by the Federal Communica-
> tions Commission for license renewal, and another reported that its
> application for renewal weighed forty-five pounds. The chairman
> of the board of a large pharmaceutical firm claimed that his com-
> pany prepared 27,000 government forms or reports a year at a cost
> of $5 million. ("We spend," he added, "more man-hours filling out
> government forms or reports than we do research for cancer and
> heart disease combined.") (1977, 7–8)

OMB estimated the total federally imposed paperwork burden at 1.5
billion hours in 1980 (Skrzycki 1998a, G2). Whatever the effect of the
1980 act, in 1994 the cumulative burden remained astronomical.[26] According to OMB, it consumed 6.5 billion hours per year, and business
organizations claimed that federal paperwork cost roughly 9 percent
of the annual gross domestic product (Strauss et al. 1995, 872). Much
of it, of course, is duplicative; some is so unintelligible that even well-
educated individuals hire lawyers and accountants to deal with it. Most
pertinently here, it is generated by the agencies, primarily the Internal
Revenue Service, in the course of exercising delegated legislative authority and implementing programs authorized by Congress.

Congress's strategy for dealing with the federal paperwork burden
involves a mix of treating the agencies as extensions and relying on
OMB's discretion for coordinated enforcement (see U.S. House of Representatives 1995). First, the acts tell the agencies what to do and, broadly,
how to do it. The 1995 act seeks to reduce the paperwork burden by 36
percent between 1996 and 2001—a goal that is very unlikely to be met

(Gugliotta 1997, A13). Before agencies collect information, they are required by the act to estimate the burden that forms and other instruments will impose and to evaluate the need for the information they seek. The act mandates testing through pilot programs, where appropriate. Agencies must also use the *Federal Register* for notice and comment regarding their intent to collect information. The act instructs them to consult with affected parties as well.

Second, after the agency goes through these steps it can submit its proposal for collecting information to OMB's Office of Information and Regulatory Affairs (OIRA). The submission must include considerations of whether the information sought is duplicative or burdensome, creates special hardships for small entities, and is clearly identified or defined. The agencies also have to indicate whether the information will be collected and managed in accordance with existing practice. In most cases, clearance by OIRA is required before the collection device can be used.

Relying on OIRA for enforcement and vesting a great deal of discretion in it deviates from Congress's general post-1946 approach to regulating agencies' procedures generically. FACA places some reporting and control functions in the president and OMB; however, the general legislative approach has been to rely on judicial, rather than executive, policing. Congress set the tone for this approach with the APA by refusing to establish an office of administrative procedure, as recommended in the attorney general's *Report*.[27]

Enforcement by OIRA ran into problems almost immediately, perhaps exacerbated by the "divided government" that followed President Ronald Reagan's election in 1980. Congress believed that OIRA would be well suited to reducing paperwork burdens through central clearance because it could coordinate agencies' requests and thereby reduce duplication and eliminate unnecessary forms. The act specifically does not increase OMB's overall authority regarding agencies' "substantive policies and programs" (Section 2, 1980 and 1995).

By 1983, Congress was so dissatisfied with OIRA's overall performance in the regulatory and paperwork arenas that it let the unit's authority lapse (Strauss et al. 1995, 873). OIRA was reauthorized by Congress in 1986, but only after requiring that in the future its head be subject to Senate confirmation (Paperwork Reduction Reauthorization Act, 1986). Under the present act, OIRA has sixty days to clear an agency request. (Requests must also be published in the *Federal Register* for comment.) If it fails to act, the agency request is automatically approved for one year. A disapproval is binding, with two exceptions: it is subject to judicial review if challenged as arbitrary and capricious; and independent regulatory agencies can override OIRA's rejection by a majority vote of their commission or board members (see Lubbers 1997, 116). The 1995 act also strengthens a public protection provision established in 1980, namely, that no one can be penalized for failing to respond to an information collection instrument that was not subjected to the required clearance process (Section 3512).[28]

From the perspective of treating agencies as extensions of the legislature, the paperwork reduction model has clear limitations because OMB is essentially part of the presidency. However, where coordinated government-wide clearance is required to achieve Congress's policy objectives, there may be few or no alternatives. As noted in Chapter 1, Willoughby (1934, 115) delineated the executive function as "seeing to it that all . . . laws are properly complied with by [the government's] several parts."

Protecting Small Entities

SBREFA, already discussed in the context of congressional review of agency rules, takes a substantially different route toward reducing administrative intrusiveness. In addition to requiring Reg-Flex analyses to eliminate undue burdens on small businesses and other entities, it seeks to ensure that enforcement is fair. It extends the scope of judicial review to include the content of Reg-Flex analyses, and relies on Small Business Regulatory Fairness Boards and an ombudsman in the Small Business Administration to guard against excessive or abusive implementation (see Sargentich 1997, 127–134).

Thomas Sargentich (1997, 137), a leading administrative law scholar, describes SBREFA in terms that are reminiscent of the charges levied against the Walter-Logan Act: "It adds numerous new procedural requirements, a greater analytical burden on agencies, heightened prospects of searching judicial review, and broadened possibilities to stall and perhaps derail regulatory efforts as a result of challenges to agency action." But from the legislative side, SBREFA, like the Paperwork Reduction Acts, reaches back to long-standing concerns and speaks to Congress's continuing effort to steer the exercise of delegated legislative authority, place checks on it, specify its substantive content, and ensure fair—if sometimes inefficient—procedure.

Conclusion: Legislative-Centered Public Administration

In 1946, Congress redefined its role in federal administration. In opting to treat federal agencies as its extensions, it developed a new, enduring, and expandable vision of public administration in which the legislature plays a central part. Administrative procedures are not simply matters of business practice. They can embody core political and constitutional values. Consequently, Congress has a large responsibility for prescribing them.

Legislative-centered public administration seeks to harmonize federal administrative arrangements with constitutional theory and design. It goes beyond a separation-of-powers contest between Congress and the president for institutional influence over the agencies, though it can be mistaken for such.[29] In passing Walter-Logan and then the APA, Congress was certainly apprehensive about its constitutional role in the increasingly larger and more powerful administrative state. It was also motivated by concern that it had lost its coequality, not to mention earlier dominance, in government. But the contest with the executive has been very much over core values—participation, transparency, and limited intrusiveness—as well as institutional power.

As noted in the previous chapter, legislative-centered public administration's means of folding the administrative state into the constitutional scheme was rejected by the mainstream. From Woodrow Wilson's seminal essay on "The Study of Administration" (1887) to the PCAM's *Report* (1937) and beyond, American public administration has been ill at ease with the separation of powers and, in some respects, individual rights (Waldo 1984; Rosenbloom and O'Leary 1997). The contemporary "reinventing government" and New Public Management approaches to public administration continue to define it as a business endeavor that should be overwhelmingly centered in the executive branch (see Osborne and Gaebler 1992; Masser 1998).

Most notably, Vice President Al Gore's National Performance Review (NPR) echoes familiar themes in calling for "liberating agencies from congressional micromanagement" and freeing them from one-size-fits-all regulations (Gore 1993, 34, 3).[30] Remarkably, the NPR views public administration as "not about politics," but rather as making "improving the way government does business a permanent part of how government works, regardless of which party is in power" (Gore 1993, iv). It seeks to empower agencies to deal efficiently, responsively, and fairly with individuals as customers. But like orthodox American public administration, it is skeptical about the direct contributions representative democracy can make to administration: "When they vote, citizens seldom have much chance to influence the behavior of public institutions that directly affect their lives: schools, hospitals, farm service agencies, social security offices" (Gore 1993, 6). Indeed, "the power that matters in a self-governing democracy is the power we can exercise 'over-the-counter,' on a daily basis, whenever we interact with our government, whenever we seek to make our needs known" (Gore 1995, 93).

The legislative-centered public administration Congress developed partly in the course of fashioning administrative law starts from a wholly different premise. There is no politics-administration dichotomy. Nor can constitutional structure and procedure be separated from administration. Public administration includes legislative functions, and therefore it should be informed by legislative values. Congress's diagnosis of federal administration as a threat to the rule of law and potentially totalitarian or despotic was more than florid political rhetoric. It was the basis for a sustained institutional effort to enact a law governing administrative procedure—a law that has formed a basic platform for congressional regulation of federal administration for more than a half-century. At bottom, the APA's fundamental premise is that when there is a serious conflict, legislative values must trump administrative or business concerns. If necessary, efficiency, economy, and even managerial effectiveness should be subordinated to participation, transparency, and the protection of individual rights. In one way or another, the APA, FACA, NRMA, and SBREFA promote participation in rulemaking. FOIA and Sunshine look toward transparency and an informed electorate as vital to American democracy. The APA and the Privacy Act are designed to protect individual rights from unfair or invasive administrative action. The Paperwork Reduction Acts attempt to prevent administrative convenience from unnecessarily burdening the society.

Nor is administration solely, or even predominantly, the purview of the president and political executives. Administration includes all three functions of government—legislation, execution, and adjudication—and so it is subordinate to all three branches. Because Congress is constitutionally responsible for legislation, it is also responsible for how agencies legislate—and, under the rulemaking review procedures in SBREFA, what they legislate as well. Judicial review protects the rule of law, the fundamental fairness guaranteed by procedural due process, and other constitutional rights. The executive is responsible for coordinating policy implementation and improving administration within these parameters and others, such as paperwork reduction and Reg-Flex analyses established by Congress.

Based on the legislative histories and content of the key federal administrative law statutes, this is Congress's institutional understanding of public administration. It has been remarkably constant. At odds with more than a century of dominant American public administrative thought, legislative-centered public administration is nevertheless constitutionally legitimate under the current separation-of-powers and "nondelegation" doctrines.

It is inherently moot whether Congress's format for legislative-centered public administration generates satisfactory agency performance and/or adequately makes federal administrative procedure comport with American democratic-constitutionalism. The model was significantly strengthened in the 1970s and again in the 1990s to further protect the values of open participation in rulemaking, transparency, and reduced intrusiveness. The legislative-centered public administration founded in 1946 is not immutable, nor does it show signs of being transitory. If anything, Congress is currently addressing the long-standing charge that "one size fits all" regulation is inappropriate by tailoring and applying laws to the specific circumstances of individual agencies. This may well blur the boundaries between Congress and administration even further. As the following chapter explains, Congress's ability to engage in specific tailoring flows directly from another major step it took in 1946—developing the wherewithal to supervise its extensions.

3 | Supervising the Agencies
Developing Congress's Capacity for Continuous Oversight

Congress Wins a Victory Over Congress. . . . This legislative miracle [the Legislative Reorganization Act of 1946] was a great victory for better government.   —Robert La Follette, Jr. (1946, 11)

The Legislative Reorganization Act of 1946

Congress's decision to structure the procedures used by agencies when exercising delegated legislative authority was a key component of its 1946 response to the administrative state. Equally important, the substantive aspects of administrators' use of legislative power had to be monitored in order for Congress to reposition itself successfully vis-à-vis federal agencies. Today, congressional oversight of administration is taken for granted, though it is often criticized for being uneven—sometimes too lax, sometimes overburdening (see Aberbach 1990; McCubbins and Schwartz 1984; Gore 1993, chap. 1). But in 1946, providing for systematic, continuous oversight by standing committees was considered a fundamental change in Congress's constitutional role.

Just as delegation fueled support for the Administrative Procedure Act (APA), it created a compelling logic for strengthening Congress's capacity for oversight, as Senator Robert La Follette, Jr. (Progressive-WI) explained:

> Keeping a watchful eye on the administration of the laws it has enacted is another important function of our National Legislature. But Congress lacks adequate facilities today for the continuous inspection and review of administrative action. The time has long since passed when we could anticipate every situation that might arise and provide for it in minute regulatory legislation.
>
> With the expansion of Federal functions during the twentieth century, Congress has perforce created many commissions and

agencies to perform them and has delegated its rule-making power to them. But it has failed to provide any regular arrangements for follow-up in order to assure itself that administrative rules and regulations are in accord with the intent of the law. (La Follette 1946, 45)

The question was not whether Congress should exercise better oversight, but rather how to accomplish it.

Congress's answer was contained in the Legislative Reorganization Act (LRA) of 1946. The act's goals included improving the legislative process generally, but better oversight was a major component. The committee structure in both houses was radically revamped. The number of standing committees in each chamber was severely reduced. House and Senate committees were given parallel jurisdictions, *and the overall committee structure was designed to follow that of federal administration generally* (U.S. Congress 1946c, 10017). Members of Congress were assigned to fewer committees in the expectation that they might develop greater specialization in one or a few policy areas. The congressional staff was reorganized, professionalized, and expanded in order to enhance the expertise available to the members.

Most importantly from an administrative perspective, the standing committees were charged with exercising "continuous watchfulness" over the agencies. They would replace the sporadic use of special investigating committees as Congress's main vehicle for oversight. That any of this occurred is testimony to Congress's collective sense that its organization was so outdated and irrational that it was not "equipped to perform adequately its main functions of determining policy, supervising the administration of the laws, controlling Federal expenditures, and representing the people" (La Follette 1946, 11).

Like the APA, the 1946 LRA was a beginning. It was conceived as a platform for further modernizing and revitalizing Congress in the future (Kefauver and Levin 1947, chaps. 2 and 17). It was subsequently amended or augmented by additional reorganizations and specific statutes intended to improve the legislative process, congressional budgeting, and oversight. Among these were the Legislative Reorganization Act of 1970, the Congressional Budget and Impoundment Control Act of 1974, the Inspector General Act (1978), the Chief Financial Officers Act (1990), and the Government Performance and Results Act (1993).

Taken together, the LRA and the measures that built on it enable Congress to supervise much federal administration and even give agencies managerial direction in some contexts. Consequently, they reinforce some key tenets of legislative-centered public administration and add others. Administration is a continuation of the legislative process. The primary purpose of congressional direction of administration is to improve the *legislative function* by providing feedback, reducing slippage through maladministration, and securing more faithful implementation of statutory goals. Measures for this purpose often pose collateral challenges to the executive, but members of Congress tend to view them as internal institutional and procedural reforms. Administrative legitimacy flows at least as much from supervision by elected representatives as from scientific and managerial expertise or direction by political executives. The claims of orthodox public administration notwithstanding, Congress has a major and constitutionally appropriate superintending role in federal administration.

The congressional reorganization was proposed by a Joint Committee on the Organization of Congress, which was first established in 1944 and then reconstituted in 1945. The LRA became law on August 2, 1946. Its stated purpose was "To provide for increased efficiency in the legislative branch of the Government." The act enjoyed broad bipartisan support in both houses, passing the Senate on June 10, by a margin of 49 to 16, and the House on July 25, by 229 to 61. It contained a wide variety of provisions that are not germane to the discussion here. Much of its thrust was to improve the lawmaking process. Other matters addressed ranged from the registration of lobbyists to remodeling the Capitol's restaurants. Titles IV and V, the Federal Tort Claims Act and the General Bridge Act, are discussed in the next chapter.

Despite the margin of victory, the act "was a non-partisan victory that upset all predictions. It came after a bitter uphill fight in both the Senate and House to shake Congress loose from two decades of inertia" (Kefauver and Levin 1947, 220). La Follette (1946, 11), its chief sponsor and floor manager in the Senate, considered its enactment nothing short of miraculous.

There was virtually no vocal opposition to the principle that Congress should exercise oversight of the agencies, though there was substantial discussion regarding its proper limits and how it could best be organized. For the most part, criticism of the act focused on its provisions for members' salary increases and pensions, which several legislators thought inappropriate in view of the huge federal debt (e.g., U.S. Congress 1946c, 10083–10084, 10098–10104). A provision to place many congressional employees under a civil service–like personnel system headed by a director was dropped in the face of stiff resistance in the Senate (see U.S. Congress 1946c, 6561). There was also some perplexity about the desirability of putting all of the reforms on a statutory basis when many of them could have been accomplished individually in each house, without the participation of the other or the approval of the president (e.g., U.S. Congress 1946c, 6538–6539, 6457–6458, 10064). A few members were concerned that the reorganization would make Congress more bureaucratic (e.g., U.S. Congress 1946c, 6556, 10086, 10010). Supporters attributed the remaining opposition to committee chairmen whose committees and attendant perquisites would be eliminated in the reorganization (see Galloway 1946, 123; U.S. Congress 1946c, 10046, 10055). Repositioning for "continuous watchfulness" began with a critical—perhaps even harsh—organizational self-assessment.

The Need to Resuscitate Congress

The reorganization was very much motivated by Congress's negative view of its capacity to legislate, oversee federal administration, and budget effectively. There was a general sense that it had lost its way, if not its constitutional purpose. At the time, a leading supporter of change, Congressman Estes Kefauver (D-TN), could seriously ask, "Is Congress Necessary?" (Kefauver and Levin 1947, chap. 1). He and his coauthor, Jack Levin, claimed that "some of its members give serious thought to the possibility that Congress might *not* survive the next twenty years" (Kefauver and Levin 1947, 5).

La Follette, who co-chaired the Joint Committee on the Organization of Congress with Representative A. S. Mike Monroney (D-OK), joined several members in considering the need for change to be truly dire. He warned his colleagues that failure to update Congress's "archaic organization" could "be tragic for our representative form of Government" (U.S. Congress 1946c, 6370). Similar views were expressed by Senate Minority Leader Wallace White, Jr. (R-ME) and by Monroney, who was the floor leader for the Legislative Reorganization Act in the House (U.S. Congress 1946c, 6531, 10039).

Congress's inability to exercise effective oversight of administration was broadly viewed as a fundamental institutional failure. La Follette believed it promoted "a widespread congressional and public belief that a grave constitutional crisis exists" (U.S. Congress 1946c, 6344). Even strong opponents of the LRA, such as Senator John McClellan (D-AR), agreed that Congress needed to develop "sufficient persuasion and influence to supervise their [the agencies'] administration of the law," noting, "We do not have that power now" (U.S. Congress 1946b, 6555). Senators James Mead (D-NY) and Claude Pepper (D-FL) were among several legislators who expressed similar concerns about inadequate oversight (U.S. Congress 1946c, 6371, 6367). Congressman Thomas Lane (D-MA) called Congress's oversight "negligible" (U.S. Congress 1946c, 10053).

The need for better oversight was clear. So was the prime reason for its failure—Congress's chaotic organizational structure. The committee system, in particular, was widely considered dysfunctional. There was a "hodgepodge" of thirty-three standing committees in the Senate and forty-eight in the House, plus a number of special and joint committees that brought the total to about one hundred units. Jurisdictions were "haphazard," and many committees operated as "isolated bastions" of "entrenched patronage, privilege—and inefficiency" (Kefauver and Levin 1947, 114).

The number of committees alone was significant. It required members of the House and Senate to serve on several committees simultaneously and caused innumerable scheduling conflicts that made high attendance levels difficult or even impossible. On average, there were about six committee seats per senator. However, four senators served on nine committees, nine senators on eight, and sixteen on seven (Galloway 1946, 63; U.S. Congress 1946c, 6344). There were 970 committee seats in the House, for an average of 2.2 seats per member (U.S. Congress 1946c, 10017). Again, however, the work was not evenly distributed: one member served on nine committees, and fifty-nine served on four or more (Galloway 1946, 63).

The problems endemic in the committee system also went beyond numbers. As noted by George Galloway (1946, 173), staff director of the Joint Organization Committee, in addition to overlaps, the pace of work varied widely, coordination between the two chambers was ineffective, and a number of committees were inactive ("ornamental barnacles on the ship of state").

During the floor debates on the Legislative Reorganization Act, several members frankly criticized these defects. For instance, according to Senator Joseph Guffey (D-PA), the Committee on Mines and Mining was "a joke, and as chairman of it, I say that knowingly. It is almost similar to the Committee on Manufactures. I have been on that committee for 12 years, and it has never had a meeting" (U.S. Congress 1946c, 6525). Several members condemned the inefficiencies. "It is necessary to go over and over the same ground," La Follette complained, "because members leave a committee to go to some other committee while a particular subject matter is threshed out and finally concluded, then they return later, and ask to have the matter gone all over again" (U.S. Congress 1946c, 6532). Congressman Earl Michener (R-MI), looking at the same problem from the perspective of the administrators, expressed concern for the "innumerable executive and agency representatives, who spend weeks appearing before different House and Senate committees dealing with the same subject, and are compelled to tell their stories and make their cases over and over again" (U.S. Congress 1946c, 10047).

Reorganization

Once the committee system was viewed as the main impediment to modernizing Congress, a general solution was evident: the number of standing committees should be reduced; the committees should have fixed, non-overlapping subject-matter jurisdictions; in the aggregate they should comprehensively cover all areas of public policy; to the extent practicable, committee jurisdictions in the House and Senate should correspond to one another; and the number of committee assignments per member should be limited (generally to one in the House and two in the Senate). Although subcommittee proliferation was perhaps inevitable, it should be resisted (U.S. Congress 1946c, 6533, 6540). Special committees, which increase the workload of members and span jurisdictional boundaries, were to be avoided.

Reorganization along the above lines would strengthen Congress's ability to formulate public policy and to legislate. But effective oversight by the standing committees required more. There would have to be some relationship between committee jurisdictions and agency missions in order to facilitate legislative specialization in administrative operations and to promote effective communication between Congress and the administrators. In Congress's view, administration had become so central to government that legislative organization should now parallel administrative organization. This is another way in which the legislative and administrative components become fused. It may initially look as though congressional organization is an extension of administrative organization, but the intent is to subordinate agencies to standing committees.[1]

Although it took years for Congress to undertake the reorganization, the whole plan had an elegant simplicity. Representative Lane captured its essence in a single paragraph:

The committee [on organization] has proposed changes . . . to secure a firm follow-through between legislative decision and executive action. . . . Most important of these is a simplified system of standing committees corresponding with the major areas of public policy and public administration. First, the correlation of the committee systems of the two Chambers with each other would facilitate joint action on specific measures by means of joint hearings. And the coordination of the congressional committee system with the pattern of the administrative branch of the National Government would, as the report states: "Improve the performance by Congress of its legislative and supervisory functions, provide direct channels of communication between the two branches, promote more harmonious and unified action in the development of public policies, and go a long way to bridge the gap between the legislative and executive branches of the Government." (U.S. Congress 1946c, 10054)

After some debate, the number of standing committees was reduced to fifteen in the Senate and nineteen in the House. As Table 1 shows, nine committees in each house had identically titled counterparts in the other, and most of the remainder bore similar names. The act devotes about thirteen pages to spelling out committee jurisdictions.

"Continuous Watchfulness" of the Agencies

The Legislative Reorganization Act's provision for standing committee oversight of administration is its most important contribution to Congress's treatment of the agencies as extensions. Section 136 reads:

To assist the Congress in appraising the administration of the laws and in developing such amendments or related legislation as it may deem necessary, each standing committee of the Senate and the House of Representatives shall exercise continuous watchfulness of the execution by the administrative agencies concerned of any laws, the subject matter of which is within the jurisdiction of such committee; and, for that purpose, shall study all pertinent reports

Table 1 Congressional Committees, 1946 and 1996

HOUSE	SENATE
1946	
Agriculture	Agriculture and Forestry
Appropriations	Appropriations
Armed Services	Armed Services
Banking and Currency	Banking and Currency
Post Office and Civil Service	Civil Service
District of Columbia	District of Columbia
Expenditures in the Executive Depts.	Expenditures in the Executive Depts.
Education and Labor	Labor and Public Welfare
Foreign Affairs	Foreign Relations
Interstate and Foreign Commerce	Interstate and Foreign Commerce
Judiciary	Judiciary
Ways and Means	Finance
Public Lands	Public Lands
Public Works	Public Works
Rules	Rules and Administration
Merchant Marine and Fisheries	
Un-American Activities	
Veterans' Affairs	
House Administration	
1996	
Agriculture	Agriculture, Nutrition and Forestry
Appropriations	Appropriations
Banking and Financial Services	Banking, Housing, and Urban Affairs
Budget	Budget
Commerce	Commerce, Science, and Transportation
Economic and Educational Opportunities	Labor and Human Resources
Governmental Reform and Oversight	Governmental Affairs
International Relations	Foreign Relations
Judiciary	Judiciary
National Security	Armed Services
Natural Resources	Energy and Natural Resources
Rules	Rules and Administration
Small Business	Small Business
Veterans' Affairs	Veterans' Affairs
Standards of Official Conduct	Ethics
Intelligence	Intelligence
Ways and Means	Finance
Transportation and Infrastructure	Environment and Public Works
House Oversight	Indian Affairs
Science	

Sources: Legislative Reorganization Act of 1946; Smith and Lawrence 1997, 170–171.

and data submitted to the Congress by the agencies in the executive branch of the Government.

The meaning of "continuous watchfulness" was intentionally imprecise, but its potential scope is revealed in the legislative history of the reorganization.

Several supporters of reorganization envisioned a broad role for Congress in federal administration. Their models involved adapting parliamentary practice to the American separation of powers. Kefauver favored a number of changes to draw the agencies closer to Congress. As noted in the previous chapter, he anticipated the Small Business Regulatory Enforcement Fairness Act of 1996 (SBREFA) by a half-century in asserting that the committees should be afforded the opportunity to sign off on agency rules and regulations in order to ensure that they follow legislative intent. He also favored requiring periodic administrative reports, with "advance information on plans that involve national policy and will require further legislative action" (Kefauver and Levin 1947, 145).

Kefauver envisioned a fusion of legislative and administrative operations. He wanted the agencies to "enlarge the number of departmental offices in the Capitol . . . [and] locate these offices next door to the rooms of the committees having jurisdiction over them," believing that "this would save much leg work, promote closer cooperation between the legislative and executive branches, and facilitate committee work" (U.S. Congress 1945b, 16). These offices would "provide continuous service to the committees and to individual members" and "should be headed by a top official of the particular executive unit with authority to speak for the proper Cabinet member or the agency director" (Kefauver and Levin 1947, 149).

Kefauver also proposed a regular "report and question" period during which administrators would answer questions "face to face on the floor of the Senate and House" (Kefauver and Levin 1947, 70–71). The report and question period was backed by Senator William Fulbright (D-AR), as well (Galloway 1946, 212; see pp. 212–221 for a discussion).

Along similar lines, La Follette proposed a Joint Legislative-Executive Council. Never enacted, it depended, first, on the creation of majority- and minority-party policy committees in each house. The policy committees would set the parties' agendas and promote party responsibility. Second, the president's cooperation would be necessary. The council would have been composed of the majority policy committee of each house, the president, and the cabinet. La Follette explained it as a device for avoiding deadlocks by facilitating coordination and collaboration (La Follette 1946, 45; Galloway 1946, 221–222; U.S. Congress 1946c, 6345).

It is against this background that the Legislative Reorganization bill initially used the term "continuous surveillance" in the oversight provision. However, Senator Forrest Donnell (R-MO) was concerned that it might be read to authorize a degree of congressional involvement in administration that, in his opinion, would be excessive. He noted that the dictionary definition of "surveillance" included "control" and "superintendence," as well as "watching." On the floor of the Senate, Donnell asked La Follette whether the intent was "that it shall be the duty of each standing committee to exercise a superintendence and a control over the action of the administrative agencies, or . . . merely to provide that there shall be a continuous state of watchfulness on the part of the committee?" (U.S. Congress 1946c, 6445).

La Follette's response can be taken as the Joint Organization Committee's view of how oversight should function. He anticipated broad, almost constant committee involvement in monitoring agencies. Although he called it "watchfulness," his description of the oversight intended suggested that in practice the committees could supervise the agencies' use of delegated legislative authority:

> if the standing committee is given this responsibility and mandate, and is given a staff of experts, it will be in touch with the various activities of the departments or agencies of the Government over which it has jurisdiction, and it will endeavor by cooperation, by meetings and exchange of views and gathering of information, to make certain, insofar as possible, that the agency or department, in exercising the broad delegation of legislative power which is contained in almost every act, is exercising it as was intended by Congress. . . .
>
> It will have no power to tell the head of a department or agency, "We abrogate this regulation," but it will become familiar, as the process goes along from month to month and year to year, with the manner in which the department or agency is administering the power bestowed upon it. It will then be very likely, I believe, if the committee finds that the agency or department is going beyond the intent of Congress, to introduce legislation to correct the situation. (U.S. Congress 1946c, 6445)

La Follette went on to suggest that the relationship between committees and agencies would not necessarily be adversarial. Over time, he noted, "the members of the particular committee and its staff will also become very much more familiar than they are today with the problems which the executive arm of the Government confronts in carrying out broad delegations of legislative power" (U.S. Congress 1946c, 6445).

Donnell's skepticism placed the concept of agencies as legislative extensions in bold relief. He deemed it highly inadvisable that Congress should be either "an adjunct to the executive department or . . . have upon itself the responsibility of seeing that there is a proper administration of the law." He thought it would be especially unfortunate if it appeared that "the standing committees . . . shall be in effect an operating branch of the Government and shall undertake to control the exercise of power by the administrative agencies" (U.S. Congress 1946c, 6445).

Donnell's position reflected the views of orthodox public administration as expressed by the President's Committee on Administrative Management (1937) and others (as noted in the previous chapters). Like the orthodoxy, it rested ultimately on a dichotomy between politics and administration. Such a dichotomy, in turn, cannot exist where administrators make public policy pursuant to broad delegations of legislative authority (see Lowi 1969). In defending his view, Donnell had to rely on an outdated legal formalism that was at odds with actual governmental practice as well as prevailing constitutional theory: "My recollection is very clear on the proposition that the Supreme Court of the United States has held time and time again that Congress has no power to delegate its legislative authority" (U.S. Congress 1946c, 6446).[2]

Given this understanding, Donnell was adamant that "it is very important to observe the line between legislation on the one hand and executive duties on the other hand." He did not like the word "review" because it suggested "placing both the privilege and the responsibility on the Congress of practically undertaking to administer the laws which it enacts" (U.S. Congress 1946c, 6446). However, he strongly endorsed "watchfulness" or "inspection" and subsequent correction of administrative abuses, if necessary, through legislation. In part, he was motivated by concern that "it would be unfortunate if the public should get the idea that they could go to various committees of the Congress and undertake to reverse the action of the specific departments" (U.S. Congress 1946c, 6445).[3]

Senator Albert Hawkes (R-NJ) raised the counterargument that

Congress should go beyond "watchfulness" to take "necessary action to correct the evil of maladministration or incorrect administration of the law" (U.S. Congress 1946c, 6446). However, La Follette was willing to accept a semantic change. He used "review and inspection," "oversight," "continuous review," and keeping "watch over" more or less interchangeably, noting, "I do not think it makes much difference" (U.S. Congress 1946c, 6446; La Follette 1946, 45). He apparently believed that any of the terms would enable the committees "to exercise the power which we have, namely, to correct abuse of the law or misinterpretation of the intent of Congress." Correction could be by legislation, "if the abuse were of importance," but presumably by less formal means in other cases. In his view, this would not cause Congress to "transgress" "the field of administering and executing the laws," which it had no right to do (U.S. Congress 1946c, 6446).

Other senators did not speak to Donnell's amendment to change "surveillance" to "watchfulness," which passed without a recorded tally (U.S. Congress 1946c, 6447). The provision received little attention in the House, where Monroney explained that the point was for the committees "to keep a continuing review" of the agencies (U.S. Congress 1946c, 10040).

The history of the provision shows that, whatever its precise parameters, "continuous watchfulness" could easily accommodate more than Donnell wanted. Neither La Follette nor Monroney viewed it as a limitation on the ability of committees to correct inappropriate administration by means other than legislation. Even if Donnell's amendment is read as slightly weakening the provision, the mandate remained powerful. As Joel Aberbach, a leading contemporary expert on congressional oversight, notes in his comprehensive empirical study, *Keeping a Watchful Eye* (1990, 30): "In 1946 Congress set a very high standard for itself. . . . The implied standard calls for oversight to take up a significant share of any committee's time and effort. It requires active review of agency behavior defined in broad terms and comprehensive study of the reports and data that agencies submit to Congress—both formidable tasks."[4]

Moreover, oversight by standing committees was viewed as a very significant change in Congress's constitutional functions. Donnell's view notwithstanding, it was explained by La Follette and Monroney as following from delegation and a core component of Congress's overall responsibility for legislation. In Monroney's words: "We think that only half the job of a standing committee is finished when it passes the legislation. We feel that the other half should be in seeing how that legislation is carried out and seeing if the agencies are living up to the mandates of the Congress and living within the restrictions which we provide" (U.S. Congress 1946c, 10040).

Staffing

"Continuous watchfulness" by the standing committees would be bolstered by new staffing arrangements. As noted earlier, the Joint Organization Committee favored establishing a civil service system for many congressional personnel. It anticipated that professional committee staff would be politically neutral experts who would develop great specialization in policy and administrative matters. Their positions, and those of many other congressional employees, would be shielded from patronage by a "Director of Congressional Personnel."

The proposed directorship encountered a great deal of vocal opposition in the Senate, where it was denounced as creating a congressional "strong man," "superlord," "generalissimo," "czar," or "dictatorship" (U.S. Congress 1946c, 6372, 6454, 6460, 6529). Sensing a protracted struggle with senators who were unwilling to forfeit patronage and/or concerned about bureaucratization, La Follette agreed to its elimination (U.S. Congress 1946c, 6395, 6440–6442, 6458–6464, 6468–6469, 6518, 6561, 6556). Nevertheless, much of the original intent was preserved.

The 1946 LRA provided that, with the exception of the Appropriations Committees, each standing committee would have four professional staff members, appointed by a majority of the committee, on a permanent basis, "without regard to political affiliations and solely on the basis of fitness to perform the duties of the office" (Section 202). Termination was by majority vote of the standing committee. Professional staff were permitted to work on committee business only. The Appropriations Committees could appoint a larger number, as necessary. Each committee was also authorized to employ up to six clerical staff. To ensure objectivity, or perhaps loyalty, no professional staff member was allowed to take employment in the executive branch within one year of leaving Congress. (This was a significant reduction from the bill's initial five-year restriction. See U.S. Congress 1946c, 6564, for La Follette's explanation.)

Congress clearly expected that the committee staff would be the workhorses for "continuous watchfulness." As Senator Pepper noted, "no one" would be in a better position to understand congressional intent and monitor its implementation (U.S. Congress 1946c, 6367).

Pepper was among several members who, along with Representative George Bender (R-OH), anticipated that the staff would work "in close contact with executive agencies" (U.S. Congress 1946c, 10060). Congressman Everett Dirksen (R-IL) thought they might be used as investigators who "must go and live in the structure of Government and find the weaknesses and then . . . sit at the elbows of the Members of Congress as they are assembled in committees and say: 'Ask him this question; ask him that question; ask him how he justifies this expense or that procedure'" (U.S. Congress 1946c, 10051). La Follette left no doubt that agency actions violating the intent of Congress would "come within the province of both the standing committees and their staffs" (U.S. Congress 1946c, 6367).

It should be noted in passing that the work of the committee staff would be augmented by that of two other congressional units. The comptroller general, who heads the General Accounting Office, was given discretionary oversight authority to undertake expenditure analyses of the agencies to help "Congress to determine whether public funds have been economically and efficiently administered and expended" (Section 206). Additionally, the 1946 LRA reorganized and strengthened the Legislative Reference Service in the Library of Congress to assist the committees in analyzing legislative proposals and other matters before them. The act called for the appointment of a number of senior specialists in the service, including those with expertise in public administration (Section 203).

A Legislative Budget

The Legislative Reorganization Act of 1946 contains a number of provisions intended to give Congress greater control of federal spending. After enactment of the Budget and Accounting Act of 1921, the president's proposed budget, also called the "executive budget," tended to frame congressional budgetary discussions (see Galloway 1946, 245–266, for an analysis of Congress and the federal budget as of 1945). It is fair to conclude that over the years leading up to the reorganization, Congress had lost a substantial degree of control over federal spending. Budget activity was "splintered" in each house, with separate committees looking at receipts and expenditures in the absence of a coordinated effort to match the two (Galloway 1946, 254).

Oversight was problematic as well. Agencies not only ran deficits, but they also transferred funds among appropriations and across fiscal years

(Galloway 1946, 253). One result, as Senator White noted, was that "no one knows, as a matter of fact, until long afterward, how much money any particular agency of the Government . . . has spent" (U.S. Congress 1946c, 6519).

However, federal budgeting is complex, and Congress made only marginal headway in gaining a better handle on it in 1946. Although La Follette (1946, 46) considered the Legislative Reorganization Act "a first promising step" toward better congressional control of federal spending, at best it was a limited and tentative one.

The act's main approach was to create a "legislative budget." It provided that the House and Senate tax and spending committees would meet jointly "and after study and consultation, giving due consideration to the budget recommendations of the President, report to their respective Houses a legislative budget for the ensuing fiscal year, including the estimated over-all Federal receipts and expenditures" (Section 138). The budget report was to set a maximum spending limit, which could be adopted or modified by concurrent resolution. However, the enforcement provisions "were struck from the bill as it passed the Senate by the House leadership as a price of its admission to the floor of the House" (Galloway 1946, 343). The act also looks toward greater coordination between the House and Senate Appropriations Committees.

At the time, these arrangements were complicated by the Employment Act of 1946, which became law on February 20, well before floor debate on legislative reorganization began. Under the Employment Act, the president is required to transmit to Congress, at the beginning of each regular session, an "Economic Report" that focuses on current and future employment, production levels, and purchasing power (Section 3). The Employment Act also created a congressional Joint Committee on the Economic Report, composed of seven members each from the House and Senate, to study the Economic Report and make recommendations to Congress for coordinating programs and responding to the president's recommendations (Section 5).[5] Logically, the Joint Committee's advice would be relevant to the spending limits adopted in the LRA's concurrent resolution, but at the time no one was quite sure how the two laws would work in tandem (see U.S. Congress 1946c, 6464–6465). (The Employment Act is discussed in greater detail in Chapter 4.)

In addition, the 1946 Legislative Reorganization Act originally contained a provision prohibiting agencies from transferring funds from one account to another. This was deleted after acting director of the Bureau of the Budget, Paul Appleby, pointed out that over the years various appropriations acts had authorized limited transfers. He argued that it would be best to leave the matter to congressional discretion in the future. La Follette agreed that the provision was more in the nature of a recommendation, since one Congress cannot bind another (U.S. Congress 1946c, 6519).

Building on the Reorganization: Enhancing Congress's Ability to Supervise the Agencies

The Legislative Reorganization Act of 1946 was a major step in the development of a formidable congressional capacity to supervise the decisions and actions of federal agencies. Today, the extent of Congress's influence over administration, and especially the appropriateness of its use, is the subject of heated scholarly and political discussions (see Aberbach 1990, chap. 2; Gore 1993, 13, 34). One person's "oversight" is often another's "micromanagement." Congress's behavior is often uneven because there are inherent tensions between its needs as an institution and those of its members for the achievement of their political and personal goals (Aberbach 1990, 22–23, 28–29). However, it is clear that if the 1946 reorganization is used as a baseline, Congress now has a much greater ability and proclivity to exercise oversight. Since 1946, each of the major components of the reorganization discussed above has been strengthened—considerably, in some cases. Like the APA, the act framed a key part of Congress's overall response to the rise of the federal administrative state and subsequently provided a platform for further developing an institutional role that had been mapped out in 1946.

The Committee Structure for "Continuous Watchfulness"

The standing committee structure in each house has endured. The number of committees has fluctuated over the years, but as of 1996 there were twenty in the House, just one more than in 1946 (see Smith and Lawrence 1997, 170; Rieselbach 1986, 64–65). At nineteen, the number in the Senate was greater by four (Smith and Lawrence 1997, 171). Even after considerable adjustment in 1995 by the newly elected Republican majority in the House, several bore names similar or identical to those of 1946 (see Table 1). They also had related jurisdictions (Smith and Lawrence 1997, 170–171; Evans and Oleszek 1997, 196; Hall and McKissick 1997, 213–221).

The standing committee structure evolved in response to a mix of institutional and political pressures (see Evans and Oleszek 1997, 193–195). However, it would still be familiar to La Follette, Monroney, and the others who organized it in 1946. Moreover, the committees' oversight mission was strengthened by the Legislative Reorganization Act of 1970 (see U.S. House of Representatives 1970, 4432–4433; U.S. Senate 1967, 17). The act amended the "continuous watchfulness" provision by calling on the standing committees to "review and study, on a continuing basis, the application, administration, and execution of those laws, or parts of laws" under their subject-matter jurisdictions (Section 118). With some exceptions, the standing committees are required to report biennially to their respective chambers. The purpose of the change, as the wording suggests, was to oblige the committees to engage in greater and deeper oversight.[6]

Whatever the direct impact of the change in wording, oversight was definitely enhanced by a proliferation of subcommittees. About a decade after the legislative reorganization of 1946, the number of subcommittees stood at 99 in the House and 105 in the Senate. The number rapidly expanded in the 1960s and early 1970s, peaking at 172 in the House and 174 in the Senate in 1976 (Loomis 1996, 80). This growth was part of an overall decentralization of power in both houses, which was largely the product of a generational change in membership, incumbents' individual electoral interests, and a related weakening of the party leadership in each chamber (Rieselbach 1986, 20–23, 47–52). The power shift was partly written into the Legislative Reorganization Act of 1970 (see Rieselbach 1986, 49–50, 56).

Subcommittee proliferation created new power centers. In 1973, as Morris Fiorina (1977, 63) observed, "On average, one of every two Democrats in the House was chairman of a subcommittee, while every Senate Democrat chaired an average of two subcommittees."[7] In the same year, House subcommittees obtained substantial autonomy through a "bill of rights" (see Rieselbach 1986, 50; Fiorina 1977, 64). They were authorized to select their own leaders and write their own rules. Their jurisdictions were fixed, rather than being subject to manipulation by standing committee chairs. They were guaranteed adequate staff and budgets, and could hold hearings and develop legislation on their own. In 1974 the Democratic Caucus in the House required each committee with more than twenty members to establish at least four subcommittees (Rieselbach 1986, 50).

The subcommittees were only partly created to enhance oversight, but they enabled Congress to take a strong hands-on approach to the agencies. Legislative distrust of the president, political executives, and federal agencies was substantial during the late 1960s and 1970s. As discussed in the previous chapter, this was the Vietnam-Watergate period in which the Freedom of Information Act (1966) and strengthening amendments thereto (1974) were enacted, along with the Privacy Act (1974) and the Government in the Sunshine Act (1976). Ongoing interaction between subcommittees and subunits of departments and agencies gave rise to a "subsystem" politics that became central to federal policy making and administration (Ripley 1975, 251–252).

At the same time, as Fiorina (1977, 68) points out, "formal liaison operations (centered in the office of the cabinet secretary)" gave the members of Congress "a direct line from the top into the bureaucracy." (In 1947, Kefauver may not have considered then extant telephones as a substitute for proximity!) Whether these top- and middle-level relationships constituted watchfulness or collaboration in the pursuit of mutual benefits (or both), they were very clearly "continuous" (see Fiorina 1977; Arnold 1979).

Toward the end of the 1970s, the number of subcommittees began to decline substantially, eventually reaching eighty-six in the House and sixty-nine in the Senate in 1996 (Smith and Lawrence 1997, 170–171; see also Loomis 1996, 80). The change was spurred by a sense that Congress had become *too* decentralized to act in a strong, coherent, institutionally responsible manner, or to cope effectively with what had become known as the "imperial presidency" (Rieselbach 1986, 57–70). A degree of recentralization and greater party control was prescribed, with notable effect by the 1990s—especially after the Republican ascendancy in the House in 1995 (see Smith and Lawrence 1997; Evans and Oleszek 1997; Dodd and Oppenheimer 1997; Sinclair 1997; Loomis 1996, 81–82). The high degree of interaction between myriad subcommittees and bureaus did not yield the institutional capacity to set a national policy agenda proactively or to rein in the presidency.

Willoughby's 1934 admonition not to confuse federal administration with the Constitution's executive function is particularly helpful in this context. The failure to heed it is partly responsible for widely divergent assessments of congressional oversight during the 1960s and 1970s (see Aberbach 1990, 24–28). Congress's ability to control, steer, or even "micromanage" administrative bureaus, programs, and procedures may ultimately be related to its strength relative to the presidency. However, the relationship is attenuated and the result of disaggregated legislative activity.

Viewing Congress's action in 1946 as simply a separation-of-powers contest between the legislative and "executive" (as opposed to Willoughby's "administrative") branches fails to recognize the extent to which Congress was motivated by a desire to ensure that its own *legislative* functions—both those delegated and those retained—were appropriately organized and implemented. Efforts by Congress to improve its own operations—including the efficacy of delegation and oversight—are not necessarily posited on a challenge to presidential power. La Follette's (1946, 11) characterization of the 1946 LRA as a victory by Congress over Congress is noteworthy. If, "on balance, members [of Congress] seem content to protect or enhance their own agency contacts rather than to engage in severe interbranch conflicts" (Rieselbach 1986, 104), then such behavior would be highly compatible with the goals of 1946. The fact that it appears inconsistent to those looking through a traditional three-branch lens, such as Rieselbach (1986), underscores Willoughby's point.

Committee Staff and Oversight

Congress's supervision of federal administration was also bolstered by a dramatic increase in committee staff. In 1947 there were 182 committee staff in the House and 222 in the Senate. By 1965 the figures stood at 571 and 509, respectively. However, the numbers virtually exploded in the 1970s, reaching almost 2,000 in the House and topping 1,200 in the Senate (Davidson and Oleszek 1985, 241). The Legislative Reorganization Act of 1970 specifically authorized an increase of two professional staff per committee, bringing the total to six in most cases (Sections 301 and 302). Much of the growth went hand in hand with the rise in the number of subcommittees, but by the early 1990s a concomitant contraction had yet to occur: in 1991, House committee staff stood at 2,201 and Senate committee staff at 1,030. In 1995 the Republicans rapidly brought these figures down to 1,246 and 732, respectively, after gaining control of the House and thereby becoming the majority party in both chambers (Oppenheimer 1997, 379–381). The reductions were related to an overall 12 percent downsizing of federal civilian personnel between 1993 and 1996 (U.S. General Accounting Office [GAO] 1998b, 1). For Republicans calling for smaller government, they were painless. As Bruce Oppenheimer (1997, 379) explains: "Because Democrats were moving into the minority, nearly all the dismissed committee staffers would be those who worked for them. Republicans, as the majority party, would have more staff than before, despite the overall reductions."

Congress's 1946 vision of how committee staff might interact with the agencies was largely on the mark. The members of Congress rely heavily on the staff. Collectively, as well as individually in some cases, the staff became highly influential in the legislative and oversight processes (Fox and Hammond 1977; Malbin, 1977). Aberbach (1990, 84) reports that 64 percent of top-level Senate committee staffers have either fairly regular, weekly, or more frequent contact with cabinet and subcabinet administrators, whereas 54 percent of top House staffers do. Interaction between top-level staffers and high-level career civil servants is considerably greater, with 92 percent in the Senate and 83 percent in the House reporting fairly regular or more frequent informal discussions (Aberbach 1990, 85). Aberbach (1990, 85) characterizes the communication levels between the staffers and administrators as "very extensive."

Agency sources account for a great deal of the information obtained by standing committees (Aberbach 1990, 88). Overall, Aberbach (1990, 91) found that 48 percent of the standing committees have "well-developed" information networks, whereas 43 percent have "intermediate" networks. The Appropriations Committees are most likely to have well-developed networks (82 percent), followed by subject-matter committees (46 percent).

Interestingly, Aberbach (1990, 91) found that only 18 percent of the specialized oversight committees have well-developed networks, though 71 percent have intermediate networks.[8] He concludes that their approaches to obtaining information are "more casual" than those of Appropriations Committees, which must review funding annually, and the subject-matter committees, which frequently deal with reauthorizations (Aberbach 1990, 92). In a sense, when it comes to review and study on a *"continuing basis,"* they are less diligent because they are out of the normal loops.

Though Aberbach's findings regarding differences between oversight and other committees cannot be considered definitive, they lend support to a point La Follette made in 1946 and help to demonstrate why the reformers wanted oversight to become part of Congress's *routine* business. In 1946, Senator McClellan offered an amendment to the Legislative Reorganization bill that would have established a Joint Committee on Administrative Practices and Efficiency to shoulder most of Congress's oversight responsibility and effort (U.S. Congress 1946c, 6564–6565). La Follette opposed the amendment because having a single point of contact with administrators, rather than many, would insufficiently fuse the legislature and the agencies. In his words, "no one committee can possibly give oversight to the actions of the myriad agencies and departments of Government and make certain that they are keeping within the bounds of the intent of Congress in delegating power to them to issue rules and regulations which have the force of law" (U.S. Congress 1946c, 6565). Oversight had to be built into the daily operations of Congress's standing committees.

Finally, Aberbach (1990, 94) found that despite frequent contacts and developed information networks, 45 percent of the committees use a reactive approach to oversight. They tend to respond to information that more or less arrives on its own, such as newspaper articles. By contrast, 34 percent of the committees engage in active monitoring and 22 percent in intermediate monitoring. Again, evaluation depends on expectations and baselines. Aberbach (1990, 95) concludes that the overall picture is "mixed": "Reactive monitoring is more typical than other styles (modal) but not overwhelmingly so. Many committee units report a very active style, and the majority of all but the oversight units are active or intermediate monitors."

Oversight Activity

The committee and subcommittee structure, adequate staff, frequent contacts with administrative personnel, and information networks create a strong capacity for legislative oversight, but they do not guarantee it. How extensive and effective is oversight?

Assessments are likely to vary, especially with regard to effectiveness (e.g., see Rieselbach 1986, 104; Aberbach 1990, 97–104). The volume of activity is certainly great. For instance, Vice President Al Gore (1993, 34) complained that "in fiscal year 1993, Congress required executive branch agencies to prepare 5,348 reports." Based on Aberbach's (1990, 35) findings, it is reasonable to assume that committees spend roughly 20 percent of their hearing and meeting time on oversight. This aggregates to over two thousand oversight days per year (Aberbach 1990, 35). Of course, such activity can be dysfunctional. Gore (1993, 34) charges that much of the reporting is "duplicative," traps administrators in a "blizzard of paperwork," and diverts everyone from "looking at results." But Aberbach's systematic study comes to the conclusion that Congress has achieved (or perhaps surpassed) the 1946 goal for continuous watchfulness:

> The nature of congressional oversight is rather impressive. Oversight is not only more frequent than it was before, it is based on a widespread and often aggressively operated intelligence system. It involves a variety of motivations and techniques, sensibly joined. It seems to have an effect on administrators, so much so that it often makes them uncomfortable. It seems fair to say that oversight addresses problems and checks, and even corrects, many errors affecting at least the more organized and articulate members of the polity. As a result, congressional oversight probably improves policy at the margins. Not bad for a maligned system. In fact, not bad for any system. (Aberbach 1990, 198)

Oversight Plus: The Government Performance and Results Act of 1993

"Continuous watchfulness" suggests that congressional oversight will tend to be more reactive than proactive. It was envisioned primarily as a means of preventing agencies from straying too far from congressional intent. "Review and study, on a continuing basis" is somewhat more forward-looking, but serves the same purpose. From the perspective of treating agencies as legislative extensions, two problems are immediately evident.

First, congressional intent is often unclear. How can agencies be expected to remain within the bounds of congressional intent when delegations are vague or essentially standardless, as in *Industrial Union Department, AFL-CIO v. American Petroleum Institute* (1980) (discussed in Chapter 2)? During committee hearings on the Walter-Logan Act and related proposals, some administrators indicated a strong desire to adhere to congressional intent, but admitted considerable difficulty in deciphering it (e.g., U.S. House of Representatives 1939, 54, 185–188, 360, 487).

Second, whether or not committees gather information actively in Aberbach's (1990) terms, oversight is at best present tense. In most cases it is after-the-fact. Committees respond with corrective intervention after agencies begin to wander substantially from congressional intent or otherwise go astray. A proactive dimension would strengthen Congress's ability to steer agencies toward the realization of its objectives; that is, to direct its extensions.

The Government Performance and Results Act of 1993 (GPRA) offers a powerful solution to these two problems. Its overall purpose is to make federal administration "results oriented" and to facilitate performance budgeting.[9] It mandates that agencies formulate five-year strategic plans with specific objectives. They must also develop indicators, preferably quantitative, that will measure progress toward these goals. The agencies are required to use the indicators in annual performance reports to Congress. Much of this activity is in conjunction with the Office of Management and Budget (OMB).

However, Congress is also deeply involved. Most significantly, GPRA provides that, "When developing a strategic plan, the agency shall consult with the Congress" (Section 3[d]). Because what one measures is often what one gets, Congress logically also has "a vital role regarding performance measurement development" (U.S. GAO 1997a, 13). Consequently, it has insisted on being involved in the choice of performance indicators as well. In a provision that strongly punctuates the point that agencies are legislative extensions subject to congressional supervision, GPRA specifically protects Congress's ability "to establish, amend, suspend, or annul a performance goal" (Section 8[a]). Strategic planning and goal setting are ordinarily considered *managerial* functions. The act leaves no doubt that any answer to the question posed in Chapter 1— "Whose bureaucracy is this, anyway?"—must include Congress.

GPRA, also known as the "Results Act," is clearly forward-looking. It proactively provides Congress with input, by a means other than legislating, at a key stage in agency decision making. It can also help overcome the collective action problem that often forces Congress to delegate broadly. Winning legislative coalitions can typically be formed more readily for general objectives than for specific ones; that is, it is easier to vote for "the public interest" or the "extent feasible" than to say precisely what such goals encompass or how the burdens and benefits associated with achieving them should be distributed. Even where agreement is readily available, legislating in detail can be time-consuming, tedious work that may ultimately fail by "handcuff[ing] administrators" (Warren 1988, 369–370). Broad delegations also have political benefits. Members of Congress can take credit for supporting popular legislation, and then perhaps win votes for righting agency missteps in implementation (Fiorina 1977, 48–49; see also Rieselbach 1986, 62).

But what stifles or entices Congress as a whole may be more readily achieved by its working units. By requiring that agencies formulate specific goals in consultation with it, Congress is in effect assigning the responsibility of proactively putting specifics into broad legislation to its committees, subcommittees, and/or GPRA work teams. These specialized units are in a much better position than Congress as a whole to determine specifically what an agency's objectives should be. They are expert, relatively small, and in frequent contact with the administrators. Majorities (or even consensus) are more likely to be formed at the committee, subcommittee, or work team level than among the 535 members. In a roundabout way, GPRA de facto authorizes Congress's subunits to define legislative intent in a way that can bind agencies. Once congressional units endorse agency strategic plans, "Federal managers" will no longer be "seriously disadvantaged in their efforts to improve program efficiency and effectiveness, because of insufficient articulation of program goals" (GPRA, Section 2[a][2]).

The committee–agency relationship GPRA envisions can promote the kind of communication between standing committees and agencies sought by the legislative reformers in 1946. Committees and subcommittees can adjust broad legislative objectives to the particular circumstances of each agency charged with implementation. Administrative discretion in key matters such as establishing priorities and defining goals is now proactively subject to direction by congressional committees, subcommittees, and/or work teams.

Moreover, these legislative units may have a great deal of flexibility in defining, redefining, and adjusting legislative intent in response to political, economic, social, ecological, and other changes. Under the Supreme Court's holding in *Chevron v. Natural Resources Defense Council* (1984), when a statute fails to speak precisely to a question at issue, agencies are permitted to adopt any reasonable interpretation of its terms. They can also alter their interpretations over time or interpret the same words differently depending on the policy context. Congressional committees and subcommittees will presumably be accorded at least equal judicial deference within GPRA's framework for strategic planning. Therefore, GPRA should position them to modify legislative intent with respect to agency goals periodically as the plans are revised. As startling as it may sound, new legislation will not necessarily be a prerequisite for updating congressional intent in a way that binds the agencies.

GPRA evokes Kefauver's suggestion regarding the location of departmental offices adjacent to committee rooms more than Senator Pat McCarran's (D-NV) belief that specific tailoring for agencies is a prescription for failure (see Chapter 2). Congress is so much stronger now, due in part to the 1946 reorganization, that it is much more likely to have the wherewithal to supervise individual agencies effectively. Like SBREFA, GPRA fills a substantial gap in Congress's treatment of agencies as extensions. Legislative delegations will continue to empower agencies broadly, but also be subject to narrowing in consultation with relatively small groups of the members.

Congress passed GPRA by overwhelming margins and with minimal debate. It was largely the work of Senator William Roth (R-DE) and policy entrepreneurs in the public administration community.[10] No particular, collective congressional intent can be attributed to its enactment simply because there is no evidence that the members knew or cared much about it. However, the act speaks very strongly to the concept that agencies are legislative extensions and, accordingly, should be subject to congressional direction through means other than legislation alone. It is premised on the need to improve both "congressional decisionmaking" and the "internal management" of the agencies *in conjunction with one another* (Section 2[b][5][6]). It is a stunning instantiation of the fusing of Congress and federal administration.

GPRA was strongly supported by the Clinton administration because it appeared to dovetail with Vice President Gore's effort to make agencies results-oriented as part of his overall National Performance Review (NPR) (Gore 1993; U.S. Senate 1993, 3). It was also embraced by public administrative reformers imbued with the desire to "reinvent government" (Hatry and Finger 1998, vii–xii). GPRA's goal of linking spending decisions to performance sounds much like the NPR's objective of "Creating a Government That Works Better & Costs Less" (Gore, 1993). However, congressional involvement in the act's implementation caught the executive and at least some of the "reinventers" off guard.

In 1997 the Republican leadership in Congress, including the Speaker, House and Senate majority leaders, and chairs of the Appropriations, Budget, and Government Operations Committees, put to rest any notion that agency plans should first be submitted to OMB for approval and then forwarded to Congress for perfunctory review. They made it clear that the act requires broad congressional participation in the formulation of strategic plans (Barr, 1997b, A19). In a letter to OMB, they insisted that agency draft plans are only "the starting point" for "discussions with Congress" and indicated that the agencies should also "come to a reasonable degree of agreement with the committees as to what performance measures will be used to gauge program success" (Barr 1997b, A19).

Congress is seeking to use GPRA in a coordinated fashion that enhances the legislature's overall ability to steer federal administration. At House Majority Leader Dick Armey's (R-TX) initiative, "departmental teams, composed of representatives from relevant House authorizing committees, as well as the appropriations, budget, and oversight committees, were specifically established to help coordinate committee consultations and simplify the provision of congressional views on agency strategic plans" (Barr 1997a, A19; U.S. GAO 1997b, 14). In August 1997 the GAO recommended that Congress proceed even more broadly by playing a decisive role in coordinating agency plans: "The Congress could work with . . . interagency coordinating groups to ensure that congressional data needs are met within any common performance measurement model." According to the GAO, such "consultation will also reinforce earlier strategic planning consultations intended to clarify and harmonize missions" (U.S. GAO 1997a, 13).

Though congressional leaders have been disappointed with the quality of agency plans and performance measures, they retain a keen interest in using GPRA to exert congressional direction over agencies (Harris, 1997, 5). In June 1998, Armey, then-Speaker Newt Gingrich (R-GA), and sixteen House committee chairs put additional pressure on OMB to work with agencies in making plans more useful for congressional decision making (Barr 1998, A4).

Assuming that Congress continues to demand better compliance with the intent of GPRA, the act can be a powerful proactive means for ensuring that the agencies function more faithfully as legislative extensions. Because organization should match mission, congressional participation in agency strategic planning may eventually have an impact on administrative structure as well. Not only is GPRA consonant with the oversight goals of 1946, it has the potential to fuse Congress and the agencies along the lines favored by La Follette and, especially, Kefauver.

Money

The Legislative Budget

Congress's ability to supervise the agencies depends in large part on its power to authorize and monitor administrative spending. A legislative budget is potentially an important tool for accomplishing this aspect of Congress's constitutional role. However, the provisions for it in the 1946 LRA failed almost immediately. In 1947 Congress was unable to adopt a spending ceiling as required. The following year a ceiling was established but then ignored. The process fell into disuse and was formally rescinded by the Legislative Reorganization Act of 1970. The main problems were lack of staff, inadequate technology for determining an appropriate expenditure level, inability to enforce spending limits, and poor coordination among the various committees involved (U.S. House of Representatives 1979, 27).

In the early 1970s Congress sought to rebuild the system, retaining some of the core premises from the 1946 effort. The result was the Congressional Budget and Impoundment Control Act of 1974. The act reinstituted the legislative budget, placed checks on presidential impoundments, and created the Congressional Budget Office (CBO) to assist Congress in analyzing federal spending and developing annual budgets.[11]

Broadly speaking, the impetus for the act was threefold. First, deficits were almost perennial, occurring in twenty-five years between 1941 and 1973, and increasingly perceived as economically harmful (Schick 1980, 51). Second, Congress was frustrated by President Richard Nixon, who successfully vetoed a number of appropriations and impounded substantial sums on policy rather than efficiency or economy grounds (Schick 1980, 45–48). Third, Nixon made congressional spending an issue in his 1972 reelection campaign, accusing the legislature of having "institutional faults when it comes to Federal spending" (Schick 1980, 44). These charges struck a responsive chord with many members of Congress.

Much of the congressional debate on the 1974 act rehearsed points made in 1946. Several members charged that Congress had not performed its constitutional functions appropriately in failing to control either budget formulation or execution. As Senator Sam Ervin (D–NC) explained, "Increasingly, Congress has relinquished power over what is spent as well as over what is not spent. The budget tells us what must be spent regardless of current policy, and the President tells us what will not be spent, regardless of what has been appropriated" (U.S. Congress 1974, 7139). Senator Charles Percy (R–IL) undoubtedly also spoke for many members in asserting that the act would reverse this situation. He thought it "represents one of those historic turning points in the evolution of our institution, a reversal of the accelerating erosion of the congressional purse power, a reassertion of our correct role in the American plan of government" (U.S. Congress 1974, 7144).[12]

Congress's institutional position vis-à-vis the presidency was certainly a major concern. However, to a large extent the members defined

Congress itself as the problem and its own reform as the solution to its loss of authority over budgeting. Allen Schick, an authority on federal budgeting, emphasizes that it would be a mistake to view the 1974 act as simply part of an inter-branch contest. Basing his observation partly on his direct participation in drafting the act,[13] Schick (1980, 49) wrote: "In developing budget reform legislation, Congress gave much more attention to the redistribution of power among its taxing, appropriating, and authorizing committees than to its relationships with the executive branch." Perhaps it could not be otherwise when, in Representative Alphonzo Bell's (R-CA) words, members of Congress knew that "this executive usurpation would not have been possible without correlative congressional abdication" (U.S. Congress 1973, 39350).

Like the 1946 reorganization, the 1974 Congressional Budget and Impoundment Control Act grew out of a collective sense that reform, though perhaps painful, was necessary to redress institutional failure. To an extent, the act piggybacked on the 1946 experience. Congressman Jamie Whitten (D-MS) provided tangible continuity: "I have worked rather hard on this bill, but I think one of the reasons I was asked to serve as one of the cochairmen was because I was one of the few who was here when we tried this experiment in 1946 and 1947. As I have said before, we did not learn what to do but we learned what would not work" (U.S. Congress 1973, 39348). Greater centralization and capacity building were in order.

The 1974 act is complex in details but straightforward in basic features. (The act is over forty pages long; see Schick 1980, 83–562, for a comprehensive analysis.) It established, in addition to the CBO, a Budget Committee in each house. Together these three units brought about four hundred additional staff to congressional budgeting (Joyce 1996, 68). The Budget Committees propose tax and spending levels annually. Discipline is provided by a "first concurrent resolution," in which Congress sets the level of total budget outlays and total new budget authority for the coming fiscal year (Section 301). The resolution comes later in the year than the similar device called for in 1946, and it is enforceable. With some exceptions, tax and spending bills cannot be considered in either house until the first concurrent resolution is adopted.

After the annual appropriations bills are drafted, the Budget Committees introduce a second concurrent resolution, which reaffirms or revises the first resolution (Section 310). Legislative work on the annual budget cannot be finalized until the second resolution and the various appropriations bills are reconciled (see Thurber 1997, 327).

The CBO, which "is regarded as having the best budget numbers in town," brings a great deal of expertise to the congressional budget process (Reischauer 1990, 22). Its main budgetary functions are making economic forecasts, analyzing the executive budget, providing baseline budget projections, and estimating the cost of public bills reported by Congress. It also does complex "scorekeeping," that is, keeping "track of all the spending and revenue legislation that is considered each year, so that the Congress can know whether it is acting within the limits set by the annual budget resolutions" (Reischauer 1990, 8). At the request of congressional committees, the CBO undertakes program analyses pertaining to federal spending and economic matters. There is virtually universal agreement that the CBO has greatly strengthened congressional budgeting.

The 1974 act also enhances Congress's control over impoundments. At the broadest level, impoundment involves a competition between two core constitutional powers. It is where Congress's power of the purse, arguably its greatest, meets the president's obligation to "take Care that the Laws be faithfully executed" (Articles I, section 9, and II, section 3). As noted above, in 1946 Congress sought greater control over the budget. But the executive also needs flexibility to adjust to changing circumstances in order to avoid waste or otherwise dysfunctional spending. The scale and tenor of Nixon's impoundments convinced Congress that budget execution was too important to leave to the executive alone.

The Congressional Budget and Impoundment Control Act tries to arrive at a balance between congressional control of spending and executive economizing. It regulates executive "recisions" and "deferrals." Recisions are terminations of funding for programs or projects. The act allows them for "fiscal policy or other reasons," but requires that the president send a recision message to both houses detailing the amount, purpose, and likely impact on the targeted programs or objectives (Section 1012). Putting inertia to work for the legislature, Congress has forty-five days to approve a proposed recision by a recision bill (which may take the form of a joint resolution) (Section 1011). If the recision is not approved, the funds must be released as budgeted. In practice, the forty-five "days" are computed in such a way that the period may actually be much longer (Schick 1980, 408).

Deferrals are executive actions that delay or preclude obligated spending. They cannot extend beyond the end of the current fiscal year. Deferrals may be proposed by "any officer or employee of the United States," though they must be transmitted by the president to Congress along with an explanation similar to that accompanying recisions (Section 1013). Under the act, either house can override a deferral by passing an "impoundment resolution" of disapproval at any time (Section 1011). In contrast to recisions, therefore, deferrals are tacitly ratified rather than defeated by congressional inaction.

In general, the 1974 impoundment provisions were viewed as a significant improvement in congressional control over budget execution. In 1980, Schick concluded that "the Impoundment Control Act has established a workable, if burdensome, procedure for review of executive impoundments. . . . Congress has been able to prevent the President from unilaterally withholding funds, and the executive branch has been able to manage its financial affairs without undue rigidity" (1980, 406).

Nevertheless, as deficits continued to grow, pressure mounted to give the president greater recision authority. This culminated—at least for the present—in the Line Item Veto Act of 1996, which the Supreme Court declared unconstitutional in *Clinton v. City of New York* (1998).[14] The act effectively would have required a two-thirds majority in each house to override a president determined to cut specific spending items.

In assessing the Congressional Budget and Impoundment Control Act as a whole, Philip Joyce, an expert on the federal budget who spent several years at the CBO, reached this conclusion:

> The Congressional Budget Act has met some of its goals, but not others. The Budget Act has led to a reassertion of the congressional role in budgeting, an expansion of the budgetary and economic information available to the Congress, an increase in the attention of the Congress to the *whole* budget, and the control of presidential impoundment power. The Act is not considered to be as successful in two other respects. First, deadlines for enacting budget resolutions and the passing of appropriation bills have routinely been missed. Second, and perhaps more significantly, there was nothing in the law that forced the Congress to deal with the alarming deficits that had appeared by the mid-1980s.
>
> The major lasting effect of the Congressional Budget Act has been to swing the pendulum back in the direction of legislative control, nearer to where it had been prior to the passage of the 1921 [Budget and Accounting] Act. (1993, 40)

As deficits mounted, the 1974 act was augmented first by the Balanced Budget and Emergency Deficit Control Act of 1985 (better known as the Gramm-Rudman-Hollings Act) and then by the Budget Enforcement Act of 1990. Gramm-Rudman-Hollings set annual deficit targets in an effort to eliminate the deficit. The Budget Enforcement Act employed a PAYGO (pay-as-you-go) approach requiring tax and spending legislation to be deficit-neutral (Joyce 1993, 41; Thurber 1997, 328–331). Both failed to control the deficit. Targets face the difficulty noted earlier of one Congress trying to bind another. PAYGO has worked on its own terms, but deficits rose as the economy performed poorly and previously obligated mandatory spending grew (Joyce 1993, 41). Annual deficits were finally erased by the vibrant economic upswing that took hold in the mid-1990s.

Accountability

After 1974, Congress had better information and stronger processes for formulating budgets and keeping track of spending. But there was still a blind spot in its ability to supervise agency spending. Knowledge of how departments and agencies were using their appropriations was limited. Oversight hearings were useful in this regard, but not comprehensive. Agency accounting systems were not standardized, and some were clearly inadequate. In 1990 Congress addressed these problems with the Chief Financial Officers Act, which seeks to improve federal accounting and financial reporting in a variety of ways.

The Chief Financial Officers Act was a congressional initiative that enjoyed strong bipartisan support (McMurtry 1991, 1; Gore 1993, 7; U.S. GAO 1998d, 22). It followed the savings and loan crisis of the late 1980s, revelations of widespread misuse of federal funds at the Department of Housing and Urban Development, as well as GAO and OMB identification of seventy-eight "high risk" programs involving at least $97 billion, and possibly much more (U.S. House of Representatives 1990, 14). The House Committee on Government Operations attributed these problems to mismanagement and financial disarray:

A primary cause is the deplorable state of the Federal Government's own management infrastructure—particularly its financial management systems—which are critical for rooting out fraud, waste, and abuse. The Federal Government operates with many antiquated systems that do not provide adequate information required for effective management, program funding, and revenue-generating decision-making. There are hundreds of separate Federal agency accounting systems, making efforts to monitor and audit programs unnecessarily difficult. (U.S. House of Representatives 1990, 14)

The act seeks to remedy these problems by restructuring OMB so that it will devote greater attention to federal financial management systems and by providing for the appointment of chief financial officers (CFOs) and deputy CFOs in nine agencies and all fourteen departments.

Among the act's purposes is "the production of complete, reliable, timely, and consistent financial information for use by the executive branch of the Government and the Congress in the financing, management, and evaluation of Federal programs" (Section 102[b][3]). The act establishes within OMB a deputy director for management, who is appointed by the president with the advice and consent of the Senate (Section 201). However, from the congressional side, the CFOs and their deputies are the key actors.

The CFOs do not sit at the elbows of the members of Congress, but they do "go and live in the structure of Government and find the weaknesses," in Representative Dirksen's 1946 phrase. CFOs in the departments, the Environmental Protection Agency, and the National Aeronautics and Space Administration are presidential appointees requiring Senate confirmation. Agency heads appoint the remainder and all deputy CFOs from the career service.

The CFOs and their deputies are charged with overseeing the financial management of all departmental or agency programs and operations, as well as developing and maintaining integrated agency accounting and financial management systems (Section 902). In a general sense, they inherited a detailed auditing role that the comptroller general performed until it became controversial and infeasible during the New Deal (see Polenberg 1966, 132–133). The CFOs report directly to the department or agency heads. With some restrictions, the act guarantees their access to all agency documents, materials, and other records that are pertinent to their mission.

Additionally, the act relies on OMB to promote greater standardization of accounting procedures and financial statements. It provides for audits by inspectors general or external auditors. The comptroller general can review these audits or conduct independent ones at his[15] discretion or on the request of any congressional committee. The act contains a number of reporting requirements to OMB and Congress. In 1996 it was augmented by the Federal Financial Management Improvement Act, which requires annual audits to indicate whether covered departments and agencies are using the required standardized accounting procedures.

Research, Evaluation, Audit, and Investigation

Oversight by congressional committees does not preclude other means of monitoring federal agencies. Since the reorganization of 1946, Congress has improved its capacity for understanding, evaluating, and checking administration by reorienting the Legislative Reference Service and the GAO, as well as by institutionalizing the use of inspectors general.

The Congressional Research Service

The 1970 Legislative Reorganization Act transformed the Legislative Reference Service into the Congressional Research Service (CRS) (Section 203). The change was intended to provide Congress with its own think tank for public policy analysis and in-depth research. Today the CRS includes a staff of experts in American public administration, government, and law; economics; environment and natural resources policy; domestic social policy; foreign affairs and defense; and science policy. The CRS works both proactively and reactively. It develops and provides members of Congress and congressional staff with a variety of policy, legal, and other analyses. It also organizes seminars and responds to over a half-million requests for information annually (see Mosher 1984, 156; *U.S. Government Manual* 1995/1996, 57).

The General Accounting Office

The GAO was founded in 1921 as a congressional watchdog over federal agency spending. Prior to the 1970 Legislative Reorganization Act, it was primarily engaged in financial audits. Its mission had been broadened somewhat by the 1946 LRA, as noted previously. After the appointment of the legendary Elmer Staats in 1966, the GAO began to undertake a number of program evaluations (Mosher 1984, 143–146). In 1970 the directional shift was put on a statutory footing: the comptroller general was charged with reviewing and analyzing the results of government programs and conducting cost-benefit studies (Section 204). The Congressional Budget and Impoundment Control Act expanded this role further by requiring the comptroller general to assist committees "in developing a statement of legislative objectives and goals and methods for assessing and reporting actual program performance" as well as "in analyzing and assessing program reviews or evaluation studies prepared by and for any Federal agency" (Section 702[a]). It sought to institutionalize the change in focus from audits to evaluation by specifically authorizing the comptroller general to create an Office of Program Review and Evaluation within the GAO.

By 1981 the GAO had undergone a "profound" transformation in organizational culture and structure. The agency was professionalized and no longer characterized by the "green eyeshade" technical audits of vouchers, which had once been its staple (Walker 1986, 137). From the perspectives of 1946, the key point is that the GAO was drawn closer to Congress and its committees. Once largely tangential, it became central to legislative oversight (Mosher 1984, 151). Mosher describes the development of a lasting symbiotic relationship between Congress and the GAO in the 1970s:

> The expanding congressional assertiveness and concern about oversight were entirely congruent with GAO's own aspirations, especially as they were remolded by Staats. . . . For Congress, GAO had unique advantages as a source of information: It had direct and immediate access to the operations of the executive agencies both in Washington and the field, and from long years of study in the many different fields of federal work, it had background data, personal acquaintance, and long memories, both institutional and individual. In return, Congress could help GAO by applying its powers and prestige to agencies that were reluctant or slow to provide GAO with information. (1984, 155)

Writing in 1992, Charles Bowsher, who succeeded Staats as comptroller general, indicated that, if anything, the relationship between GAO and Congress had become even stronger. He claimed "considerable success" in working more closely with committees and noted that the proportion of GAO's work done at their specific request had increased from 40 to 80 percent over the past decade (Bowsher 1992, 6). By the GAO's count, about 75 percent of its recommendations are accepted by the agencies within four years (Bowsher 1992, 7).

Mosher (1984, 152) might have added that the GAO offers an expansive menu of services to congressional committees, which now include assigning staff to work with them, reviewing and drafting bills, supplying questions to be asked during hearings, providing testimony, and giving informal briefings on studies in progress. As he summed up the transformation of the GAO, it went from watchdog to *"bird dog:* it scents, points, searches, and retrieves its prey, which is useful information, and delivers it to the hunter (the Congress)" (1984, 162).

Inspectors General

No officials charged with finding administrative weaknesses go and live inside the agencies quite like the inspectors general (IGs). Placed in twelve departments and agencies by the Inspector General Act of 1978 and currently operating in sixty, the IGs have been characterized as "congressional 'moles' within their agencies" (Moore and Gates 1986, 10; Gore 1993, 31). The Office of the Inspector General is charged with conducting and supervising audits and investigations; promoting administrative efficiency, economy, and effectiveness; and preventing and detecting fraud and abuse (Section 2). More broadly, IGs keep Congress and the agency heads "fully and currently informed about problems and deficiencies relating to the administration of . . . programs and operations and the necessity for and progress of corrective action" (Section 2).

Under the 1978 act, each IG appoints one assistant for auditing and another for investigations. The IGs are directly subordinate to the agency heads or their deputies. They have full access to administrative records, reports, and so forth. They are also empowered to investigate employee complaints of violations of law or regulations, mismanagement, gross waste of funds, abuses of authority, or substantial and specific dangers to the public health and safety (Section 7).

The IGs are clearly creatures and agents of Congress. The Inspector General Act was a congressional initiative to create "a strong right arm" (see Light 1993, chap. 4). It enjoyed especially strong bipartisan support in the House, where it passed by 388 to 6 (Light 1993, 67). But it is also in the tradition of the "joint custody" of federal administration mentioned in Chapter 1 (see Rourke 1993).

The 1978 act provides for presidential appointment of the IGs, with Senate confirmation. Appointment is without regard to political affiliation. There is no fixed tenure and the president can fire IGs at will, with the proviso that Congress be informed of the reasons. IGs established by subsequent legislation are appointed and dismissed by the agency heads (see Light 1993, 26).

Presidents have been somewhat ambivalent toward the IGs. President Jimmy Carter initially opposed the 1978 act, but then signed and embraced it (Moore and Gates 1986, 31). Upon taking office in 1981, President Ronald Reagan fired all the IGs. However, he proceeded to rehire about half of them, and sought to replace the rest with "meaner junk-yard dogs," as his press secretary, James Brady, put it (Light 1993, 102; Moore and Gates 1986, 33).

In 1993 the NPR made "reorienting the Inspectors General" a key component of its overall reform effort (Gore 1993, 31). According to the NPR, the IG offices had some fifteen thousand federal employees doing the wrong job: "At virtually every agency he visited, the Vice President heard federal employees complain that the IGs' basic approach inhibits innovation and risk taking. Heavy-handed enforcement—with the IG watchfulness compelling employees to follow every rule, document every decision, and fill out every form—has had a negative effect in some agencies" (Gore 1993, 32). The NPR wants the IGs to devote more time to evaluating managerial control systems aimed at preventing waste, fraud, and abuse while simultaneously promoting effective and efficient service (Gore 1993, 32).

The IGs' own view of their appropriate role has also fluctuated over time. Paul Light (1993, chaps. 5 and 6) found that the IGs were more likely to identify Congress as their primary audience during the Carter administration, but were drawn more closely to the executive under Reagan. As one might expect, after this change occurred a substan-tially higher proportion of IGs identified congressional interference as a source of frustration (Light 1993, 127).

Joint custody violates the orthodox administrative principle of "unity of command" (Gulick 1937, 85), and it cannot make living in the agen-cies easy. But performing oversight for Congress is the IGs' core mission. Failure to do so responsively will inevitably attract the legislature's attention—perhaps much more so than the impenetrable IG reports (Light 1993, 226).

From Watchfulness to Supervision: Summing Up

Congress has done a great deal since 1946 to move from "continuous watchfulness" to a strong capacity for supervising the agencies. The standing committee mandate and resources for oversight have been ex-panded considerably. The formal mission was broadened in 1970, and many more staff have been added to assist with it. Committee members and staff do interact with agency personnel on a frequent, if not con-tinuous, basis. Their involvement in administrative matters, which was both a challenge and something of an issue in 1946, is now accepted as legitimate and routine. Congress's oversight has also been substantially enhanced by the transformation of the GAO and the placement of IGs and CFOs in the agencies. GPRA moves the congressional role in administration well beyond review and study. It calls for direct legislative participation in the core managerial processes of strategic planning and performance evaluation. The CRS provides Congress with a better analytic capability regarding all aspects of federal administration. The CBO does the same with respect to budgeting and fiscal matters. The legislative budget is imperfect, but no longer a dead letter. Congress also has new tools to check impoundments. All of these developments fit nicely within the broad effort Congress began in 1946 to redefine its position vis-à-vis federal administration.

Are There Constitutional Limits to Legislative Supervision of Federal Agencies?

Taken together, the APA and the Legislative Reorganization Act of 1946 constituted a fundamental shift in Congress's relationship to the agencies. Delegation of legislative authority would be accompanied by the statutory regulation of administrative procedures for its use as well as by continuous watchfulness of its substantive interpretation and implementation. The agencies would be treated as extensions of Congress for legislative functions and appropriately supervised by its standing committees. Both statutes served as platforms for additional legislation and practices that support their objectives. The resulting structures are elaborate and provide powerful controls on administrative activity.

Insofar as delegations are constitutional, administrative law in general does not raise separation-of-powers issues (though particular requirements or procedures sometimes may). But what about oversight by committees, their participation in the formulation of strategic plans, and Congress's relationship to specific administrators such as the IGs and CFOs? The purpose of these arrangements is to intrude on administrative practice—so much so in the case of IGs that the Department of Justice initially argued that "the continuous oversight of Executive agencies contemplated by the [IG] bill is not a proper legislative function but is rather a serious distortion of our constitutional system" (see Light 1993, 63). Are there constitutional barriers to Congress's ability to steer federal administration by means other than legislation?

At first the question may appear settled. In 1946 Congress rejected the advice of the public administrative orthodoxy and the President's Committee on Administrative Management by opting for a much greater role in regulating administrative processes and in overseeing agency decisions. It finessed Senator Donnell's charge that the tripartite structure of the federal government would be compromised, and has been developing the 1946 framework ever since. But there has always been some concern that Congress's post-1946 hands-on approach to federal administration is somehow constitutionally inappropriate.

There is a fairly straight line from Louis Brownlow's fear in 1947 that presidential power might be "usurped" by Congress, its houses, and/or its committees, to contemporary criticism of "micromanagement" (Brownlow 1949, 116; see Chapter 1). For instance, supporters of GPRA worry that "Congress must take care to respect the constitutional boundaries between it and the executive agencies." By this they mean that "the design and operation of the management systems to deliver services is primarily the responsibility of the executive branch. Congress should be careful in carrying out its oversight roles to avoid micromanagement. . . . The ability of Congress to pass legislation and to control appropriations should assure that advice of its members and committees will be taken seriously by executive branch agencies" (Hatry and Finger 1998, 30).[16]

Vice President Gore's NPR is also highly critical of "micromanagement," though mostly on policy rather than constitutional grounds:

Congressional appropriations often come with hundreds of strings attached. The Interior Department found that language in its 1992 House, Senate, and conference committee reports included some 2,150 directives, earmarks, instructions, and prohibitions. As the federal budget tightens, lawmakers request increasingly specific report language to protect activities in their districts. Indeed, 1993 was a record year for such requests. In one appropriations bill alone, senators required the U.S. Customs Service to add new employees to its Honolulu office, prohibited closing any small or rural post office or U.S. Forest Service offices, and forbade the U.S. Mint and the Bureau of Engraving and Printing from even studying the idea of contracting out guard duties. (Gore 1993, 13)

Gore's complaint leaves no doubt that Congress has inserted itself into much federal administration. But perhaps to the dismay of those who identify administration as an executive domain, such congressional controls are perfectly acceptable under contemporary constitutional law.

They do not even approach the current limits, the most pertinent of which were established by the Supreme Court in the 1980s.

In the well-known case of *Immigration and Naturalization Service v. Chadha* (1983), a comfortable majority[17] on the Supreme Court held that the legislative veto was unconstitutional. The device dates back to 1932 and had been used in almost two hundred statutes (*Chadha* 1983, 944–945). The version at issue allowed either house to overturn decisions by the attorney general suspending the deportation of aliens. However, the Court's opinion was broad enough to encompass a two-house veto as well.

In dissent, Justice Byron White argued that the legislative veto filled a key congressional need:

> Without the legislative veto, Congress is faced with a Hobson's choice: either to refrain from delegating the necessary authority, leaving itself with a hopeless task of writing laws with the requisite specificity to cover endless special circumstances across the entire policy landscape, or, in the alternative, to abdicate its lawmaking function to the Executive Branch and independent agencies. To choose the former leaves major national problems unresolved; to opt for the latter risks unaccountable policymaking by those not elected to fill that role. (*Chadha* 1983, 968)

However, the majority countered that "convenience and efficiency are not the primary objectives—or the hallmarks—of democratic government, and our inquiry is sharpened, rather than blunted by the fact that congressional veto provisions are appearing with increasing frequency" (*Chadha* 1983, 944).

Opting to enforce constitutional integrity, the Court held that the veto violated the requirement that Congress present all legislation to the president for potential veto. Additionally, the one-house veto was at odds with the Constitution's bicameralism. The majority concluded that "there is no support in the Constitution or decisions of this Court for the proposition that the cumbersomeness and delays often encountered in complying with explicit constitutional standards may be avoided, either by the Congress or by the President" (*Chadha* 1983, 959).

When it was decided, *Chadha* was viewed as a major constraint on Congress. However, according to Samuel Krislov (1994, 38), the legislative veto is "still dying after all these years" because Congress has largely circumvented or ignored the Court's holding. Certainly the dire consequences predicted by Justice White have not materialized. Congress retains plenty of leverage over agency actions, and has added to it with GPRA and SBREFA. But *Chadha* does stand for the principle that there are some lines Congress cannot cross, no matter how much government has changed since the founding or how convenient shortcuts might be.

Chadha was followed by another constitutional integrity case, *Bowsher v. Synar* (1986). The Court's 5–4 decision there is something of a tease for those who believe congressional "micromanagement" violates the separation of powers. Some of the Court's language suggests that the central premises of legislative oversight and GPRA might be unconstitutional, but broad statements to such effect are repeatedly followed by others that limit their applicability. Consequently, they pose no real threat to today's relationship between Congress and federal agencies.

Bowsher addressed a complex set of procedures in the Gramm-Rudman-Hollings Act authorizing the comptroller general to enforce deficit reduction targets by ordering budget cuts. The majority opinion, written by Chief Justice Warren Burger and joined by Justices William Brennan, Lewis Powell, William Rehnquist, and Sandra Day O'Connor, held that the scheme violated the separation of powers. Ironically, their logic was most succinctly explained in Justice White's dissent: "The Court's decision . . . is based on a syllogism: the Act vests the Comptroller with 'executive power'; such power may not be exercised by Congress or its agents; the Comptroller is an agent of Congress because he is removable by Congress [for cause, through joint resolution, rather than by impeachment and conviction only]; therefore the Act is invalid" (*Bowsher v. Synar* 1986, 765).[18] However, the majority's phrasing was far more complicated.

Opponents of "micromanagement" could be cheered by the majority's view that "the Constitution does not contemplate an active role for Congress in the supervision of officers charged with the execution of the laws it enacts" (*Bowsher v. Synar* 1986, 722). But they would be disappointed upon finding that "supervision" in this context means "subject to dismissal": "Congress cannot reserve for itself the power of removal of an officer charged with the execution of the laws except by impeachment. To permit the execution of the laws to be vested in an officer answerable only to Congress would, in practical terms, reserve in Congress control over the execution of the laws" (*Bowsher v. Synar* 1986, 726).

In another statement that would seriously limit Congress's role in federal administration, the majority asserted that "once Congress makes its choice in enacting legislation, its participation ends. Congress can thereafter control the execution of its enactment only indirectly—by passing new legislation" (*Bowsher v. Synar* 1986, 733–734). But here "control the execution" refers specifically to "placing the responsibility for execution . . . in the hands of an officer who is subject to removal only by itself, Congress." This is constitutionally prohibited because Congress, "in effect, has retained control over the execution of the Act, and has intruded into the executive function" (*Bowsher v. Synar* 1986, 734).

A concurring opinion by Justice John Paul Stevens, joined by Justice Thurgood Marshall, has much the same quality. Unlike the majority, Stevens considered ordering budget cuts to be a legislative function (*Bowsher v. Synar* 1986, 751–752). However, he found the act unconstitutional because "Congress may not exercise its fundamental power to formulate national policy by delegating that power to one of its two houses, to a legislative committee, or to an individual agent of the Congress such as the Speaker of the House of Representatives, the Sergeant at Arms of the Senate, or the Director of the Congressional Budget Office" (*Bowsher v. Synar* 1986, 737).

If Stevens's language seemed to pose a threat to the committees' authority to steer agencies on policy matters, then this possibility was dispelled in short order. By "power to formulate national policy," Stevens meant *legislating:* "Even though it is well settled that Congress may delegate legislative power to independent agencies or to the Executive, and thereby divest itself of a portion of its lawmaking power, when it elects to exercise such power itself, it may not authorize a lesser representative of the Legislative Branch to act on its behalf" (*Bowsher v. Synar* 1986, 757–758).

Worse yet for those seeking bright fault lines in the separation of powers, Stevens argued: "One reason that the exercise of legislative, executive, and judicial powers cannot be categorically distributed among three mutually exclusive branches of Government is that governmental power cannot always be readily characterized with only one of those three labels. On the contrary, as our cases demonstrate, a particular function, like a chameleon, will often take on the aspect of the office to which it is assigned" (*Bowsher v. Synar* 1986, 749). The system is anything but static: "Obligations to two branches are not . . . impermissible, and the presence of such dual obligations does not prevent the characterization of the official with the dual obligations as part of one branch" (*Bowsher v. Synar* 1986, 746). Executive agencies can have legislative functions, such as rulemaking; legislative employees, such as members of the Capitol Police force or the Librarian of Congress, can exercise executive ones.

Justice White's dissent picked up on the fluidity of the separation of powers as well, accusing the majority's view of being "distressingly formalistic" (*Bowsher v. Synar* 1986, 759). In his opinion, Congress's power to remove the comptroller general was statutorily constrained and largely hypothetical. Consequently, "Realistic consideration of the nature of the Comptroller General's relation to Congress thus reveals that the threat to separation of powers conjured up by the majority is wholly chimerical" (*Bowsher v. Synar* 1986, 774). Justice Harry Blackmun, who also dissented, agreed with White's analysis of the removal issue. For justiciability reasons he would have refused to consider the constitutional issues until such time—if ever—that Congress actually dismissed the controller general.

Bowsher was followed by *Morrison v. Olson* (1988). As discussed in Chapter 2, *Morrison*'s view of the separation of powers is so fluid that it led a dissenting Justice Antonin Scalia to proclaim incredulously, "There are now no lines" (*Morrison v. Olson* 1988, 726). Whether the lines might have been clearer had Congress not repositioned itself vis-à-vis federal administration in 1946 is a moot point. The indisputable fact is that while legislative-centered public administration may conflict with orthodox and contemporary public managerial values, it is wholly constitutional. Administrative reformers who ignore or resist this legal reality run considerable risk of failure (see Chapter 5).

Recapitulation

In 1946, Congress reconceptualized federal agencies as legislative extensions. Accepting that they would continue to exercise delegated legislative authority, Congress adjusted its constitutional role to place greater emphasis on regulating administrative procedures and monitoring agency behavior. Over the next half-century, Congress considerably reinforced its attention to both administrative law and oversight. The APA has been augmented by several statutes; ultimately, SBREFA brings substantive control of rulemaking full circle back to Congress. It is likewise with the 1946 LRA's goal of "continuous watchfulness." Congress took on a stronger mandate in 1970. It increased its oversight activity. It gained professional staff, researchers in the CRS, evaluators in the GAO, agents in the form of CFOs and IGs, and much greater budget capacity. GPRA also brings some closure: by participating in the development of strategic plans, congressional committees, subcommittees, and work teams can define the legislative intent of broad delegations in a way that binds agency management. "Continuous watchfulness" has been expanded into supervision. The goals of 1946 for establishing a greater congressional role in federal administration have been surpassed.

The unfolding of 1946 also yields a legislative-centered public administration. Because such public administration focuses on agencies' legislative functions, it emphasizes the need for administrative operations to embrace core legislative values: representativeness, openness, participation, responsiveness, and public accountability. It views legislative supervision of agencies as a requirement for legitimizing administrative authority. It does not consider the constitutional separation of powers to be a barrier to direct legislative participation in managerial activities such as strategic planning and performance evaluation. The standard managerial value set—efficiency, economy, and internal organizational effectiveness—tends to take on secondary importance when clear conflicts arise.

Contemporary legislative-centered public administration joins today's public management in seeking results. However, it views procedural and reporting requirements as well as legislative intervention in agency decision making as producing, rather than encumbering, proper results. Legislative steering is regarded as wholly appropriate to ensure the faithful use of delegated power. Ultimately, results must match legislative intent, which may be defined and redefined not only through legislation but by other forms of legislative input as well. Administrative performance is important, but subordination to legislative values and controls is essential. Consequently, supervision can be forward-looking. It can mandate managerial systems, such as those for accounting, as well as other administrative procedures. If committees or subcommittees and their staff become the main point of legislative contact with agencies, it is because they are the best means available.

Legislative-centered public administration, like its executive-centered counterpart, can divert administrative decision making from universalistic criteria and lead to excessive controls. This matter is considered in the concluding chapter. However, it also harmonizes modern public administration with American democratic-constitutionalism. Just as it would be too facile to dismiss the APA as "red tape," it is overly simplistic to condemn legislative participation in administration as "micromanagement."

There was one additional key component of the congressional repositioning of 1946: attention to the legislators' home districts. Congress divested some particularly unproductive constituency- and district-oriented functions to the agencies. It improved its ability to help constituents resolve problems involving federal administration. It also gained greater control over federal public works. These reforms strengthened the members' prospects for continuing incumbency and contributed to the long-term viability of Congress's 1946 response to the rise of the administrative state.

4 | Constituency Time
Casework, Public Works, and Incumbency

The Congress of today is performing a volume of work which it was never designed to perform but which it cannot avoid.
—Senate Minority Leader Wallace White, Jr. (R–ME)
(U.S. Congress 1946c, 6532)

A Crushing Workload

In addition to increasing the federal government's scope and administrative apparatus, the New Deal and World War II dramatically expanded the scale of two historic congressional functions: constituency service and the authorization of public works. Both were tremendously time-consuming. The members of Congress considered them to be central legislative responsibilities and vital to their continued incumbency. However, by 1946 they were being performed at significant opportunity costs to the legislature as an institution. They seriously diminished the time available for considering legislation, engaging in oversight, performing other core functions, and even visiting the home districts. Dealing more efficiently with casework and gaining better control over public works were major components of Congress's response to the federal administrative state in 1946. The members' ability to do so in a way that promoted their own incumbency contributed to the staying power of the institutional redefinition embodied in the Administrative Procedure Act (APA) and the Legislative Reorganization Act (LRA). Treating the agencies as legislative extensions and supervising them posed no threat to reelection.

In 1946, coping with constituency and district service[1] was considered an acute problem, as Representative A. S. Mike Monroney (D–OK) explained:

Congress is badly jammed up with an extraneous work load that cuts the time for legislative action down to about 20 per cent of the work day. Most members who testified before our hearings [on the 1946 Legislative Reorganization Act] estimated that fully 80 per cent of their time was consumed with purely nonlegislative activities. District problems, complaints, letters from constituents, visits, and conferences with groups from the home state or groups interested in legislation—all cut down on the time that members ought to devote to the study and understanding of legislation. (Monroney et al. 1949, 29–30)

Similarly, Senator Robert M. La Follette, Jr. (Progressive-WI) estimated that "from one-half to three-fourths of the time of the average member nowadays is consumed with running errands and knocking on departmental doors on behalf of constituents" (La Follette 1946, 46).

The workload posed a serious dilemma. Without some adjustment, the central objectives of the 1946 reforms would fail. Congress would be unable to legislate, delegate, and exercise continuous watchfulness effectively. Consequently, it would fail to strengthen its institutional position in the administrative state. If Congress spent an inordinate amount of time on constituency and district service, its roles in initiating, framing, and steering the implementation of public policy would necessarily be limited. However, in the members' view, neglect of casework and public works would invite electoral defeat.

In 1946 Congress sought to solve its workload problem by making constituency and district service more efficient and effective. Because both functions typically involve federal agencies, congressional strategies for improving them necessarily bore on federal administration. In practice, these strategies reinforced other elements of the 1946 legislation discussed in the previous chapters. Congress transferred some particularly unproductive forms of constituency service and infrastructure decision making to the agencies. It began to rely more heavily on personal staff to perform the growing body of remaining casework and, in effect, to institutionalize routine intervention in administration on behalf of constituents having problems with federal agencies. Congress also attempted to bring greater rationality, effectiveness, and legislative control to the allocation of public works spending, much of which was by the agencies.

As with Congress's efforts to use the agencies as extensions for the performance of legislative functions and to exercise more effective oversight, the main impetus behind the measures discussed in this chapter was to strengthen the legislature in an institutional sense. However, they were also calculated to serve the members' ability to represent their constituents and districts in a more direct fashion. Congress collectively sought to match its organization and processes to the changed scope of that part of its mission involving constituency and district service. It reached the view that its institutional arrangements should facilitate legislative intervention in federal administration for casework and district service. This added another element to legislative-centered public administration. The members' representational roles encompass direct intercession in administrative decisions affecting individual constituents and specific district interests.

Today such intervention is commonplace, but there was no place for it in the "apolitical," executive-centered public administrative orthodoxy of the 1930s and 1940s. The assertion of particular constituent and district interests poses a clear danger to public administrative decision making based on general principles developed to promote the public interest (Gellhorn 1966, 77–82). At a time when public administration rested much of its claim to legitimacy on its scientific quality, the clash was particularly severe.

This chapter completes the story of how and why Congress responded to the administrative state in 1946. It begins with a fundamental—the members' abiding interest in incumbency (see Fiorina 1989, 101–110). It then explains Congress's effort in 1946 to adjust its relationship to the agencies in order to enable the members to provide better service to their constituents and to gain greater leverage in bringing public works projects to their home districts. The chapter concludes with a consideration of how these reforms, along with others adopted in 1946, contributed to incumbency and, thereby, to the remarkable durability of Congress's institutional redefinition of 1946.

Constituency and Incumbency

The Seventy-ninth Congress was not particularly strong in terms of incumbency. The longest period of service belonged to Congressman Adolph Sabath (D-IL), whose first term began in 1907. Another eleven members of the House had been elected prior to 1920. The Senate's leader in seniority was Kenneth McKellar (D-TN), first elected in 1916. Only one other senator, Arthur Capper (R-KS), had been elected prior to 1920. At the other end of the scale, about half of the senators were in their first terms and just over one-third of the representatives were in their first or second (see U.S. Congress 1946b, 162–176). However, the overwhelming majority of members wanted to retain their jobs: 398 representatives and 30 senators sought reelection in November 1946

(Ornstein, Mann, and Malbin 1996, 60–61). By this measure, the interest in incumbency was obviously quite strong.

To some extent, the idea of a "career" Congress was incorporated into Section 602 of the 1946 LRA. It set up a congressional retirement system. Pensions were established for those who would serve at least six years, reach the age of sixty-two, and agree to contribute a share of their salaries to the retirement fund. The provision was controversial, but it survived by votes of 166 to 63 in the House and 43 to 22 in the Senate (U.S. Congress 1946c, 10104, 6575).

Proponents viewed the retirement system as strengthening Congress's attractiveness as an organization in which to spend a career. Representative Jennings Randolph (D-WV) explained that, from a career standpoint, being a member of Congress "has a peculiarly hazardous nature" because it "does not lead to something else. There is no other Congress that you can get a job in for example. There is no way you can be promoted to chairman of the board of directors" (U.S. Congress 1946c, 10103).

La Follette argued that a retirement system would strengthen Congress by attracting talented candidates and providing those who reached the "upper-age brackets" with the feeling "that they have the opportunity to retire after years of faithful service." He suggested that it would be difficult to achieve the main goals of the LRA for committee specialization and effective oversight without substantial incumbency (U.S. Congress 1946c, 6570).

By contrast, opponents contended that congressional pensions were wholly indefensible in view of the government's long string of budget deficits and huge accumulated debt (U.S. Congress 1946c, 10100–10104). They also thought a retirement system would bureaucratize Congress (U.S. Congress 1946c, 10087, 10100). However, no opposition was expressed to the idea of long service in Congress per se.

Regardless of their positions on the retirement scheme, the members strongly agreed that casework and district service were keys to incumbency. The belief that reelection required constant attention to the home district ran deep in 1946. For instance, Representative Estes Kefauver (D-TN) recalled his experience as a freshman paying a courtesy visit to the Speaker, Will Bankhead (D-AL). Kefauver asked, "What is the secret of long tenure? How do members get reelected term after term without substantial opposition?" Bankhead unhesitatingly replied, "It is a simple one. Give close and prompt attention to your mail" (Kefauver and Levin 1947, 170–171).

Representative Monroney, a chief sponsor of the 1946 LRA, put it the other way around. Failure to provide constituency and district service was a prescription for electoral defeat: "Former Representative Ramspeck suggested that the Congress be divided into halves, with one half of each state delegation serving as errand boys and Washington contact-men, and the other half serving as real legislators and devoting their time exclusively to this end. This proposal met with no favor from members, however, for all realized that the service-giving branch would find reelection easy, while the voting member, without the contacts, would find election almost impossible" (Monroney et al. 1949, 30).

Kefauver shared the sentiment: "There's nothing . . . in any rules of the Senate or House which obligates a member to help someone's Aunt Minnie get a job with the Veterans Administration, or to arrange a sightseeing trip when Grandmother visits Washington. But in nine cases out of ten, a senator or representative must do these things if he is to stay in office" (Kefauver and Levin 1947, 188). Apparently the term "casework" had not yet come into the congressional lexicon. Kefauver referred to what is now known as casework as acting as a "*personal* representative" or "W.R."—Washington Representative—as opposed to an "M.C."— Member of Congress (Kefauver and Levin 1947, 10, 186).

"Pork barrel," of course, was considered a tried-and-true approach to reelection. Federal spending for public works is a venerable legislative tradition that reaches back at least as far as the rivers and harbors acts of 1824 (Fitzgerald and Lipson 1984, viii). Though the scope was now much greater, there was nothing new about bringing "pork" to the home district as a means of promoting incumbency. Projects could be defended as improvements, necessary infrastructure, or developmental. During the New Deal they were candidly considered a means of creating employment and an alternative to the "dole" (U.S. Congress 1945a, 9117).

The new development was a subtle change in the orientation of public works policy. In the late 1930s and early 1940s, the federal government subscribed to economist John Maynard Keynes's theory that government could mitigate the undesirable effects of the normal business cycle by engaging in counter-cyclical fiscal policy (see Keynes 1936; Bailey 1950, chap. 1). Deficit spending could reduce unemployment; surpluses would combat inflation.

For members of Congress in 1946, the chief issue posed by Keynesian economics was implementation. The New Deal had shifted some of the impetus for public works from the legislature to the executive. Unless Congress took action, the trend was almost certain to accelerate as public works spending became part of national economic policy making, which was dominated by the presidency. This would reduce the members' ability to use public works as an electoral resource, as well as further weaken Congress's institutional position in the administrative state.

According to Kefauver and Levin (1947, 7–11), the need to gain a better grip on public works was substantial. They listed public works as one of three core legislative functions, the other two being legislation and constituency service. However, obtaining "a fair share of benefits" for the home districts had become daunting. The members had to "assemble influential delegations 'from back home' and marshal imposing charts and statistics to impress some executive department with the claim of their particular constituency" (Kefauver and Levin 1947, 9–10). The Employment Act of 1946, which is discussed later in this chapter, was viewed almost universally in Congress as a means of redressing the balance and putting public works under firm legislative control.

By the 1970s, political scientists had amassed considerable evidence that constituency and district service were strongly related to congressional incumbency (Fiorina 1977, 1989). The strategies for incumbency developed in 1946 seem to have worked rather well (see the discussion below). However, their payoff was not immediate. The election of 1946 ushered in the famous Eightieth Congress. The Republicans took control of both chambers with a net gain of fifty-six seats in the House and thirteen in the Senate (Vogler 1988, 80). The partisan change has been attributed to voter concern with the economy, particularly inflation and disruption associated with the military demobilization (Vogler 1988, 79–80). The election certainly could not be considered a referendum of any sort on Congress's effort to reposition itself vis-à-vis federal administration. The APA, the LRA, and the Employment Act were largely bipartisan measures, and with the exception of the Employment Act, it is unlikely that their main features figured significantly, if at all, in the voters' choices.[2] Moreover, the electorate returned Democratic majorities in 1948, partly as a result of President Harry S. Truman's attack on the "do-nothing" Republican Congress in his surprisingly successful presidential campaign (Shannon 1963, 515; Truman 1956, 2:206–209, 222; Vogler 1988, 80).

By subsequent standards, incumbents fared poorly in the 1946 and 1948 congressional elections. The voters returned 75.4 percent of the House membership in 1946 and 72.9 percent in 1948. Figures this low would not be seen again until 1992. In the Senate, 56.7 percent of those seeking reelection in 1946 were successful, as were 60 percent in 1948.

Comparable losses for incumbent senators occurred only in 1978 and 1980. Since 1950, incumbents have typically held more than 80 percent of the seats in the House. Senate incumbency has varied to a greater extent, with the success among those seeking reelection ranging from 55.2 percent in 1980 to 96.9 percent in 1990 (Ornstein, Mann, and Malbin 1996, 60–61).[3]

In 1946 incumbency was a strong motive for improving constituency and district service. But even absent an interest in being reelected, many members would have provided such representation. As Kefauver and Levin pointed out, casework and public works were central legislative functions. The key question was how to improve them. Congress's collective answer is explained in the remainder of this chapter.

Loadshedding: Torts and Bridges

As discussed in Chapter 1, by 1946 many members of Congress thought that the legislature had failed to keep pace with the vast changes in the scope and structure of the federal government. Evidence from the floor debates on the Legislative Reorganization Act indicates that, as a whole, Congress felt truly inundated—even oppressed—by the increased workload it faced.[4] Senator Styles Bridges (R-NH) claimed that at least ten senators had actually died from overwork, and Senator Albert Hawkes (R-NJ) agreed that "the load is too heavy for any normal man in the world to carry" (U.S. Congress 1946c, 6559, 6561). From an organizational perspective, loadshedding was clearly in order.

It was accomplished by Titles IV and V of the 1946 Legislative Reorganization Act. Title IV is better known as the Federal Tort Claims Act (FTCA), and Title V as the General Bridge Act.[5] Both transfer traditional, but particularly inefficient, constituency and district service functions to the agencies as part of an overall effort to preserve the members' time for more productive legislative activity.

The Federal Tort Claims Act

The FTCA allows individuals to sue the federal government in the district courts for money claims arising out of "damage to or loss of property or on account of personal injury or death caused by the negligent or wrongful act or omission of any employee of the Government while acting within the scope of his office or employment, under circumstances where the United States, if a private person, would be liable to the claimant" (Section 410). It authorized claims of $1,000 or less to be settled by the agencies at their discretion.

In terms of political theory, the FTCA was a significant measure because it waived a substantial amount of the United States' traditional sovereign immunity for common-law torts. However, it also retained important limits. The FTCA prohibits punitive damages and jury trials. It contains a number of agency exemptions and general exceptions. The government cannot be held liable for the performance or nonperformance of discretionary functions or for the behavior of employees who have exercised due care pursuant to a statute or regulation, even if it is invalid. (Federal governmental liability for constitutional torts is based on constitutional interpretation rather than the FTCA.)[6]

Originally, the act also barred claims "arising out of assault, battery, false imprisonment, false arrest, malicious prosecution, abuse of process, libel, slander, misrepresentation, deceit, or interference with contract rights" (Section 421[h]). However, this provision was changed in 1974 to allow recovery for torts intentionally committed by federal law enforcement officers.[7]

The logic behind the FTCA was compelling. The "only justification" for sovereign immunity from the torts at issue seemed to have been "historical" (U.S. House of Representatives 1945, 3). Compensation had been by private bills in Congress, if at all. This was a particularly inefficient and ineffective form of constituency service, one that La Follette referred to as a "time-consuming chore" (U.S. Congress 1946c, 6370). Drafting, sponsoring, and considering such bills was onerous, while success was elusive. From 1927 to 1945, the number of private bills introduced for tort compensation apparently ranged from 1,644 to over 2,300 per Congress (U.S. House of Representatives 1945, 2).[8] Overall, about 20 percent of all private claims bills were passed, with success ranging from about 11 to 33 percent in any given Congress (U.S. House of Representatives 1945, 2). Reported payouts per Congress were from $562,000 (Seventieth Congress) to $1,355,767 (Seventy-eighth Congress) (U.S. House of Representatives 1945, 2).

Aside from the obvious workload problem, the private bills may have caused as much disaffection as support among constituents. An individual's disappointment at not receiving compensation could well outweigh his or her gratitude for having the bill introduced in the first place. Moreover, the number of requests for such bills was sure to rise. As the House Judiciary Committee observed, "With the expansion of governmental activities in recent years, it becomes especially important to grant to private individuals the right to sue the Government in respect to such torts as negligence in the operation of vehicles" (U.S. House of Representatives 1945, 3).

There was limited opposition to the FTCA. A few members of Congress were opposed to the waiver of sovereign immunity (U.S. Congress 1946c, 6373, 10072). Fairness was also a concern. Senator Walter George (D-GA) thought that a claimant seeking $1,000 would need a "bomb-proof claim" to receive fair treatment from an agency (U.S. Congress 1946c, 6373). He feared that the courts would be flooded with suits and also contended that since the legislature is responsible for tax policy, it ought to control expenditures as well. Congressman Errett Scrivner (R-KS) was opposed to the absence of a limit to the compensation that could be awarded by the district courts (U.S. Congress 1946c, 10092). The latter point was countered with the argument that a fixed limit would invite suits for that amount (U.S. Congress 1946c, 10093). (Subsequently, a $10,000 limit was set, but then eventually abandoned.)

The General Bridge Act

The General Bridge Act was pragmatic loadshedding, pure and simple. It overrode existing law requiring congressional approval of the construction of *every* bridge over a navigable stream in the United States. Blanket legislative approval was given to whatever the chief of engineers and the secretary of war might conclude with regard to such bridges (Section 502).

La Follette explained that "cranking up the legislative machinery in order to grant to a railroad or corporation the right to build a bridge across a navigable stream" was an unnecessary "time-consuming and costly procedure" (U.S. Congress 1946c, 6370). An apparently exasperated Congressman Everett Dirksen (R-IL) elaborated: "You could introduce a thousand bills, you could fill this Chamber with bills and never get a bridge until after the War Department had explored every engineering aspect of it. It has got to go there anyway, it has to have the approval of the War Department engineers, so why have the Consent Calendar of this House cluttered from one year's end to the other with a hundred bridge bills when the work has to be done by the War Department engineers?" (U.S. Congress 1946c, 10095).

Two members of the House Committee on Interstate and Foreign Commerce, which had jurisdiction over the bridges concerned, spoke against the measure. Representative Clarence Lea (D-CA), the committee chairman, was reluctant to yield whatever leverage over the War Department Congress still retained. He reminded his colleagues that "there are two distinct lines of work of the members of the House. One is as to their legislative duties and the other is a very important part of a Congressman's work, and that is contact with the departments of Government" (U.S. Congress 1946c, 10094). Lea thought it would be "a great advantage" to be able to apply to the committee when seeking approval for bridges in their districts. Representative Virgil Chapman (D-KY) unabashedly appealed to the legislators' interest in incumbency: "Scores of Members have bridges in their respective districts that are pointed out by their constituents as monuments to the public service of the Congressman who introduced the bills that authorized their construction" (U.S. Congress 1946c, 10094).

However, like the private bills for torts, legislating approval of bridges was apparently considered an unnecessary "nuisance" by most members (U.S. Congress 1946c, 10095). If one wanted to maximize constituency or district service, there were much better ways of doing so.

Additional Measures and Significance

In passing, another loadshedding measure should be mentioned. Section 207 of the 1946 LRA gave the heads of the War, Navy, and Treasury Departments authority to correct military records in order to remove errors or injustices.

The loadshedding in these areas was comprehensive and complete. The LRA provided that "No private bill or resolution (including so-called omnibus claims or pension bills), and no amendment to any bill or resolution" dealing with a matter covered by the FTCA, the General Bridge Act, or the section on military records "shall be received or considered in either the Senate or the House of Representatives" (Section 131). Moreover, only the FTCA contains significant agency reporting requirements (Section 404).

Compared to the APA and other sections of the 1946 LRA, these loadshedding measures were rather limited steps in the development of legislative-centered public administration. Their main significance was Congress's endorsement of the principle that functions it had traditionally performed, but no longer wanted to, could be accomplished more effectively by the agencies through administrative means. Legislative-centered public administration treats some governmental functions as interchangeable in the sense that they can be handled by either legislators or administrators. Legislation is only one means of compensating torts or approving the construction of bridges. If the same functions can be performed by the agencies more efficiently or effectively, with lower opportunity costs and no damage to legislative values, then transferring them may be a sound organizational decision.

Once one rejects complete compartmentalization of functions and accepts some degree of interchangeability, it is reasonable to believe that Congress can strengthen itself by relying on the agencies to do part of its work. The relationship between the power of Congress and the executive branch is not necessarily zero sum. Representative Chapman missed the point with his charge that the General Bridge Act was a "supine surrender of legislative prerogatives" and a "shameless abdication of legislative responsibility" (U.S. Congress 1946c, 10095). The overwhelming majority of members saw the act as a means of increasing Congress's power by enhancing its capacity to deal effectively with its core constitutional responsibilities.

Legislative loadshedding to the agencies provides another dimension to the question raised in Chapter 1, "Whose bureaucracy is this, anyway?" Clearly, it is partly the legislature's. Loadshedding is a special form of delegation because it is planned, proactive, and essentially voluntary. Unlike much delegation of legislative authority, it does not evolve ineluctably or perhaps unavoidably over time as Congress finds itself unable or unwilling to write precise standards for implementation into legislation. In today's organizational terminology, loadshedding is deliberate congressional "outsourcing" to the agencies. Here again, it is more accurate to view the agencies as functional extensions of Congress than as constitutionally separated from it.

The theory behind congressional loadshedding in 1946 was clear enough, but what about the practice? The main purpose of these provisions was to save Congress's time so that it could provide more effective representation, including constituency and district service. The Joint Committee on the Organization of Congress's *Report* on the 1946 Legislative Reorganization Act includes a section on "Saving Congressional Time" that notes the desirability of having a regular annual recess to "insure the return of Members to their constituents for that refreshment of contact and exchange of opinion and experience so essential to responsive representative government" (U.S. Congress 1946c, 10048). La Follette emphasized that the members needed to "see at first hand how the governmental machine which they have helped to create is operating in their States and districts" (U.S. Congress 1946c, 6465).

The efficacy of the loadshedding is difficult to judge. It is uncertain whether much time was saved, and if so, impossible to determine whether it was well invested in other legislative activities. Almost 10,800 bills were introduced in the Eightieth Congress, about the same number as in the Seventy-seventh. Eventually, in the mid- to late-1960s, the number topped out at over 26,000. The number of private bills enacted dipped from 593 and 549 in the Seventy-seventh and Seventy-eighth Congresses, respectively, to 458 in the Eightieth. But the number then jumped to over 1,000 for each of the next three Congresses and did not decline to below 500 until the late 1950s.[9] Nowadays, it is reasonable to expect some 10,000 bills to be introduced per Congress. However, since 1981 the number of private bills enacted per session has ranged only from 8 to 56 (Ornstein, Mann, and Malbin 1996, 158, 160, 165).

In 1946 the members may well have had higher expectations from loadshedding than appear to have been realized. In any case, they clearly recognized that time was only part of the answer to their workload problem. Congress also needed to strengthen its capacity for constituency and district service directly.

Staffing Up for Casework

It is difficult to overstate Congress's preoccupation with casework in 1946. Constituency service was a traditional function, and a well-accepted legislative role, but it had a "Frankenstein" element: the new scope had transformed it into something voracious, increasingly burdensome, and almost menacing.

Perhaps Senate Minority Leader Wallace White (R-ME) was best situated to assess the change. Forty-five years earlier he had served as a secretary to his grandfather, who was also a member of Congress. White noted that if his grandfather "received as many as 15 letters in the morning's mail he thought he was being oppressed by the people of his State." White's grandfather never kept copies of letters sent or received, a fact which his grandson said "illustrates the leisurely pace of our legislative machinery of 45 years ago" (U.S. Congress 1946c, 6531). He went on to say, perhaps tongue in cheek, that "No Senator or Representative would suggest that he does not wish to hear from his constituents, or go to this department and that department and spend a half a day in trying to straighten out some matter for a constituent. We all express eagerness and pleasure in undertaking such tasks" (U.S. Congress 1946c, 6532). There was no subtlety in Senator Alben Barkley's

(D-KY) response: "Much of what we must do is drudgery" (U.S. Congress 1946c, 6537).

Pleasure or drudge, virtually everyone in Congress agreed that casework had to be done. Senator John McClellan (D-AR) asked, "To whom else can our constituents go? . . . To whom else can they appeal? . . . I assume there is no other way to proceed, in many cases" (U.S. Congress 1946c, 6549). By authorizing more committee staff to help with lawmaking (as discussed in the previous chapter), the 1946 LRA opened up more time for the members' personal staffs to engage in constituency service and other functions. It was foreseeable that the number of personal staff and their capacity for casework would grow. Eventually, the personal staffs would be better organized, more or less in keeping with a proposal made in connection with the act.

The original legislative reorganization bill provided for each senator and representative to employ an administrative assistant "for nonlegislative duties." The need for such a staff member was explained by Congressman Walter Judd (R-MN):

To me this is the single, most valuable part of the bill, from the standpoint of the Congressman's work. If the purpose of this bill is, as has been said, to save our time and to increase our efficiency, no single thing can do more toward that end than to enable us to get a capable high-grade individual who can do far more than clerical work. He can exercise initiative, prepare material for our use, and take responsibility, especially in handling matters with the executive departments, thereby freeing us for our primary responsibilities, namely, to study national problems and devise and enact wise legislation to deal with them. (U.S. Congress 1946c, 10084)

With specific reference to casework, La Follette noted that "a large part of that responsibility could be passed on to the administrative assistant, at least in the initial stages of the efforts of constituents . . . to have their problems properly presented to officials of sufficient power in the agencies . . . to deal with them." He emphasized that the intent was to enable constituents to "get more service," not to "shove this load off onto someone else, and to disregard our responsibility" (U.S. Congress 1946c, 6369).

The Senate supported the provision for administrative assistants, but it was defeated in the House (see U.S. Congress 1946c, 10084–10085; La Follette 1946, 46; Kefauver and Levin 1947, 186). The House leadership was convinced that it would be financially imprudent to "vote ourselves an administrative assistant at this time." They believed that although the volume of work facing each of the ninety-six senators might justify such a position in that chamber, the need for administrative assistants in the House was uneven and the provision would be wasteful in some cases. The assistants were voted down 32 in favor to 162 opposed (U.S. Congress 1946c, 10085).

Their demise was decidedly temporary. Administrative assistants were authorized for the Senate offices by the First Supplemental Appropriation Act of 1947 (Kofmehl 1977, 167). In the following year, ninety-three senators' offices employed administrative assistants (Fox and Hammond 1977, 22). Although the titles may vary, the basic position has remained ever since.

The use of administrative assistants or equivalent positions developed more slowly in the House. Representatives hired personal staff within a framework of caps on salary, number, and top pay. However, by 1977 the House had adopted the essence of the 1946 proposal (Kofmehl 1977, 180).

With administrative assistants in place in the Senate and more personal staff all around, Congress quickly realized its objective of relying on them more heavily for casework. Writing with reference to the Eightieth through the Eighty-third Congresses (1947–1953), Kofmehl (1977, 173) concluded that the personal staff "relieved their Senators from eighty-five per cent of the work on departmental business." Subsequent studies in 1965–1966 and 1975–1976 confirmed that the staff remained deeply involved in casework (Vogler 1988, 225). Available research makes precision impossible, but on average during the mid-1960s to the mid-1970s the personal staffs were apparently spending at least 25 percent of their time on constituency service, and perhaps as much as 66 percent (Vogler 1988, 225; Fiorina 1977, 59). On average, the elected members reported spending 28 percent of their workweek on it (Fiorina 1977, 59).

Both the size of the personal staffs and the volume of casework have grown over time. In 1947 there were 1,440 personal staff in the House and 590 in the Senate (Davidson and Oleszek 1985, 241).[10] Twenty years later, the figures stood at 4,055 and 1,749, respectively. By the early 1990s, the combined total would reach almost 12,000 (Ornstein, Mann, and Malbin 1996, 131, 133).

Much of the increase in staff was driven by constituency service. The demand for casework grew from 5.6 percent of the voters in 1958 to

17.2 percent in 1978 (Fiorina 1989, 87). Causality has worked in both directions. Over the years since 1946, constituents grew accustomed to contacting their representatives and senators with problems and requests; the members have also sought to generate casework by advertising their desire and ability to provide service (Ornstein, Mann, and Malbin 1996, 127; Fiorina 1977, 49). As the amount of casework increased, the proportion of personal staff stationed in the home districts expanded, reaching about 47 percent in 1994 (Ornstein, Mann, and Malbin 1996, 127, 135). In 1984 some congressional offices received 5,000 to 10,000 requests for casework, numbers double those of a decade earlier (Vogler 1988, 219).

The extent to which casework contributes to incumbency will be considered later in the chapter. There is no doubt that its chief purpose is often to get a member reelected, not to repair either an alleged injustice to an individual constituent or a systemic administrative failure. Nevertheless, casework also affects the relationship between the members and federal administration.

Casework is an important feature of legislative-centered public administration. First, it places legislators in the role of protecting the public from specific instances of inappropriate administration. Other than "representative" in the sense of advocate, there is no agreed-upon term for this role. It lacks the organizational structure and institutionalized processes of a classic ombudsman (see Gellhorn 1966, 9–10). It differs significantly from the intervention of a "patron" or "boss" in machine politics because it does not require a significant level of personal connection or obligation on the part of the individual seeking assistance. Nor is there an expectation that outcomes may be corrupt (Heidenheimer 1989). It is not supervision or oversight as those terms are normally used. Nevertheless, it is clearly a major congressional activity. The electorate and the elected share a mutual expectation that casework will be performed.

The legislator as protector has become a significant part of the overall U.S. administrative culture. One need not accept a perceived injustice at the hands of administrators, go to court to fight it, or wait one's turn for the agency to get around to reviewing its action. People who might never think of cutting in line in other contexts may have no problem asking their legislator to jump the queue for them, go in, and straighten things out. Administrators are expected to answer to legislators promptly when they are charged with failing a member of the public in some way (see Gellhorn 1966, 77–78). Given the inevitability of substantial numbers of real and imagined administrative mistakes in modern government, acting as protector makes legislators direct participants in the relationship between the citizen and public agencies (Gellhorn 1966, 66–73). If legislators have a responsibility to intervene on behalf of their constituents, then they should also have the staff and other resources to do so.

Second, a closely related key fact is that *casework is treated as legitimate by everyone involved: the public, the legislators, and the agencies.* In 1946 Congress began to improve its capacity for casework in response to the public's demand for help in dealing with federal administration. The agencies accepted casework inquiries, if somewhat begrudgingly.[11] By the mid-1960s, if not earlier, "congressionals" routinely received priority attention in federal administration (Gellhorn 1966, 77–78). Their processing is institutionalized: obviously insincere, picayune, and meritless inquiries are answered along with the more significant ones (Gellhorn 1966, 69–70; Dodd and Schott 1979, 269–270). When warranted by law or the appropriate use of discretion, the agency may make an adjustment. Walter Gellhorn (1966, 79), an administrative law scholar, estimated that individuals receive a more favorable outcome in about 10 percent of the cases—a staggering number in view of the total volume. In some instances, "agencies become sensitized to problems occurring at the middle and lower levels of the bureaucracy . . . and even search for patterns behind the complaints" (Dodd and Schott 1979, 269).

Orthodox, executive-centered American public administrative thought does not incorporate such a legislative role, or anything approaching it. According to the orthodoxy, administrative agencies are repositories of substantive and managerial expertise, which they employ in pursuit of the public interest. They develop cost-effective, standardized techniques for prioritizing and processing inquiries and complaints. The treatment of individual cases should be based on universalistic criteria, not on the particularism of who may be calling attention to the complainant's problem (Thompson 1961, 172–173; Hummel 1977, 24–25). If legislative intervention is allowed to distort administrative processes, public administration will forfeit some of its claim to legitimacy based on politically neutral scientific expertise. Consequently, an aggrieved party should be required to exhaust his or her potential remedies within the administrative framework before seeking redress from the outside. Appeals beyond the administrative hierarchy, if necessary, should go to adjudicators, not legislators.[12] Casework is not just unwanted intervention; it can actually undermine some of orthodox public administration's basic premises.

Third, once casework is accepted as legitimate, it follows that members of Congress also have a role in righting maladministration. Although far from routine, casework sometimes reveals such ineptitude, abuse, or other ills that Congress feels a need to change an agency's administrative fundamentals, including its authority, organization, processes, and leadership. For instance, abuse and poor administration uncovered through casework played a significant role in Congress's enactment of both the "Taxpayers' Bill of Rights" in the 1986 Tax Reform Act and the Internal Revenue Service Restructuring and Reform Act of 1998 (see Burnham 1989, 305; Roth and Nixon 1999).[13]

Legislative responsibility to correct serious administrative failures reveals the force of Lewis Meriam's (1939) and W. F. Willoughby's (1927, 1934) contentions that Congress is the author of federal administrative authority, structure, procedure, and business practice (see Chapter 1). There is, of course, no compelling reason not to intervene *before* serious failure occurs. Therefore, in the context of casework as well as in the formal exercise of "continuous watchfulness," legislative-centered public administration can accommodate a large and proactive supervisory role for Congress.

"Reengineering" District Service

The Employment Act of 1946 became law on February 20, several months before the APA and the LRA. Written largely by members of Congress, it was an integral part of the overall discussion about how to strengthen the legislature and redefine its position with regard to federal agencies (U.S. Congress 1945a, 8954, 9055, 11987, 12025). The act's main policy objective was to promote employment by coordinating federal spending, primarily on valuable public works, with the business cycle. Congress wanted to be prepared with a rational jobs program to counter the next serious economic downturn, which economists were predicting would occur sometime after 1950 (U.S. Congress 1945a, 8967; Bailey 1950, chaps. 1 and 2). Politically, the act was a ratification of New Deal fiscal policy, which departed from the norm of seeking to balance the budget annually and relied on deficit spending to combat the depression.

The initial bill, which emphasized "full employment," faced opposition from conservative legislators who feared it was a precursor to a federally planned economy (Bailey 1950, 130). A few charged that it was a measure straight out of the Soviet Constitution (U.S. Congress 1945a, 9065, 11975, 12006). After debate, compromise, and parliamentary maneuver, the final version's convoluted "Declaration of Policy" reflected the policy balances that had been reached:

The Congress hereby declares that it is the continuing policy and responsibility of the Federal Government to use all practicable means consistent with its needs and obligations and other essential considerations of national policy, with the assistance and cooperation of industry, agriculture, labor, and State and local governments, to coordinate and utilize all its plans, functions, and resources for the purpose of creating and maintaining, in a manner calculated to foster and promote free competitive enterprise and the general welfare, conditions under which there will be afforded useful employment opportunities, including self-employment, for those able, willing, and seeking to work, and to promote maximum employment, production, and purchasing power. (Section 2)

As reported out of the conference committee, the act passed by a vote of 322 to 84 in the House and unanimously in the Senate (Murray 1946, 30; U.S. Congress 1946c, 986).

Aside from the declaration of policy, which was symbolically important, the act had three main features. First, it required the president to submit an Economic Report to each session of Congress. The envisioned report would focus on the state of the economy and make recommendations for dealing with employment and purchasing power. Second, it created a three-member Council of Economic Advisers to study the economy and advise the president. The advisers are appointed by the president, subject to Senate confirmation.[14] Third, it established a congressional Joint Committee on the Economic Report, composed of seven members each from the House and Senate. Now called the Joint Economic Committee, appointment is by the presiding officer in each chamber and reflects, insofar as feasible, their partisan balances. The Joint Committee's chief function under the act is to analyze the president's report and make recommendations to Congress.

On one level, the act was intended to strengthen Congress's ability to monitor the national economy and budget in response to its overall conditions. Had the legislative budget provisions of the 1946 Legislative Reorganization Act been implemented effectively, the Joint Committee's recommendations might have become central to federal budgeting.[15] On a second level, Congress viewed the act as a means of gaining greater control over public works, which would be the main vehicle for deficit spending. In terms of the congressional response to the administrative state, this objective was more important.

Congress faces a huge collective action problem when dealing with public works. The appetite of the members for projects in their districts is likely to be larger in the aggregate than the economy can efficiently bear. Moreover, there is little or no incentive for an individual member to abjure pork unless such action will have a significant impact on total federal spending. Constituents are likely to be more sanguine about subsidizing projects elsewhere when they see some tangible returns in their own districts as well. It is no accident that public works acts have been labeled "Christmas tree" bills (Ferejohn 1974, 2). But when the members logroll, some projects will inevitably be marginal or wasteful. Taxes, deficits, and/or inflationary pressures will mount. What is apparently good for each member will be bad for Congress as an institution, which will appear wasteful and inept. The total sum of benefits to each district may be detrimental to the national economy as a whole.

The obvious solution to this problem is to impose discipline on the members with regard to at least three factors: overall spending, timing, and the selection of public works projects.[16] That is precisely part of what proponents of the Employment Act promised it would do.

Supporters of the act had considerable trouble in presenting it as a measure for controlling spending. It essentially called for deficit spending during economic downturns, but contained no real barrier to providing public works when the treasury was flush. As Senator Robert Taft (R-OH) explained: "It is a very difficult program to carry out, because . . . the pressure for public works is just as strong when times are good as at any other time; and if we get a large public-works program going in the height of prosperity, then when there is a desire to extend it and to put more people to work in hard times, the opportunity is greatly limited" (U.S. Congress 1945a, 9030).

Proponents insisted that Congress would be up to the task, especially with the Joint Committee on the Economic Report in place. For instance, Senator Robert Wagner (D-NY) asserted that the committee would be able "to develop a full employment program adjusted to changing needs and changing conditions." He did not think implementation would be problematic, since "it all depends on Congress" (U.S. Congress 1945a, 8954, 8959). Similarly, Senator Joseph O'Mahoney (D-WY) emphasized that the act "does not authorize the Executive to spend a dime" (U.S. Congress 1945a, 9055).

Proponents' statements regarding timing may have been more convincing. For instance, Congressman Wright Patman (D-TX) explained that even assuming that all the proposed projects were meritorious, it would be unwise to build them at a time when government spending would contribute to "ruinous inflation" as opposed to when people "actually need the employment" (U.S. Congress 1945a, 11990).[17]

Controlling the timing of public works had a potentially major political advantage as well. As the following exchange in the House candidly indicates, the Employment Act could turn pork into virtue:

> Mr. [Brooks] Hays (D-AR). For example, here are two types of public-works programs; one is for flood control, that might be of an emergency character. We want to create these protective levees, and so on, regardless of [economic] conditions. But there are other programs, such as the erection of county agricultural buildings that occur to me as worth-while enterprises.
>
> As one of the proponents of that kind of program, I agree that they ought to be geared to the employment situation. Is it the gentleman's opinion that under this program . . . it would be possible for us to plan . . . the construction of buildings of that kind and other public works so that we would do it in those periods in which it is beneficial from the standpoint of the Nation's economic life?
>
> Mr. Judd. Yes, precisely.
>
> Mr. Hays. And that we can therefore avoid some of the criticisms of pork-barrel legislation if this developed?
>
> Mr. Judd. That is certainly one of the objectives of this legislation. (U.S. Congress 1945a, 12011)

As Patman, Hays, and Judd suggested, timing and the selection of projects were related. The objective, in Representative Charles Savage's (D-WA) words, was to "plan in advance so that we will not have to suddenly force ourselves into a slipshod system in a hurry to take care of unemployment" in a wasteful way (U.S. Congress 1945a, 12021). Senator Barkley reiterated the point that only Congress would be able to choose the projects: "No matter what the national budget may provide, no matter what the recommendations of the President may be, no matter what his annual [economic] report may contain . . . under this bill no project can be carried out or begun unless Congress later on separately, by other legislation, shall authorize specifically the things which are to be done" (U.S. Congress 1945a, 9131). Senator O'Mahoney also emphasized that the legislation was "a bill to restore the functions of Congress" (U.S. Congress 1945a, 9055).

Bringing economic rationality to district-oriented public works presents monumental challenges. It is fair to say that Congress did not succeed in 1946. Pork not only remained a staple of congressional politics, but it expanded well beyond public works to grants, tax expenditures, and other distributive policies (Nivola 1997; Fitzgerald and Lipson 1984, vii–xxxv). Examples are legion, but two recent ones should efficiently indicate public works' enduring popularity in Congress.

First, in 1993 the number one choice of a majority of the 110 *new* members in the House was a seat on the Public Works and Transportation Committee (Cooper 1993, A13). This was before the sustained economic upturn of the mid- and late-1990s, but after federal budget deficits became a major political issue in the 1980s. It also followed the enactment of major legislation, including the Budget Enforcement Act of 1990, aimed at reducing deficits and eventually balancing the budget. Lest anyone think that the new members' interest was in chopping waste, when asked whether any of his pet projects were pork, one freshman member candidly replied, "There ain't much beef up here" (Cooper 1993, A13).

A second contemporary example of Congress's continuing interest in district service is the much criticized Transportation Equity Act for the Twenty-first Century (1998). It is over 400 pages long and authorizes projects totaling $218 billion over six years, including 1,400 line items costing $9 billion. A newspaper focused on Congress, *The Hill,* suggested that "Perhaps no better example of a pork-laden bill has ever passed." Representative Dan Miller (R-FL) said the bill had "more pork than a Memphis barbecue." Among the items were bike paths in Rhode Island ($5.85 million), traffic signs to the Devil Rays' stadium in Tampa ($1 million), a "Native Roadside Vegetation Enhancement Center" in Iowa ($760,000), the restoration of cobblestones in Memphis ($700,000), and a highway exclusively in Canada that would benefit Alaskans ($120 million) (Friedly 1998, 4).[18]

There is considerable systematic evidence that Congress fared better in gaining greater control over the selection of projects. In the 1950s it strengthened this objective of the Employment Act by requiring formal standing committee clearance of some public works projects (Rhode 1959, chap. 2). Previously, formal committee clearance was limited to some of the military's real estate dealings. The first instance was in a

1944 naval public works act (Rhode 1959, 9). In 1954 the Public Buildings Purchase Contract Act extended formal committee clearance to the acquisition of space by the General Services Administration and the Post Office, both of which had to obtain approval from the House and Senate Public Works Committees before appropriations could be made (Rhode 1959, 21–22). The Watershed Protection and Flood Prevention Act of 1954, as amended in 1956, required the Department of Agriculture to obtain prior approval from the Agriculture Committees in Congress for all proposed watershed projects involving a federal contribution of over $250,000 or a structure between 2,500 and 4,000 acre-feet (Rhode 1959, 26). Anything physically larger required approval by the Public Works Committees. A similar type of provision gave the Committees on Interior and Insular Affairs authority to nullify water-storage projects proposed by the secretary of the interior under the Small Reclamation Projects Act of 1956 (Rhode 1959, 27).

Although there was some presidential resistance to formal committee clearance requirements, the Eisenhower administration eventually accepted their legitimacy when tied to Congress's appropriations powers (Rhode 1959, chap. 2). The constitutional demise of the legislative veto in *Immigration and Naturalization Service v. Chadha* (1983) throws considerable doubt on the legitimacy of some types of formal clearance. However, it has certainly not prevented Congress from formally requiring "reports" and "consultation," which in practical political terms may be very similar (see Kirst 1969; Davidson and Oleszek 1996, 331–334).

At some point after the enactment of the Employment Act and the variety of clearance arrangements adopted in its wake, the relative positions of Congress and the agencies in the public works arena changed. Senators and representatives were no longer the supplicants Kefauver (and others) described. Today, the agencies often court them. For instance, R. Douglas Arnold's empirical study of the distribution of military employment, Model Cities grants, and water and sewer grants found that

> bureaucrats appear to allocate benefits strategically in an effort both to maintain and to expand their supporting coalitions. When it furthers their purposes, they broaden their program's geographic scope and increase the number of shares of benefits so that more congressmen can be brought into their supporting coalitions. When necessary, they allocate extra shares of benefits to leaders and to those who are crucial coalition members. But the allocational

strategies that bureaucrats select are not the same for all programs. Each is specially tailored to fit a program's peculiar situation in Congress, to compensate where general-benefit strategies have proven weak, and to reward those congressmen who are especially important to a particular coalition's success. (Arnold 1979, 207)

John Ferejohn's 1974 comprehensive empirical study of rivers and harbors legislation from 1947 through 1968 reached a similar general conclusion: "The distribution of the Corps of Engineers' projects is related to the distribution of influence over the Corps of Engineers within the Congress" (233–234). Congress also has considerable influence with regard to the allocation of defense-related public works. Demand by the members coupled with the distributive strategies of administrators in the Department of Defense could largely explain why, in 1975, "fewer than 75 of the 435 members of the House of Representatives [did] *not* have a major defense plant or a military installation in their district" (Dye and Zeigler 1975, 331).

More recent studies conclude that legislative-administrative relationships involving distributive policy are stable, entrenched, and relatively free of presidential involvement (Vogler 1988, 304–306). In fact, Congress became so dominant that in the area of defense spending it imposed constraints on the ability of individual members to protect some federal installations in their districts through logrolling or other means. The Defense Base Closure and Realignment Act of 1990 sought to take district service politics out of military downsizing and consolidation decisions. It presents Congress with an all-or-nothing choice regarding proposed base closings. Under the act, the secretary of defense was authorized to make recommendations with respect to closures and realignments in 1991, 1993, and 1995. These recommendations were submitted to Congress and to a Defense Base Closure and Realignment Commission (DBCRC). The latter was a presidentially appointed eight-person unit created by the act. After holding public hearings on the secretary's recommendations, the DBCRC reported to the president, who could accept or reject but not alter its recommendations. Presidential disapproval triggered a DBCRC second report. If this were also disapproved, no closures would occur for that year. Presidential approval was followed by submission of the recommendations to Congress, which had up to forty-five days to reject them *in their entirety* by joint resolution. If the members of Congress had not become so adroit at blocking individual base closings, there would have been no reason to adopt such elaborate and inflexible procedures.

The Defense Base Closure and Realignment Act is testimony to the achievement of one of Congress's main goals in 1946. Several members argued that the Employment Act would have the great virtue of placing Congress in charge of public works. Even though the act has not operated the way its proponents claimed it would in terms of economic policy making, the idea that Congress should be in control of the distribution of projects has prevailed—perhaps sometimes too strongly, as in the case of military base closings. As Congress gained greater leverage over public works, a mutually supportive relationship between legislators and administrators developed. Here again, there is a strong tendency for Congress and the agencies to become fused in their decision making.

Conclusion: 1946 and the "Career" Congress

Following 1946, service in Congress increasingly began to resemble a career. John Hibbing (1991, 2) is among several political scientists who systematically study the reasons why "the likelihood of a new member of Congress staying for an entire career has been much greater in the second half of the twentieth century than at any time previously."[19] Analysts use a variety of approaches to describe the many aspects of this fundamental change in the nature of congressional service. The average number of years spent in the House and Senate has increased, as has the success of incumbents standing for reelection. For a time, districts with vigorous electoral competition—that is, "marginal seats"—were "vanishing" (Mayhew 1974; Fiorina 1977, 1989; Ornstein, Mann, and Malbin 1996, 67, 68). As an organization, Congress became "institutionalized" and "professionalized" (Polsby 1968; Fiorina 1977, 5).

Determining what caused the development of a career Congress can be likened to working with a "giant jigsaw puzzle" (Shepsle 1978). There are many interconnected pieces, and the career Congress itself is only one section of the overall picture. Although the whole puzzle has yet to be put together, Congress's response to the administrative state in 1946, including the attention it devoted to constituency and district service, is certainly a significant segment of it.

Some of the pieces have already been assembled. In 1946 Congress accepted as a fact that it would necessarily continue to delegate much of its legislative authority to federal agencies. It sought to control the use of that delegated authority by structuring administrative procedures and exercising "continuous watchfulness" over administration. The members were concerned with incumbency, as well as with Congress's institutional place in the constitutional scheme. They loadshed, enhanced their capacity for casework, and tried to gain greater leverage over district service in the form of public works projects. Each of these steps was thoroughly discussed and deliberate. Delegation may have become unavoidable, but Congress's overall response to the federal administrative state did not just happen or evolve. It was planned.

In explaining the development of the career Congress, Morris Fiorina (1977, 1989) largely ignores the 1946 congressional repositioning, yet explains why historically high levels of incumbency followed in its aftermath. His analysis focuses on the House, for which there are better data. Logically much of it should pertain to the Senate, though probably to a weaker degree. First, "the 'personal vote' for members of Congress has increased while the more impersonal vote, reflecting broader forces such as partisanship and national conditions, has declined" (Fiorina 1989, 91). Casework and district service are a large component of that personal vote. Second, in Fiorina's words, they "are basically pure profit" in terms of incumbency (1977, 45). Relative to 1945, they are more effectively performed and the electorate seems more likely "to evaluate representatives in terms of constituency attentiveness" (1989, 89). Third, while casework and district service make it easier to win friends, delegation reduces the likelihood of making enemies. It enables the members to avoid taking clear stances on controversial issues and on the potentially divisive trade-offs involved in much regulatory policy. After the agencies make the tough choices, the members may also be able to win some electoral support through well-publicized oversight or other intervention on behalf of district interests (1977, 48–49). In Fiorina's words, "Congressmen take credit coming and going. They are the alpha and the omega" (1977, 48).

The delegating, supervising, constituency- and district-servicing Congress promotes incumbency so well that it is seductive. Older members seem to agree that "the system is set to reelect incumbents regardless of party" and that "no congressman who gets elected and who minds his business should ever be beaten" (Fiorina 1977, 47, 62). New members are socialized into it. They are "presented with a battery of seminars, workshops, retreats, lectures, and publications all designed to teach them how to organize a congressional office; how to utilize congressional procedures; how to get reelected; and how to get publicity. . . .

Modern members seem quick to learn much of what they feel they need to know about serving (staying?) in Congress" (Hibbing 1991, 17).

The public also goes along. Turnouts for midterm House elections are likely to be in the 30 percent range (Ornstein, Mann, and Malbin 1996, 50). It is relatively easy to "love our congressmen but not the Congress" (Parker 1989, 54). Public opinion polls since the 1960s indicate that, on average, only about a third of the adult population is likely to hold a favorable view of Congress (Loomis 1996, 44; see also Davidson and Oleszek 1996, 426). Nevertheless, the electorate asks for casework, apparently appreciates federal spending in the home districts, and rewards their representatives and senators with incumbency (Parker 1989, chap. 3). Whether the voters would punish them for neglecting constituency and district service is a moot point (see Hibbing 1991, chaps. 1, 2, and 7; Rivers and Fiorina 1989). Although the impact of "home style" may be diffuse, incumbents widely believe that it counts significantly (Fenno 1978; Cain, Ferejohn, and Fiorina 1987, chap. 6). As Thomas Mann (1978, 1) notes, "Congressional elections are local, not national, events: in deciding how to cast their ballots, voters are primarily influenced not by the President, the national parties, or the state of the economy, but by the local candidates."

The development of a career Congress helps explain why the 1946 framework has endured and served as a platform for successive congressional measures to regulate administrative procedures, supervise administration, enhance the members' capacity for casework, and strengthen their influence on federal spending in the home districts. The institutional decisions made in 1946 have clearly been consonant with the members' interest in incumbency. That was not Congress's only—or even primary—goal. The legislative repositioning in 1946 was not a conspiracy,[20] but rather a deliberative introspective effort to carve out a coherent and productive place for Congress in a government that had changed drastically during the previous decade and a half. The APA, the 1946 Legislative Reorganization Act, and the Employment Act were considered separately, but they were integrally related. Congress altered its mission, organization, and, with time, career structure. By these measures, the 1946 framework was essentially a refounding of the first branch.

The fact that so much else has changed highlights the remarkable durability of the 1946 congressional response to the administrative state. During the past fifty years, legislative leadership was decentralized, then recentralized; subcommittees proliferated, then contracted; seniority, pronounced dead in 1975, survived; the legislative budget has had a number of ups and downs; the South realigned with the Republican Party; greater party discipline emerged in Congress while the importance of political parties in congressional elections declined (see Vogler 1993; Loomis 1996; Parker 1989; Fiorina 1989). Much has also happened in federal administration: reorganizations, PPBS, MBO, ZBB, civil service reform, regulatory change, TQM, downsizing, and "reinventing"[21] (see Rosenbloom 1998b).

However, as this and the two preceding chapters demonstrate, the fundamentals established in 1946 are not only still in place, they have been strengthened considerably by subsequent legislation. There are a great number of important questions one could ask about the 1946 framework. Its effects on congressional behavior and performance in the national government are subject to a variety of interpretations and evaluations, even as its origins and coherence are largely ignored. Such work is better left to specialists on Congress and the legislative process. Here, the primary concern is with the significance of the legislative-centered public administration that underlies Congress's 1946 response to the administrative state for American public administrative thought, practice, and reform.

5 | Legislative-Centered Public Administration
Administrative Theory, Practice, and Reform

Congress has as much right to participate in the administration of the laws as it has in their formulation. . . . Administration is neither a simple nor an automatic business. It is packed with opportunities and demands for exercises of discretion, on the part of the agency and administrative personnel involved, which should be made politically accountable as far as possible. And the greater the degree of authority given to the agency under the terms of the law enacting a particular program, the greater is the duty of Congress to participate in and supervise the agency's decisions.
    —Edward de Grazia (quoted in Gellhorn 1966, 75, n. 31)

The congressional response to the administrative state in 1946 has had profound ramifications for American public administration. However, because it involved seemingly separate policy arenas—administrative procedure, legislative reorganization, tort claims, bridges, and constituency and district service—its overall deliberateness, coherence, and impact have not been self-evident. The previous chapters explain how and why the various pieces were fashioned as well as the contributions each made to the development of a legislative-centered public administration. The objective now is to show how they fit together and how the legislative-centered public administration they framed deeply affects American public administrative theory, practice, and reform.

Legislative-Centered Public Administration

As developed in this study, legislative-centered public administration is a theoretical construct derived from the major discussions, decisions, and actions taken by Congress with regard to federal administration. Its evolution began during the New Deal as Congress felt increasingly displaced and began to search for an appropriate role in the burgeoning administrative state. It speaks to Congress's institutional interests as well as to the values that should inform administrative performance. It is part justification, part explanation of deep, institutionalized congressional involvement in administration within the parameters of the constitutional separation of powers.

Contemporary legislative-centered public administration was framed in 1946 when Congress debated and legislated fundamental changes in its institutional position with respect to the agencies. Subsequently, it was augmented as Congress further developed the 1946 platform for regulating administrative procedures, supervising agencies, and intervening in administration to provide constituency and district service. It is the equivalent of a judicial doctrine that explains judicial decisions. As they develop, such doctrines are not necessarily articulated, named, or even fully understood by the judges and attorneys who employ them. Yet, in time they often crystallize and become tangible, institutionalized ways of analyzing and resolving issues.[1] Legislative-centered public administration has reached such a stage.

Looking back over the past half-century, there is a clear line from several major contemporary statutes bearing on federal administration to proposals made as an integral part of Congress's effort to reposition itself vis-à-vis the agencies in 1946. For instance, congressional review of agency rules according to the Small Business Regulatory Enforcement Fairness Act of 1996 (SBREFA) and direct legislative participation in agency strategic planning under the Government Performance and Results Act of 1993 (GPRA) have antecedents in the debates over the Walter-Logan Act (1940) and the Administrative Procedure Act (APA) of 1946 (see Chapter 3). One Congress may not be able to bind another, but nor has any Congress jettisoned the 1946 framework or reconsidered its institutional position in the administrative state de novo. The 1946 framework was grounded in a powerful institutional logic that has been strongly reinforced not only by SBREFA and GPRA in the 1990s, but also by such major legislation as the Freedom of Information Act (1966), the 1970 Legislative Reorganization Act, the Federal Advisory Committee Act (1972), the Privacy Act (1974), the Congressional Budget and Impoundment Control Act (1974), the Government in the Sunshine Act (1976), the Paperwork Reduction Acts (1980, 1995), and the Negotiated Rulemaking Act (1990). Legislative-centered public administration is an explication of that logic.

Origins

As noted in Chapter 1, legislative-centered public administration did not begin on a blank slate in 1946. Lewis Meriam and W. F. Willoughby established some of the groundwork for it in the 1920s and 1930s. Though their ideas regarding congressional participation in administration never became mainstream, both were highly respected scholars affiliated with the Brookings Institution.

Willoughby contended that the Constitution places the administrative function with the legislature (1927, 11). Congress is responsible for administrative organization, authority, and procedure, as well as for directing, supervising, and controlling administrative activity (1927, 11; 1934, 138). It followed that Congress should be organized in a fashion that would promote the effective and efficient performance of these functions. As a matter of policy, though not necessarily of constitutional law, Willoughby thought that Congress "should not itself seek to engage in the actual performance of administrative work" because it "would tend to throw the work of administration into the field of partisan politics" (1934, 132).

Writing in 1939, after the New Deal had radically transformed both the presidency and federal administration, Meriam also argued that Congress should have a large role in federal administration. It should exercise control over the agencies "by reducing appropriations, by passing laws that require administrative officers to follow sound practices in administrative matters and, through its power of investigation, by exposing to the public instances of abuse of trust by administrative officers" (1939, 173). He called on Congress to strengthen its staff and the General Accounting Office to assist with these responsibilities (1939, 173). Unlike Willoughby, Meriam believed the Constitution clearly prohibited congressional execution of the laws (1939, 126).

When Congress developed its own version of legislative-centered public administration in 1946, it incorporated some of these earlier ideas and rejected others.[2] Overall, the congressional approach calls for a much larger legislative role than either Meriam or Willoughby contemplated. Relative to their work, it also places less importance on efficiency as an administrative value.

Major Tenets

1. Administration involves legislative functions.

Rulemaking and lawmaking are functional equivalents. Legislative (substantive) rules made by agencies have the force of law. When agencies make such rules, in effect they legislate. Congress can delegate its legislative authority to the agencies at its discretion for a wide variety of reasons: to alleviate its workload; to avoid a particularly nettlesome political issue; to focus highly specialized administrative expertise on a particular problem; for convenience; or simply because the agencies do not face the constraints of a legislature that is reconstituted every two years. Not all congressional and administrative functions are clearly distinct from one another. On the contrary, there is some interchangeability among them. Some functions can be performed by Congress directly or delegated to the agencies. Administration is not confined to executive functions.

2. When the agencies are engaged in legislative functions, they serve as extensions of Congress.

The agencies perform legislative functions for Congress, at its discretion, pursuant to delegations of its authority. The Constitution's grant of legislative power to Congress encompasses a responsibility to ensure that delegated authority is exercised according to appropriate procedures. Therefore, Congress legitimately tells the agencies *how* to perform legislative functions as well as toward what substantive policy ends. The "how" does not invade the president's constitutional obligation to "take Care that the Laws be faithfully executed" (Article II, section 3). Congress not only has the constitutional authority, but also a duty to specify the procedures, values, and decision criteria that agencies must use when they perform legislative functions.

Treating the agencies as legislative extensions goes much further in justifying congressional regulation of their processes and decision making than is contemplated by the more common "principal-agent" model advanced by Willoughby (1927, 29; 1934, 157) and others (see Gill 1995). Principals cannot ordinarily prescribe the internally and externally oriented procedures an agent will use in carrying out their purposes. But Congress tells the agencies what rulemaking procedures they must satisfy, when their decisions must be sustained by substantial evidence on the record as a whole, how to use advisory committees, which interests must be given special consideration, and, in some cases, even when their decision making must be open to the public.

Such matters are subject to congressional regulation because when agencies perform legislative functions they serve as arms of Congress and, therefore, may be subordinated to its values and prescriptions. As Willoughby pointed out (1934, 115), it is a mistake to equate administration with the executive function. Administrative agencies may perform legislative functions whether they are located in the executive branch or have independent status. Public administration is by no means solely an executive matter or responsibility. The U.S. Supreme Court said as much in *Vermont Yankee Nuclear Power Corp. v. Natural Resources Defense Council* (1978) by strongly endorsing Congress's broad authority to prescribe administrative rulemaking procedures and thereby affirming its large constitutional role in the administrative state.

3. There can be no strict dichotomy between politics and administration. Therefore, American public administration should be informed by the democratic-constitutional values that apply to the exercise of political authority.

Administrative decisions and actions are often political because they allocate benefits and burdens.[3] This is almost self-evident when agencies engage in legislative functions such as rulemaking, but it is also true in the context of enforcement, personnel and budget systems, organizational design, the location of administrative facilities, and other matters (Lipsky 1980; Shafritz et al. 1992, chap. 3; Wildavsky 1961; Seidman 1970; Arnold 1979).

Where politics is involved, the orthodox vision of administration based on the application of neutral, scientifically informed expertise in pursuit of the public interest is insufficient to legitimize agency actions or yield politically responsive decisions. In fact, to the extent that such administration is insulated from political controls or unresponsive, it may be considered illegitimate, as several members of Congress contended while debating the Walter-Logan Act and the APA.

Insofar as politics is involved in administration, agencies' operations should comport with the values of American democratic-constitutionalism. Adherence to these values will help legitimize their actions and improve administrative performance in the political system. For instance, as a general rule, democratic-constitutionalism demands that administrative operations and decisions be open to public scrutiny; that interested parties have a right to representation and participation in agencies' decision making; and that administrators respect the public, protect their rights, and avoid intruding on their privacy and autonomy.

Perhaps negotiated rulemaking comes closest to legislative-centered public administration's ideal decision-making model. The agency notifies the public of its intent to engage in rulemaking and then joins with other concerned parties in a cooperative problem-solving exercise that emphasizes information sharing, compromise, participatory decision making, and responsiveness to the legitimate concerns of all those involved.

4. Congress has very broad supervisory responsibility for federal administration.

Congress is the author or "source" of federal administration, as Willoughby (1927, 11; 1934, 115) explained. It empowers, organizes, and funds agencies, and provides for their staffing. Supervision is one of Congress's major functions. It is responsible for ensuring that administrative operations are faithful to its mandates and delegations. Congressional organization can promote effective supervision by adequately staffing standing committees and subcommittees and aligning them with executive-branch organization.

This is another area in which legislative-centered public administration goes well beyond the principal-agent model in prescribing congressional involvement in administration. The "continuous watchfulness" standard was a high one in 1946, but in many respects it has been surpassed. Congress's supervisory role justifies placing inspectors general and chief financial officers in the agencies, imposing a vast number of reporting requirements on administrators, using committee and personal staff to monitor agency behavior, and establishing direct congressional participation in the core managerial activities of strategic planning and performance measurement. Additionally, the supervisory role comprehends congressional action to establish administrative systems and criteria for accounting, reducing paperwork, collecting and releasing information, and a wide variety of other activities. Congress is an author that continually revises the script.

5. Members of Congress have an obligation to intercede in administration on behalf of their constituents' and districts' interests.

Because Congress creates, empowers, and sustains administration, it has an obligation to make sure that it functions appropriately in individual cases as well as in general. Casework is not particularistic favor-seeking or rule-bending; it is a legitimate and major legislative function. The members have an obligation to see how the administrative machinery Congress created is working, to intervene when it seems to falter in specific instances, and to redesign it when failure is endemic. Personal staff are used to perform most of the casework in order to preserve the members' time for other key legislative functions, including lawmaking and supervising the agencies. Public works spending is a legitimate congressional function, when rationally ordered. The members may intercede in administrative decisions regarding public works and the location of agencies' facilities because, as representatives, they are obligated to try to obtain a "fair share" of such benefits for their districts.

6. The role of the president and political executives in federal administration is to implement legislative mandates, coordinate agency actions government-wide, manage agencies on a day-to-day basis, and exercise discretion in pursuing the public interest when Congress has not provided specific direction.

This tenet is derivative. Legislative-centered public administration speaks overwhelmingly to the role of Congress in federal administration. It has very little to say about that of the presidency. In 1946 the possibility that Congress might itself try to implement the laws was raised, but it was not given serious consideration. The members seemed to believe that they should not cross that line. Because of its organization, Congress faces serious limitations when coordination among the agencies is necessary to achieve a policy goal. It often relies on the Office of Management and Budget for coordination, as in the case of the Federal Advisory Committee Act of 1972, the Paperwork Reduction Acts of 1980 and 1995, GPRA, and other measures. "Continuous watchfulness" and other forms of supervision involve liaison and intervention, but not active, day-to-day hands-on management by congressional committees and staff. Finally, congressional loadshedding and broad delegations of legislative authority to the agencies are based on the belief that extensive administrative discretion is appropriate.

In Willoughby's (1934, 115) view, the executive power or function involved foreign relations. Legislative-centered public administration tends to recognize a greater role for the presidency in defense, national security, and law enforcement by frequently exempting these functions from the constraints of administrative law. For example, the APA, the Freedom of Information Act, and the Government in the Sunshine Act make exceptions for one or more of these functions.

7. The primary role of the federal courts with regard to federal administration is to provide judicial review of agency actions under the terms and conditions established by Congress through administrative law.

Legislative-centered public administration maintains that Congress has a responsibility to regulate the scope of judicial review of agency actions. This was the fundamental premise behind Congress's debate and passage of the Walter-Logan Act and, subsequently, the APA. Several additional statutes, including the Freedom of Information Act, the Federal Advisory Committee Act, the Privacy Act, the Government in the Sunshine Act, the Negotiated Rulemaking Act, and SBREFA, contain explicit provisions for judicial review.

Substantively, legislative-centered public administration views judicial review of agency actions as a means of protecting individual rights and promoting fairness. Broadly speaking, administrative law calls on the courts to check harmful agency action involving unconstitutionality or illegality, abuse of discretion, improper use of procedures, delay, or irrational decision making.[4]

Coherence and Limitations

Overall, the legislative-centered public administration derived from congressional debates and lawmaking since the 1930s and 1940s provides a coherent approach to legislative participation in public administration in a separation-of-powers system. The orthodoxy, which was the only alternative theory in 1946, was unable to prescribe an adequate role for Congress in federal administration. In its view, Congress's job was to establish and empower agencies, follow the executive budget in funding them, turn the entire administrative apparatus over to the president, and hold administrators accountable after instances of real or potential maladministration came to light (U.S. President's Committee on Administrative Management [PCAM] 1937, 49–50). Ongoing congressional supervision—not to mention participation in federal administration—would interfere with efficiency and effectiveness by impairing the unity of command and obscuring responsibility. In 1937 the President's Committee on Administrative Management actually argued that the fate of democracy throughout the world depended, in part, on Congress's willingness to play such a limited role in federal administration (PCAM 1937, 2).[5]

The orthodoxy's prescriptions might have promoted more efficient and effective federal administration. However, in Congress's collective view as expressed in 1946, they would not have created better *government*. The separation-of-powers and checks-and-balances systems would have been upset. Congress might *not* have been necessary, or at least as necessary as its members thought it should be (Kefauver and Levin 1947, chap. 1).

Agencies are a center of political power in the administrative state, and a branch of government that fails to develop or maintain leverage over them will be relatively weaker for it. The overall purpose of legislative-centered public administration is to protect the vibrancy of constitutional government by strengthening Congress's participation in federal administration.

From this perspective, legislative-centered public administration solved Congress's constitutional problem coherently. Congress has broad responsibility for federal administration because the agencies perform legislative functions, act as its extensions, make political decisions, are established and empowered by it, and have a variety of substantial impacts on the people whom the members represent. Constitutionally, as Willoughby argued, administration cannot sensibly be considered an executive function solely subordinate to the presidency. There cannot be a fire wall between the author and the actors charged with carrying out its intent. To be uninvolved in ongoing administrative matters would be to abdicate a fundamental congressional responsibility. In some contexts, Congress and the agencies are more fused than separated.

When legislative-centered public administration's core premises were enacted in 1946, it was a radical theory, without precedent. It has been criticized since its inception. In 1947, Louis Brownlow (1949, 17) perceived Congress's effort to strengthen itself as a potential threat to sound administration and unity of command in the executive branch under the president. He seemed convinced that congressional regulation of administrative procedure would "interfere" with effective administration (1949, 116–117, 128). Three basic lines of criticism have been common.

First, critics of legislative-centered public administration sometimes charge that it promotes congressional usurpation of executive powers and invades the president's constitutional responsibility to "take Care that the Laws be faithfully executed" (Article II, section 3). As noted in Chapters 2 and 3, some congressional initiatives involving administrative law and supervision of the agencies have encountered this criticism. For the most part, however, the thrust of legislative-centered public administration is firmly supported by the constitutional law reaching from *Kendall v. United States* (1838) to *Morrison v. Olson* (1988). The contention that it is constitutionally suspect is particularly weak with regard to the independent regulatory commissions, which are beyond the president's constitutional reach in many respects (Moreno 1994). Upsets such as *Immigration and Naturalization Service v. Chadha* (1983) (the legislative veto) and *Bowsher v. Synar* (1986) (vesting an executive function in the comptroller general) are not inconsequential, but they have not proven fundamental.[6]

Critics from Brownlow in the 1940s to Vice President Al Gore in the 1990s have also contended that legislative-centered public administration elevates the wrong values. Brownlow (1949, 116–117) and other traditionalists charge that Congress imposes procedures and requirements that impede efficiency, economy, and effectiveness. Some agencies opposed the APA on these grounds. Gore (1993, chap. 1) and proponents of "reinventing government" or the New Public Management claim that the legislative focus on procedure and supervision makes it difficult for agencies to produce results (see Rosenbloom 1998b, 20–27).

Criticisms along these lines face two serious problems. Public administration is now widely understood to be more than a "field of business," as Woodrow Wilson and others in the orthodox tradition claimed (Wilson 1887, 18; White 1926, 57; see also Gore 1993, iv). It involves governance. Theories of public administration are likely to be political theories in important respects, since they deal with the values that should order public life (Waldo 1948, 1984). As a representative national institution operating within a system of checks and balances, Congress is well situated to make binding decisions with respect to value trade-offs. There is no perfect national administrative system. Political and administrative values are often in tension with one another (Wilson 1967; Rosenbloom 1983). If there is a conflict between representativeness, openness, or inspector general–style accountability and cost-effectiveness, Congress is the federal government's primary institution for determining which should prevail. Unless Congress's choices are obviously or egregiously wrong, they carry a good deal of facial legitimacy.

Second, it is incumbent on critics to show that administration according to the values they prefer would actually be better. This is no easy task. Diagnosis of the ills that may be caused by legislative-centered public administration does not automatically yield a prescription for cure. As suggested above, even if such a prescription is available, it may have harmful effects on other values. Robert La Follette, Jr. (Progressive-WI) once wrote, "What is wrong with Congress? There certainly is no dearth of volunteers to answer that question. If criticism alone could make for perfection, Congress would by this time be one of the most perfect of all human institutions" (1943, 92). The same is true of federal administration. If national administration in a separation-of-powers system were an easy problem, it probably would have been solved by now (see Wilson 1967; Riggs 1991, 1994).

Many will find a third criticism more persuasive. Legislative-centered public administration contains no self-regulating mechanism. It can promote both excessive and self-serving legislative involvement in public administration. Willoughby (1927, 1934) anticipated this problem when he noted that Congress places too many detailed requirements on administration, thereby giving it a "rigidity . . . that often militates against efficiency and makes it impossible for administrative officials to meet emergencies and do the things most urgently needed" (Willoughby 1927, 17). Chapters 10–12 of his book on *Principles of Legislative Organization and Administration* (1934) seek to counteract this tendency by specifying the limits of appropriate legislative involvement in administration. The Employment Act of 1946 also recognized a congressional tendency toward excess, though implicitly. Part of its purpose was to bring rationality and order to the members' appetite for public works. More recently, in 1996, Congress tried to give the president a line item veto to rein in wasteful constituency- and district-oriented spending, but its effort was ruled unconstitutional in *Clinton v. City of New York* (1998).

According to Vice President Gore, there is no doubt that Congress is excessively involved in federal administration (1993, 34). Many find the volume of casework and public works especially troubling because so much of it is in the service of promoting the members' incumbency. The members know that a great deal of casework is "unmeritorious," but they do it anyway for the sake of "public relations" (Gellhorn 1966, 69). Some may even be surprised when the agencies take it seriously (Gellhorn 1966, 69). The very term "pork" connotes excess and waste.

However, legislative excess needs to be kept in perspective. Going back to something like Brownlow's conception of the appropriate extent of legislative involvement in federal administration in order to curb it would be a drastic response. The 1946 framework and its subsequent development are not only intended to give Congress a larger role in the administrative state; they are also efforts to deal with genuine administrative problems such as haphazard rulemaking, secrecy, inadequate accountability, and the abuse of individual rights. Legislative-centered public administration operates within the constitutional system of checks and balances. Both the presidency and the courts play a role in checking it, as ultimately can the electorate. It should also be remembered that Congress has some capacity for self-imposed discipline, as in the case of the Defense Base Closure and Realignment Act of 1990 and the pay-as-you-go provisions of the 1990 Budget Enforcement Act (see Schick 1995).[7]

In sum, legislative-centered public administration is a coherent theory regarding the congressional role in federal administration under the constitutional separation of powers. In addition to being the "source" of federal administration, Congress will perforce delegate and therefore treat the agencies as extensions for performance of its legislative functions. Because administration involves political decision making, Congress is responsible for ensuring that the agencies embrace democratic-constitutional values. Congress has broad supervisory responsibility for administration and should be organized and staffed accordingly. Its representational role includes district service and casework, for which personal staff are necessary. The primary function of the presidency and political executive with respect to federal administration, especially in the domestic sphere, is to coordinate the agencies' activities and manage their day-to-day operations. The courts should serve as a check on unconstitutional, illegal, irrational, or abusive administration, largely as specified by Congress through administrative law.

Impact on Theory

Elements of legislative-centered public administration had an almost immediate, though diffuse, impact on American public administrative theory. They substantially reinforced a trend already under way in the 1940s toward broadening the field's concerns and range of values. The academic literature in the late 1940s and early 1950s included a number of works that were grounded in the 1946 legislation by viewing federal administration as incorporating legislative and judicial functions as well as being intertwined with matters of congressional organization. Such perspectives were not altogether new. They had been raised before, by Willoughby (1927, 1934) and others.[8] However, the legal basis of the 1946 framework and its immediacy made it difficult to maintain that federal administration was simply an executive endeavor, or a matter almost exclusively for presidential concern.

Although the intellectual history of American public administration is generally well understood, the contribution made by the legislative-centered perspective has been underappreciated. Consequently, a very brief review is in order.

Broadly speaking, by the 1940s federal administration had been sequentially organized according to three dominant approaches (see White 1965a–d; Van Riper 1958, chaps. 2–12; Rosenbloom 1971, chaps. 2–4; Mosher 1968, chap. 3; Kaufman 1956). From the founding until the inauguration of Andrew Jackson as president in 1829, federal administration was essentially an arm of the elites who dominated the federal government. Executive leadership was the primary administrative value.

Calling for greater participation by and representation of the common man in government and politics, Jackson ushered in the "spoils system." The elites were displaced as the political party in control of the presidency made patronage dismissals and appointments to the federal service. Representativeness was a defining value for federal administration.

The orthodoxy developed slowly after the Civil War as a political response to a number of factors. Administrative reforms would enable the federal government to deal more effectively with the nation's rapid industrialization and urbanization (Skowronek 1982). The reformers also sought to diminish the corrupting impact of political machines on the nation's politics and administration, to protect the American political culture from "imported change" by the growing numbers of urban immigrants, and to make it possible for a more fit class of political leaders to become dominant (see Rosenbloom 1971, chap. 3; Rosenbloom 1998b, 212–216; Rohr 1986, 231, n. 61).[9] Reforms for these purposes included the introduction of merit systems, restrictions on public employees' partisan political activity, city management, line item budgets, and "non-political" independent administrative authorities for managing ports, bridges, parks, and so forth.

Orthodox administrative doctrine was the product of a confluence of three broad movements: civil service reform (1870s–1890s), which focused on depoliticizing the public service through merit and political neutrality; Progressivism (1890s–1920s), which broadened reform to include electoral practices and administrative organization; and Scientific Management (1900–1930s), which considered management a science for designing work and motivational systems. The orthodoxy's chief emphasis was on building a scientifically organized, politically neutral, and highly competent civil service. Although there were some dissenters, it dominated the field.[10] The 1937 President's Committee on Administrative Management *Report* can be considered the orthodoxy's "high noon." Then, however, as Harold Seidman points out, "the clock stopped" (1970, 9).

The orthodoxy drew a strict dichotomy between politics and administration. It considered administration a design science for planning, organizing, staffing, directing, coordinating, reporting, and budgeting (known by the acronym POSDCORB). The main objective was to increase administrative efficiency, economy, and effectiveness. For the most part, the orthodoxy focused on overhead systems, including organization, personnel, and budgeting, as opposed to service delivery.

Democratic-constitutional values such as representativeness, political responsiveness, and participation were viewed as either subordinate or hostile concerns (Waldo 1984, 192). As noted earlier, with regard to the federal government, the orthodoxy prescribed unity of command in the executive branch with the president on top and a very limited role for Congress in administration.

The orthodoxy came under increasing and ultimately successful challenge after congressional delegation of legislative authority to the agencies became pronounced during the New Deal. If agencies make legislative rules and are involved in governing, then how can they be apolitical (Appleby 1945, 1949)? What kind of science or expertise enables administrators to determine the public interest or the best organizational arrangements for achieving it (Herring 1936; Simon 1946)? If "a picture of the Presidency as a reservoir of authority from which the lower echelons of administration draw life and vigor is an idealized distortion of reality," then how useful is it to advocate unity of command (Long 1949, 258)? If a general theory of public administration is inherently a political theory, then which political values should it incorporate and why (Waldo 1948)?

As an intellectual matter, the orthodoxy eventually crumbled under the weight of such questions. Much of the academic field turned to case studies in an unsuccessful effort to build a replacement theory (Rosenbloom 1995). Practitioners continued to rely on orthodox prescriptions for their common sense and conventional acceptability. Though some efforts were made at establishing a new paradigm, none succeeded.[11] Post-orthodox public administration has had no particular name.[12]

By any measure, the post-orthodox conception of public administration is much broader than the orthodoxy's, and its value set is significantly larger. A reading of the leading professional journals dealing with public administration during the late 1940s and early 1950s makes it clear that the main components of legislative-centered public administration were quickly introduced into the literature and considered important new avenues for research and theory building. Two examples are particularly striking and important.

1. Public administration is more than a field of business or management. Writing in *Public Administration Review,* Vincent Barnett noted that "Judicialization of the Administrative Process" under the APA "proceeds on the assumption that all administrative actions are really 'legislative' or 'judicial' in character" (1948, 127). His analysis shows how, based on this view, administrative law seeks to broaden the range of values that inform administrative organization and procedure. Barnett

thinks the APA's constraints are misguided, but he provides the reader with enough information and perspective to draw his or her own preliminary conclusions. He holds that the APA should be evaluated in terms of its impact on efficiency, speed, *and* fairness (1948, 126).

Also dealing with administrative law, Kenneth Culp Davis (1953) reviewed a number of public administration textbooks in an *American Political Science Review* article. He takes them to task for paying too little attention to regulatory administration, which he considers a central administrative activity. He also calls on the field to improve its discussion of administrative law.

Articles like these point to the difficulty of maintaining that public administration is simply a managerial endeavor. They make it plain that public administration is not apolitical and that managerial values may not be appropriate to its legislative and adjudicatory functions. Barnett (1948) devotes enough space to the APA's provisions for judicial review to leave one wondering what the courts would review if public administration were confined to competent, politically neutral management.

2. Congress is a major and legitimate actor in federal administration. La Follette presented the case and approach for "Systematizing Congressional Control" in a 1947 *American Political Science Review* article. Writing in the same journal, Senator Elbert Thomas (D-UT) (1949, 1182) explained that one of the objectives of the 1946 Legislative Reorganization Act (LRA) was to promote "closer cooperation with and supervision of the executive department." In *Public Administration Review,* Roland Young (1948) gave Estes Kefauver and Jack Levin's book, *A Twentieth-Century Congress* (1947), a mostly favorable review. He specifically endorsed Kefauver's plan for weekly sessions during which administrators would appear on the floor of Congress for two hours to report on their operations and answer questions (Young 1948, 143–144). Other *Public Administration Review* articles included Jesse Burkhead's (1948) analysis of the failure of the legislative budget and what could be learned from it, as well as an effort by Gladys Kammerer (1949) to apply the principles of public administration to congressional organization.

Although not specifically grounded in the APA or the LRA, Charles Hyneman's book on *Bureaucracy in a Democracy* (1950) mentions both and deals with many of the topics Congress addressed in 1946. Merle Fainsod's (1951, 122) review in *Public Administration Review* gave Hyneman high marks for "a vigorous affirmation of the doctrine of legislative supremacy," for presenting "a sharp challenge to the doctrinal orthodoxies which have dominated public administration circles over the last years," and for his "faith in congressional capacity to determine administrative arrangements." Hyneman's work eventually became standard (and difficult) reading for doctoral students and was certainly a major contribution to the field.

Emmette Redford's 1954 *American Political Science Review* article on "Administrative Regulation" followed in the same vein. Executive and legislative organization are related: "The unity within the executive branch for which Hamilton, the Brownlow and Hoover Commissions, and students of administration generally have argued can be achieved only if there is more unity in the Congress" (1954, 1113).

Perhaps no one did more to legitimize legislative-centered perspectives and areas of inquiry than John Gaus (1950). In a *Public Administration Review* article analyzing "Trends in the Theory of Public Administration" during the 1940s, he noted that one of two "particularly important sources for administrative theory . . . is that of opinion formation, parties, and legislatures, in which the problems of congressional reorganization and of American parties in the light of postwar public policy formulation have stimulated a re-examination of the relation of parties and legislatures to the chief executives and administration generally on the one hand, and to functional needs and popular participation in government on the other" (1950, 165). Partly influenced by the legislative reorganization, Gaus staked out major areas for public administrative theory and research that were well beyond the boundaries of orthodox inquiry. He was also prescient: the interface between Congress and administration, public policy formulation, and public participation in administration subsequently became major areas of study.

In time, these contributions of the legislative-centered perspective to public administrative theory became mainstream. Public administration came to address virtually all the themes and values related to the congressional repositioning of 1946: the combination of executive, legislative, and judicial functions in public administration and the values that should be attached to them; representation and participation in the administrative process; fairness; openness; the agencies as supplementary lawmakers; political responsiveness; congressional supervision and participation in administration; and judicial review. All of these are now core topics of theory and research.

Impact on Administrative Practice

The impact of legislative-centered public administration on practice has also been concrete. The 1946 framework complicates practice immensely because it requires administrators to respond to a wider range of values, which sometimes conflict with one another, and to supervision by Congress as well as the presidency. As noted earlier, it also calls on the federal courts to serve as a check on some forms of maladministration. Put differently, legislative-centered public administration brings values derived from the constitutional separation of powers into federal administrative practice and increases the extent to which agencies are subordinate to all three branches of the government.

The Separation of Powers and Administrative Values

Prior to 1946, the agencies were engaged in execution, legislation (rulemaking), and adjudication. However, they were not systematically required to adhere to legislative or judicial values when performing those functions. In Congress's view, and no doubt that of a large part of the public, federal administration faced a problem of legitimacy. The legislature seemed to be atrophying, while the agencies appeared to be increasingly powerful but unrepresentative and somewhat arbitrary and uncontrolled. It was this state of affairs that triggered demands for an administrative procedure act.

The remarkable role of the Constitution in the American political culture has been noted time and time again by political scientists and other observers (see Gitelson, Dudley, and Dubnick 1988, chap. 2; Kamen 1987). Among its qualities is an ability to legitimize the exercise of governmental power in a society that values limited government. The APA began a process of systematically applying the constitutional values associated with legislating and adjudicating to federal administrative activities involving those functions. As observed in Chapter 2, Congress was interested in legitimizing the agencies' actions as well as placing procedural constraints on them. It consciously turned to constitutional values in fashioning the procedures it would impose.

To be legitimate in the American constitutional system, the legislative process must be open to public view and debate, allow for the representation and participation of interested parties, and be responsive to the overall concerns of the polity as well as to those groups that will be adversely affected by the policies it generates. There must be formal mechanisms for holding the legislators accountable. Legislatures should also operate within a framework of checks and balances.

The APA was rudimentary in many respects, but its provisions for rulemaking, open information, and judicial review help bring these leg-

islative values into federal administration. After 1946, federal administration became more substantially infused with legislative values as
Congress augmented the APA with freedom of information, measures
promoting representativeness and openness in the advisory committee
system, government in the sunshine, protections for small businesses and
other entities, negotiated rulemaking, and formal congressional review
of agency rules.

Constitutional values were also applied to agency adjudication. Prior
to 1946, procedures were problematic. They varied widely among agencies. Some were probably fair by the standards of the day; others were
unfair enough to prompt Congress to embark on a long struggle to enact an acceptable administrative law bill. The APA's provisions adapt
constitutional procedural due process to formal adjudication by federal
administrators (Gellhorn and Levin 1997, 237). Hence the term "judicialization," which may connote more elaborate procedure than the
APA required at the outset (Barnett 1948; Warren 1996, 311–314). The
APA's goal was to guarantee fairness in administrative hearings, without
overburdening the agencies. Nevertheless, the act was immediately criticized in the public administration literature for relying on trial-like, adversarial procedures (Sherwood 1947; Barnett 1948).

Subsequent development has been mostly within the executive branch
and by judicial decisions (see Warren 1996, chap. 7).[13] However, in 1990
Congress revisited the issues associated with formal adjudications, which
had grown more complex and subject to delay over time. In the Administrative Dispute Resolution Act (1990), it authorized agencies to use a
variety of alternative dispute resolution (ADR) techniques in place of
adjudication. These include negotiation, conciliation, facilitation, media-
tion, fact-finding, minitrials, and arbitration.

The 1990 act had a sunset clause, but ADR was reauthorized and
strengthened by the Administrative Dispute Resolution Act of 1996.[14]
ADR is used in such a wide variety of settings in order to avoid full-
blown court trials that its authorization in federal administration since
1990 tends to match the society's experience with adjudication rather
than to detract from the subordination of the agencies' judicial functions
to constitutional values associated with fair adjudicatory procedure.

Execution, of course, has been considered the prime or definitive administrative function. With the exception of the Jacksonian or spoils
period, the constitutional values associated with it have generally been
Hamiltonian:

Energy in the executive is a leading character in the definition of good government. . . .

A feeble executive implies a feeble execution of the government. A feeble execution is but another phrase for a bad execution; and a government ill executed, whatever it may be in theory, must be, in practice, a bad government. . . .

The ingredients which constitute energy in the executive are unity; duration; an adequate provision for its support; and competent powers. (Hamilton 1788, 423–424)

The historical effort to achieve these values—generally rendered as efficiency, economy, and effectiveness or cost-effectiveness—eventually resulted in the "managerial presidency" (Arnold 1986). The Executive Office of the President and especially the Office of Management and Budget (OMB) within it are the main organizations for promoting them. Both units are manifestations of orthodox public administration's impact on governmental structure and process. However, they also reveal one of the orthodoxy's major weaknesses. Hamilton's "unity," which referred to a single rather than plural executive, was not the orthodoxy's "unity of command." In fact, the constitutional law established in *Humphrey's Executor v. United States* (1935) and *Wiener v. United States* (1958) places agencies exercising quasi-legislative and/or quasi-judicial functions largely outside the ambit of presidential executive orders and OMB controls (see Moreno 1994).

The value sets associated with legislation, adjudication, and execution often converge within single agencies or administrative programs. They complicate federal administrative practice because they sometimes compete or conflict with one another. In a sense, they replicate the tensions among the governmental branches that are inherent in the separation of powers. They do not make for smooth administration, but they improve its fit in the constitutional framework.

The Separation of Powers Over Administration

Legislative-centered public administration also subordinates federal administration to controls by all three branches. The answer to Francis Rourke's (1993) question—"Whose bureaucracy is this, anyway?"—is that it is ideally the public's but more immediately belongs to the president, Congress, and the courts. Rourke (1993, 687) uses the terms "dual sovereignty" and "joint custody" to explain how the president and Congress share control and influence over federal administration. He neglects the courts because his interest is in the other two branches, but the courts also play a significant role in influencing administration and directing agencies.[15]

The academic literature on control of federal agencies tends to cast the issues in terms of a separation-of-powers contest between the president and Congress (e.g., Rourke 1993; Wood and Waterman 1994, 29–30; Weingast and Moran 1983; Calvert, McCubbins, and Weingast 1989; Katzmann 1994). Frequently, like Rourke, it ignores the courts altogether. It sometimes concludes that the president has the upper hand, other times not, and observes that relative power may vary according to policy arena (Vogler 1988, 304–312). However, the empirical evidence that federal administration is under "tripartite custody" to a much greater extent now than in 1946 is overwhelming. As Chapters 2–4 explain, the case for the proposition that the 1946 framework increased the congressional share is equally strong. As noted above, the APA also enhanced judicial custody.

Tripartite custody places federal administration under the separation of powers. Like the process of bringing the separation of powers into the value sets that govern federal agencies' legislative, judicial, and executive functions, it adds complexity and causes conflict. Perhaps many administrators would empathize with Howard Phillips in *Local 2677, the American Federation of Government Employees v. Phillips* (1973), who, as discussed in Chapter 2, found himself pulled in one direction by the presidency, pushed in another by Congress, and ultimately told what to do by a court. As fifty years' worth of literature on federal bureaucratic politics shows, at the higher levels the administrator's job includes trying to reconcile competing presidential and legislative perspectives in promoting administrative programs within the framework of the rule of law (e.g., Long 1949; Bernstein 1958; Kaufman 1981; Lynn 1996, chap. 3). According to John Millett (1959, 441), this is how it should be: "We cannot look to constitutional doctrine to find an answer to the question: How do we keep the bureaucracy politically responsible in America? Rather we must look to practice. And in practice . . . all three branches of government, legislative, executive, and judicial, have major roles to play in maintaining politically responsible behavior. Each such role is different; each operates directly upon administrative agencies. In a sense, administrative agencies are responsible in varying ways to all three branches of government."

The rise of the administrative state confronted the U.S. political system with a unique problem: how to integrate a large-scale administration into a stable separation-of-powers system (Riggs 1991, 1994).[16] The President's Committee on Administrative Management had one potential solution; in 1946 Congress legislated a lasting framework for another. Congress achieved a much larger role in federal administration. But as Chief Justice Warren Burger suggested, the system is often "clumsy, inefficient, even unworkable" (*Immigration and Naturalization Service v. Chadha* 1983, 959). It is frustrating and easy to criticize. It prompts a continual search for a better way.

Lessons for Reformers

Since 1946, reform has been a normal condition in federal administration (see Light 1997). It stems from many causes: dissatisfaction with "bureaucracy"; the need to correct maladministration, abuse, and failures; the possibilities raised by new ideas, techniques, and technologies; economic and social change; politics; and more. It also has many objectives, including improving organization and performance; reducing waste, fraud, and abuse; promoting democratic-constitutional values such as representativeness, participation, openness, and individual rights; and enhancing accountability, supervision, and control.

The scope of reform varies widely from minor agency reorganizations to major efforts to reorient federal administration. The latter has never occurred in one fell swoop. Andrew Jackson initiated the spoils system, but he did not install it (White 1965b). The orthodoxy struggled for decades to achieve dominance (Arnold 1986). The present study is the first comprehensive treatment of the 1946 framework and its further development as a set of coherent reforms, united by a powerful institutional logic, that fundamentally changed federal administration over time. Legislative-centered public administration achieved substantial success by the end of the 1970s, faced something of a hiatus in the 1980s, and picked up considerable momentum in the 1990s with the enactment of GPRA in 1993 and SBREFA in 1996.

Most federal administrative reforms fall short of their mark, some decidedly so (Light 1997, 179). Many are misconceived, poorly designed, and either implemented improperly or not at all (Caiden 1991, 14–16, 151). The insight that legislative-centered public administration has become a major force in federal administration provides guidance as to what kinds of reforms are unlikely to succeed.

It is standard practice to view federal administrative reforms through a separation-of-powers lens. What strengthens the president is thought to weaken Congress. (Again, most analysts pay scant attention to the courts.) Paul Light's comprehensive study of 141 federal reforms since 1945 posits such a contest: "A recurring theme in making the government work is just who will lead the effort. Congress has clearly been ascendant in reform during the post-Watergate period, becoming the most frequent originator of reform ideas. The question . . . is to what extent reform has also shifted power to one institution or the other." Light was able to make a judgment on 106 of the reforms, finding that "69 shift power toward the president, 37 toward Congress" (1997, 205). But if Congress is ascendant, why is power over federal administration being shifted to the president? The legislative-centered perspective provides a better answer than the institutional contest model.

Congress initiates reforms that strengthen legislative-centered public administration, and it blocks those that do not. Congress is dominant when a reform involves the agencies' performance as legislative extensions or its ability to supervise them. Light calls administrative law, the Inspector General Act, and related measures "watchful eye" reforms, and concludes that "Congress has clearly been the leader" in this area (1997, 210). Moreover, Congress will oppose reform efforts to free agencies from reporting and other "watchful eye" requirements because "Congress will almost always put its need to see ahead of a manager's need to act" (1997, 213).

However, Congress is willing—perhaps even eager—to endorse reforms that strengthen the presidency insofar as they fit the legislative-centered model or at least do not weaken it. "Even after Watergate," Light observes, "Congress was still quite capable of loaning the keys to administrative reform to the presidency" with regard to paperwork reduction, and it "still shows a surprising readiness to defer to the commander in chief with regard to war on waste" (1997, 206).

In sum, an understanding of legislative-centered public administration helps to identify the areas of administrative reform in which Congress will seek institutional dominance and those in which it will not. Light's "watchful eye" reforms go to the core of the congressional role in legislative-centered public administration. Coordinating agency activities, as in paperwork reduction, and managing their day-to-day affairs with a view toward reducing waste are largely presidential functions according to the legislative-centered model. What is at stake is not institutional *power* per se, but Congress's vision, as initially framed in 1946, of its appropriate institutional *role* in federal administration.

The lesson for federal administrative reformers is evident: reforms should be formulated, designed, and implemented with sensitivity to legislative-centered public administration. Reforms that threaten its main tenets will face tough challenges and, ultimately, are likely to fail unless Congress can be brought on board. Simply asking Congress to stop or significantly reduce its roles in treating the agencies as extensions, supervising them, and intervening in their operations on behalf of constituency and district interests is unlikely to succeed. Under normal conditions, offering it some different, meaningful, workable, and comprehensive institutional role in the administrative state would seem to be a prerequisite to gaining its support. So doing, of course, would be no mean feat.

Vice President Al Gore's National Performance Review–National Partnership for Reinventing Government (NPR) presents a clear example of the frustrations reformers may face (Gore 1993). The NPR clashed strongly with legislative-centered public administration. It adopted a business model for federal administration and proposed a role for Congress not unlike that advocated by the President's Committee on Administrative Management in 1937. Rather than roll over, agree to biennial budgeting, pay greater deference to the executive budget, reduce the tools of "micromanagement" (budget earmarks, staffing floors, and reporting requirements), or deregulate federal administration, as Gore advised, Congress deepened its involvement in administration through the strategic planning, oversight, and review provisions of GPRA and SBREFA (see Gore 1993, 13, 17, 20, 34). Major federal administrative reforms depend on Congress. They require agreement with legislative-centered public administration or initiating what is likely to be a very difficult, long-term effort to find another acceptable place for Congress in the administrative state.

Conclusion: Legislative-Centered Public Administration and Democratic-Constitutionalism

The contemporary congressional role in federal administration is not accidental. It was produced by deliberation rather than happenstance. There is an underlying comprehensive logic to it. Congress creates agencies, delegates legislative authority to them, and treats them as its extensions. It regulates their procedures, supervises them, and requires federal administration to comport with democratic-constitutional values as well as managerial ones.

The congressional role embodied in legislative-centered public administration is constitutional. It follows James Madison's belief that "The interest of the man must be connected with the constitutional rights of the place" in order to prevent "a gradual concentration of the several powers in the same department" (Madison 1788, 321–322). It does not usurp the president's executive powers. Although it is not immutable, it show no signs of being transitory. In fact, except for a brief time prior to 1946, it is the only role Congress has ever played in the modern federal administrative state.

Congressional involvement in federal administration can be misguided, excessive, and uncoordinated. It may sometimes be aimed at incumbency rather than better public policy and administration. However, to dismiss the congressional role simply as interference or micromanagement is to seriously misunderstand its overall constitutional function.

Democracy requires that administration be subordinated to representative institutions. In parliamentary systems this requirement is met, at least in theory, by formally fusing legislative and executive powers. Legislative-centered public administration serves a similar function in the U.S. separation-of-powers system. It substantially fuses legislative and administrative functions with regard to rulemaking, defining and implementing congressional intent, and dealing with a variety of constituency and district interests. In so doing, it broadly subordinates administration to congressionally imposed procedural and substantive controls and values. Because Congress is the Constitution's premier representative national institution, its relationship with the agencies is very much in keeping with democratic theory.

Legislative-centered public administration may not yield the most efficient, economical, and effective administration. It operates in a separation-of-powers system that is rife with institutionalized cross-pressures (Millett 1959, 441; Riggs 1994, 66; Rosenbloom 1983). These are exacerbated by Congress's own lack of unity. However, it is one approach toward adapting or retrofitting the administrative state to the U.S. constitutional scheme. That is the context and level on which it should be evaluated.

It is easy enough to criticize some of Congress's actions with regard to federal administration. Casework and pork barrel are soft targets. It is much more difficult to build a theory that can truly replace the legislative-centered perspective. Riggs (1991, 1994) warns us to beware of parliamentary models. Given the scale of the federal government, it is clearly too late to return to the illusion of a workable dichotomy between politics and administration or the idea that the executive branch should be unified under the president because he "is indeed the one and only national officer representative of the entire Nation" (PCAM 1937, 1). Gore's (1993, 2) assurance that "The federal government is filled with good people trapped in bad systems" does not resonate well in a constitutional system of checks and balances based on the Madisonian view that "If men were angels, no government would be necessary. If angels were to govern men, neither external nor internal controls on government would be necessary. In framing a government which is to be administered by men over men, the great difficulty lies in this: you must first enable the government to control the governed; and in the next place oblige it to control itself" (Madison 1788, 322). Without being defeatist, Dwight Waldo (1984, xviii) argues that reconstructing post-orthodox public administration, of which the legislative-centered approach is such a key part, presents a problem that "*cannot be solved—*acceptably, workably—given our constitutional system, our constitutional history, and our democratic ideology." Critics of legislative-centered public administration would probably do better to work within its parameters than to reject it entirely.

This book began with the question, "What is the appropriate role in large-scale public administration for a national legislature in a separation-of-powers system?" Legislative-centered public administration offers the only deliberate answer the nation has ever tried. This study has elucidated this perspective, analyzed it, and made it accessible. The importance of the legislative-centered perspective cannot be denied. The consequences of fully integrating it into the self-conscious study of public administration are unknowable, but it should open broad new avenues of thought and understanding. The consequences of failure to take it seriously are certain: much of the field will continue to promote a constitutionally and politically untenable vision of public administration as simply an executive-centered, managerial endeavor; it will neglect the full range of values that public administration entails, and it will prescribe faulty reforms.

Appendix
Statutes Cited

Administrative Dispute Resolution Act (1990). PL 101-552. 104 Stat. 2736. November 15.

Administrative Dispute Resolution Act (1996). PL 104-320. 110 Stat. 3870. October 19.

Administrative Procedure Act (1946). PL 79-404. 60 Stat. 237. June 11.

Atomic Energy Act (1946). PL 79-585. 60 Stat. 755. August 1.

Balanced Budget and Emergency Deficit Control Act (1985). PL 99-177. 99 Stat. 1037. December 12.

Budget and Accounting Act (1921). PL 67-13. 42 Stat. 20. June 10.

Budget Enforcement Act (1990). PL 101-508. 104 Stat. 1388-573. November 5.

Chief Financial Officers Act (1990). PL 101-576. 104 Stat. 2828. November 15.

Civil Service Act (1883). PL 47–27. 22 Stat. 403. January 16.

Civil Service Reform Act (1978). PL 95-454. 92 Stat. 1111. October 13.

Congressional Budget and Impoundment Control Act (1974). PL 93-344. 88 Stat. 297. July 12.

Defense Base Closure and Realignment Act (1990). PL 101-510. 104 Stat. 1808. November 5.

Employment Act (1946). PL 79-304. 60 Stat. 23. February 20.

Ethics in Government Act (1978). PL 95-521. 92 Stat. 1824. October 26.

Federal Advisory Committee Act (1972). PL 92-463. 86 Stat. 770. October 6.

Federal Financial Management Improvement Act (1996). PL 104-208. 110 Stat. 3009. September 30.

First Supplemental Appropriation Act (1947). PL 80-1. 61 Stat. 3. January 31.

Freedom of Information Act (1966). PL 89-487. 80 Stat. 250. July 4.

Freedom of Information Act Amendments (1974). PL 93-502. 88 Stat. 1561. November 21.

Government in the Sunshine Act (1976). PL 94-409. 90 Stat. 1241. September 13.

Government Performance and Results Act (1993). PL 103-62. 107 Stat. 285. August 3.

Hatch Act (1939). PL 76-252. 53 Stat. 1147. August 2.

Inspector General Act (1978). PL 95-452. 90 Stat. 1101. October 12.

Internal Revenue Service Restructuring and Reform Act (1998). PL 105-206. 112 Stat. 685. July 22.

Legislative Reorganization Act (1946). PL 79-601. 60 Stat. 812. August 2.

Legislative Reorganization Act (1970). PL 91-510. 84 Stat. 1140. October 26.

Line Item Veto Act (1996). PL 104-130. 110 Stat. 1200. August 9.

Negotiated Rulemaking Act (1990). PL 101-648. 104 Stat. 4969. November 29.

Occupational Safety and Health Act (1970). PL 91-596. 84 Stat. 1590. December 29.

Paperwork Reduction Act (1980). PL 96-511. 94 Stat. 2812. December 11.

Paperwork Reduction Act (1995). PL 104-13. 109 Stat. 163. May 22.

Paperwork Reduction Reauthorization Act (1986). PL 99-500. 100 Stat. 1783. October 18.

Privacy Act (1974). PL 93-579. 88 Stat. 1896. December 31.

Public Buildings Purchase Contract Act (1954). PL 83-519. 68 Stat. 518. July 22.

Ramspeck Act (1940). PL 76-880. 54 Stat. 1211. September 19.

Regulatory Flexibility Act (1980). PL 96-354. 94 Stat. 1164. September 19.

Small Business Regulatory Enforcement Fairness Act (1996). PL 104-121. 110 Stat. 857. March 29.

Small Reclamation Projects Act (1956). PL 84-984. 70 Stat. 1044. August 6.

Tax Reform Act (1986). PL 99-514. 100 Stat. 2085. October 22.

Transportation Equity Act for the Twenty-first Century (1998). PL 105-178. 112 Stat. 107. June 9.

Watershed Protection and Flood Prevention Act (1954). PL 83-566. 68 Stat. 666. August 4.

Notes

1. The Problem: Repositioning Congress in the Modern Administrative State

1. Citations to all statutes mentioned in the text can be found in the Appendix.

2. The politics-administration dichotomy was challenged by E. Pendleton Herring in 1936, but it was not until the late 1940s that Waldo (1948), Appleby (1949), and Long (1949) seriously weakened its intellectual standing.

3. These statutes are discussed in Chapter 2. The Freedom of Information and Privacy Acts deal with federal agencies' release and withholding of information. The Federal Advisory Committee Act regulates the formation, representativeness, and openness of federal advisory committees. The Government in the Sunshine Act promotes open meetings in about fifty federal boards and commissions. The Paperwork Reduction Acts seek to reduce and coordinate federal agencies' requests for information from the public. The Negotiated Rulemaking Act provides for rulemaking by negotiation among concerned parties. The Small Business Regulatory Enforcement Fairness Act strengthens requirements that agency rulemaking be sensitive to the needs of small entities and also provides for formal congressional review of major rules.

4. These statutes are discussed in Chapter 3. The Inspector General Act places inspectors general in several administrative units and authorizes them to report to Congress. The Government Performance and Results Act requires agencies to establish strategic plans in consultation with Congress, among other provisions.

5. Civil Service Rule I of 1907 had already placed employees covered by the merit system under almost identical restrictions. In 1938, Senator Carl Hatch (D-NM) explained the need to bring exempted employees under such a measure: "When I look out over the country, and observe the vast, vast numbers of Federal employees who reach out and extend to every county and to every precinct in the United States, I realize that some other administration . . .

could absolutely control any political convention in which Representatives, Senators, or even a President were to be nominated" (U.S. Congress 1938, 4459). The Hatch Act was substantially revised and liberalized in 1993.

6. The other two members were Luther Gulick, a leading expert on public administration, and Charles Merriam, a well-known professor of political science. See Karl 1963 for intellectual biographies of the three committee members.

7. The U.S. Attorney General's Committee on Administrative Procedure (1941) was appointed in 1939 by the attorney general at the president's request. Roosevelt's veto message on the Walter-Logan Act (1940) cited the desirability of waiting for its report before adopting a comprehensive administrative procedure act. See U.S. Congress 1940, 13942–13943.

8. Taken from Rourke 1993.

9. Karl (1963, 164) explains that this arrangement was part of the Budget and Accounting Act of 1921, which created the federal executive budget: "Giving the executive his budget required that a watchdog be placed over his activities; but no one could decide who should hold the leash. . . . Congress attempted to compromise. . . . If it could not hold the leash itself, and apparently it felt it could not, and if it could not trust the leash in the hands of the President, then the answer was obvious. Congress gave it to the dog. The Comptroller General thereafter governed disbursement of funds, settlement of accounts and the auditing of those accounts without the responsibility of explaining his actions to any branch of the government except the various judges of the various courts of claims."

10. The key measures were bipartisan and supported either unanimously or by large majorities in each house. There were 56 Democrats, 39 Republicans, and 1 Progressive in the Senate; 239 Democrats, 192 Republicans, 1 Progressive, 1 American Labor Party member, and 2 vacancies in the House. The cumulative experience in the Senate was 745 years, with 49 senators having begun their present service in 1941 or later. House members had 3,419 years of cumulative experience. Seventy-six representatives were in their first term. The average length of service in each house was just under eight years, which is relatively short by subsequent standards (see Chapter 4). Reading the *Congressional Record* for 1946, one gets a sense that the overwhelming number of members felt that the need for reform was urgent and that some of the newer members had limited respect for past practices. As Fulbright, who joined the Senate in 1944, expressed it: "It seems to me that the fact the Senate has been a great body in the past has no application to the present, because circumstances have so changed that it does not follow at all that old procedures and old rules will result in a continuation of former efficiency" (U.S. Congress 1946c, 6531).

Among the members whose names may still be well known were Senators La Follette, Alben Barkley (D-KY, Majority Leader), Millard Tydings (D-MD), Harry Byrd, Lister Hill (D-AL, Majority Whip), Tom Connally (D-TX), Arthur Vandenberg (R-MI), Burton Wheeler (D-MT), James Eastland (D-MS), Carl Hatch, Richard Russell (D-GA), George Aiken (R-VT), Fulbright, Wayne Morse (R-OR), Warren Magnuson (D-WA), Claude Pepper (D-FL), Robert Taft (R-OH), and Robert Wagner (D-NY). Representatives included Sherman Adams (R-NH), Leslie Arends (R-IL, Minority Whip), Wright Patman (D-TX), Melvin Price (D-IL), John Rankin (D-MS), Sam Rayburn (D-TX, Speaker), L. Mendel Rivers (D-SC), John Sparkman (D-AL, Majority Whip), J. Parnell Thomas (R-NJ), Carl Vinson (D-GA), Henry Jackson (D-WA), Lyndon Johnson (D-TX), Estes Kefauver, Clare Boothe Luce (R-CT), John McCormack (D-MA), Mike Mansfield (D-MT), Wilbur Mills (D-AR), Karl Mundt (R-SD), Clifford Case (R-NJ), Emanuel Celler (D-NY), John Dingell (D-MI), Everett Dirksen (R-IL), Helen Gahagan Douglas (D-CA), Sam Ervin (D-NC), Albert Gore (D-TN), Adam Clayton Powell (D-NY), and Jamie Whitten (D-MS).

2. The Legislative Process by Other Means: Agencies as Extensions of Congress

1. Willoughby's view surfaced during hearings on the APA in 1945. David Simmons, president of the American Bar Association, suggested that "The people of America . . . desire that the Congress set up its own agencies." The idea was rejected as administratively impractical because it would overburden the members (see U.S. Senate 1946, 50–52). More modern authors, such as David Truman (1971, 439), sometimes consider administration as an extension of legislation, but primarily for implementation: "Administration of a statute is, properly speaking, an extension of the legislative process." By contrast, Cornelius Kerwin (1994, 345) states flatly that "Rule-making is the single most important function performed by agencies of government," and he defines it as "law-making."

2. See *Youngstown Sheet and Tube Co. v. Sawyer* (1952) and *In re Neagle* (1890).

3. *Morrison v. Olson* (1988, 689–690) reasons that "The analysis contained in our removal cases is designed not to define rigid categories of those officials who may or may not be removed at will by the President, but to ensure that Congress does not interfere with the President's exercise of the 'executive power' and his constitutionally appointed duty to 'take care that the laws be faithfully executed.' . . . [T]he real question is whether the removal restrictions

are of such a nature that they impede the President's ability to perform his constitutional duty."

4. Senatorial courtesy allows the senators from a state, who are members of the president's political party, to block the appointment of a person from that state to a federal post requiring Senate confirmation. Individual senators can also exercise influence by placing "holds" on appointments, which delay their consideration by the full Senate.

5. See U.S. General Accounting Office (1997b). The Ramspeck Act of 1940 specifically authorizes the practice.

6. *Panama Refining Company v. Ryan* (1935) and *Carter v. Carter Coal Co.* (1936). See generally Jackson 1941.

7. A stir was caused in the federal administrative law and regulatory communities in May 1999 when the U.S. Court of Appeals for the District of Columbia Circuit suggested that it might be time to reinvoke the nondelegation doctrine. It remains to be seen whether its opinion in *American Trucking Associations, Inc. v. U.S. Environmental Protection Agency* will be upheld on appeal or followed in other cases.

8. The Court nullified the Occupational Safety and Health Administration's standards for benzene in the ambient atmosphere of regulated workplaces on the basis that the agency had assumed, but not scientifically established, that any amount of a carcinogen presented a danger.

9. Conceivably, the cloud may lift, or at least thin out. In *United States v. Lopez* (1995), after an almost sixty-year hiatus, the Supreme Court gingerly breathed some new life into the other prong of the judiciary's resistance to New Deal legislation in the 1930s by limiting the reach of congressional power under the Commerce Clause. It is possible that it will do the same to the nondelegation doctrine.

10. Even some administrators were opposed to delegation. William Kelley, chief counsel for the Federal Trade Commission, testified before a Senate Subcommittee of the Committee on the Judiciary that "We just feel that Congress should not give to anybody, anybody, whether it is a court or administrative tribunal, the discretion to promulgate rules having the force and effect of law in *ex parte* hearings upon applications of interested parties" (U.S. Senate 1941, 293–294).

11. Legislative rules are generically like laws. They regulate behavior and establish eligibility. Interpretive rules are policy statements explaining how an agency understands various aspects of its legal mandate. Procedural rules pertain to an agency's organization and internal procedures for rulemaking, adjudication, and other functions (see Kerwin 1999, 22–29, for a discussion).

12. Related statements were made by Representatives Earl Michener (R-

MI), Clare Hoffman (R-MI), and Homer Angell (R-OR), among others (U.S. Congress 1940, 4534, 4541, 4593).

13. At one point the bill passed the Senate unanimously, but through a parliamentary maneuver it was subsequently returned to the legislative calendar for further consideration. See the statement of Senator Henry Ashurst (D-AZ), U.S. Congress 1940, 7177.

14. The theme that complexity requires delegation was widely shared. For example, see the statement by Representative Estes Kefauver (D-TN), U.S. Congress 1946c, 5767.

15. For instance, Clyde Aitchison, commissioner of the Interstate Commerce Commission, testified that congressional regulation of administrative procedures was a "retrograde step" that would undermine administrative flexibility (U.S. Senate 1946, 97). The Securities and Exchange Commission, Federal Power Commission, and Federal Security Administration also opposed the APA (Brazier 1993, 329).

16. The Senate *Report* accompanying the administrative procedure bill in 1946 also noted a lack of transparency: "Even the ordinary operations of administrative agencies are often difficult to know" (U.S. Senate 1946, 187).

17. Senator King also complained that "what amounts to legislation is being enacted day after day by appointed officials—not by the elected representatives of the people—and without consulting those who will be most affected by the legislation—contrary to the practice followed generally by Congress through its committees" (U.S. Congress 1940, 13673).

18. The U.S. General Accounting Office (1998c, 2–3, 6–8) found that in 1997 this provision was used in about half of all potentially covered rulemakings. Most of the instances involved administrative or technical matters of limited applicability. However, eleven major rules were also published without a notice of proposed rulemaking (NPRM). The use of the "good cause" exception is subject to judicial review. When informal rulemaking is avoided, agencies may nevertheless engage in practices that adhere loosely to its general intent. Under "direct final rulemaking," a rule is published and goes into effect on a specified future date unless adverse comments are filed. In the latter event, the rule is withdrawn and the agency may begin an informal proceeding. Under "interim final rulemaking" the rule is effective immediately, but subject to post-promulgation comments and potential withdrawal or revision.

19. The APA's provisions for judicial review were intended to subordinate agencies to the rule of law and to serve as a check on irrational or unfair agency decision making and action. But the act envisions public participation in rulemaking, transparency, and mandated adjudicatory and enforcement procedures, rather than judicial review, as the primary checks on agencies. It embraces a

presumption of judicial review, but exempts matters committed to agency discretion by law or precluded by statutes. The boundaries of contemporary judicial review are largely the result of judicial interpretation. For instance, it is not illogical to analyze "the reviewability of 'unreviewable' administrative action." For a cogent analysis see Warren 1996, chapter 9.

20. References herein to legislative source books follow the source book pagination. Additional information, such as the year of a statement or report, is provided in the text or citation, as necessary.

21. In fiscal 1997 there were 963 advisory committees. Executive Order 12838 (February 1993) required agencies to reduce the number of discretionary, but not congressionally mandated, committees by one-third. See U.S. General Accounting Office 1998a.

22. See also the statement by John Foster Dulles, then chair of the Committee on Administrative Law, Bar Association of the City of New York (U.S. Senate 1941, 1156), arguing that the courts might mistakenly interpret congressional inaction as informed acquiescence.

23. These included Kansas, Nebraska, Virginia, and Wisconsin (see U.S. Senate 1970, 1293).

24. SBREFA was part of the Republicans' effort to fulfill their 1994 "Contract with America" (see Cohen and Strauss 1997, 96). It enjoyed presidential and congressional Democratic Party support because, as discussed below, it contains a number of special protections for small businesses and other entities, something President Bill Clinton and the "New Democrats" wanted to take as much credit for as did the Republican-dominated Congress (see Sargentich 1997, 135).

25. See Skrzycki (1998b), who asks, "Will Congress Wake Up to Its Rule-Blocking Weapon?"

26. Strauss et al. (1995, 872, n. 6) report that by 1984 the paperwork burden had declined by 32 percent, but then began to rise again.

27. The proposed office would have been headed by a director appointed by the president with the advice and consent of the Senate for a seven-year term. Other members would be a justice of the U.S. Court of Appeals for the District of Columbia Circuit and the director of the Administrative Office of the U.S. Courts. The Office of Federal Administrative Procedure, which would not be bound by civil service rules, would appoint hearing examiners and work with agencies to establish "just and efficient" administrative practices (U.S. Senate 1970, 705–706). Such an office was opposed by the American Bar Association in 1941 (U.S. Senate 1941, 1091–1092) and was not included in the APA bill (U.S. Senate 1946, 303).

28. The current paperwork reduction format contains a number of com-

plexities, quandaries, and technicalities that do not bear on the discussion here (see Lubbers 1997; U.S. General Accounting Office 1998e). Jeffrey Lubbers, a leading expert on federal administrative procedure, predicts "numerous disputes between agencies and OIRA," "wrangles" over funding, and "less paperwork burden on the public," but also "delays in regulatory implementation" (1997, 121).

29. For some contemporary approaches see Knott and Miller 1987; McCubbins, Noll, and Weingast 1989; Ferejohn and Shipan 1990; Brazier 1993; Katzmann 1994.

30. The NPR became the National Partnership for Reinventing Government in 1998, but the "G" is usually silent.

3. Supervising the Agencies: Developing Congress's Capacity for Continuous Oversight

1. See Seidman 1970 for an elaborate discussion of how congressional and administrative organization are interrelated.

2. As noted in Chapter 2, delegations of legislative power are permissible when accompanied by an "intelligible principle." See *J. W. Hampton, Jr. and Co. v. United States* (1928) and *Schechter Poultry Corp. v. United States* (1935).

3. This is entirely plausible under the Small Business Regulatory Enforcement Fairness Act of 1996. As discussed in Chapter 2, the act provides for formal congressional review and potential disapproval of the major rules made by agencies.

4. Ogul (1976, 5) considers the standard to be "impossible to perform."

5. The choice of a joint committee was in keeping with Congress's interest in coordinating its activities and exercising better control over the agencies. The Atomic Energy Act, also passed in 1946, provides for a bipartisan congressional Joint Committee on Atomic Energy, composed of nine members each from the House and Senate. Its mission was to "make continuing studies of the activities of the Atomic Energy Commission and of problems relating to the development, use, and control of atomic energy" (Section 15[b]). This committee was given jurisdiction over all atomic energy matters coming before Congress.

6. An earlier version, the Legislative Reorganization Act of 1967, was offered by the Special Committee on the Organization of Congress, which was chaired by (now) Senator Monroney. It provided for a "Review Specialist" "to administer and coordinate the review function of the committee" (U.S. Senate 1967, 17). The 1967 bill was never enacted, and the provision was later dropped as "unworkable" (see U.S. House of Representatives 1970, 4433).

7. Fiorina's second edition (1989) includes the complete text of the original as part one, and corrections and reinterpretations of it as part two. His view of the matters cited here as "Fiorina 1977" remained unchanged.

8. The specialized oversight committees were Government Operations, Governmental Affairs, and some subcommittees of the House Commerce, Public Works, and Ways and Means Committees.

9. A results orientation focuses on administrative outputs and outcomes rather than on agency procedures or inputs such as staff and budgets. Performance budgeting seeks to connect budgetary allocations to the end product generated by agencies. Ideally, it would enable budgeters to determine the relative return for each dollar allocated. At the federal level, performance budgeting has been recommended on and off since 1949. It is easier to propose than to implement. See Lewis 1989, 155–164.

10. Among the policy entrepreneurs involved were Joseph Wholey of the University of Southern California and Harry Hatry of the Urban Institute. They secured endorsement of the GPRA bill by the National Academy of Public Administration in 1991. See U.S. Senate 1993, 8. One of GPRA's core ideas goes back at least as far as the 1940s when Kefauver and Levin (1947, 74) wrote: "Appearances before Congress would require Cabinet members and administrative chiefs to formulate clear definitions of executive policies."

11. The act is variously called by its full title or the Congressional Budget Act, the 1974 Budget Act, or the Impoundment Control Act (which is contained in Title X).

12. Similar statements were made by Representatives Robert Lagomarsino (R-CA), George H. Mahon (D-TX), William Alexander (D-AR), John Rhodes (R-AZ), and Melvin Price (D-IL). See U.S. House of Representatives 1979, 301; U.S. Congress 1973, 39343–39344, 39356, 39362, 39730.

13. Schick was at the Congressional Research Service. See U.S. House of Representatives 1979, 291.

14. In *Clinton v. City of New York* (1998) the Supreme Court held that the "line item veto" at issue enabled the president to amend or repeal statutes in contravention of Article I's procedures for legislation.

15. To date, all the comptrollers general have been male.

16. This reasoning echoes the U.S. President's Committee on Administrative Management (1937), discussed in Chapter 1. It would be difficult to find a significant federal management system that is not based on or substantially regulated by congressional action. Systems for personnel administration, procurement, information management, accounting, auditing, rulemaking, adjudication, and so on are all embodied in law. Boundaries between the executive branch and the legislature are highly permeable and, after *Morrison v. Olson*

(1988), largely ill-defined (see Chapter 2). Note the comparison with the 1949 Hoover Commission Report (U.S. Senate 1970, 854): "There is always the temptation in this system for members of the staff or of the committee to intrude into the actual administration of the statute and to attempt to influence specific policies or decisions. . . . Any such development would appear inconsistent with the traditional separation of powers." Note also the legislative-centered counterpoint. In 1946 the president of the American Bar Association, David Simmons, called for Congress to "set up its own agencies" and to "have a staff adequate and equal to that of any department of the Government" (U.S. Senate 1946, 51). The House Judiciary Committee chair, Hatton Sumners (D-TX), responded that such an approach was impractical, *not unconstitutional:* "You are going to have to go ahead and establish these great organizations of considerable size around Members of Congress and wind up with 500 or 600 other bureaus, and the Congressman will be in the center of it and he won't know much about what the folks are doing under it" (U.S. Senate 1946, 51–52).

17. The majority opinion was written by Chief Justice Warren Burger and joined by Justices William Brennan, Thurgood Marshall, Harry Blackmun, John Paul Stevens, and Sandra Day O'Connor. Justice Powell also found the statutory scheme in violation of the separation of powers, but because, in his view, it authorized Congress to engage in a judicial function. Justices Byron White and William Rehnquist dissented.

18. The Budget and Accounting Act of 1921, codified at 31 U.S. Code section 703(e)(1)(B), defines cause as permanent disability, inefficiency, neglect of duty, malfeasance, commission of a felony, or an act involving moral turpitude. Notice and a hearing are required before dismissal by joint resolution. The act does not provide for presidential dismissal of the comptroller general, which is why the Court's majority argues that he is subordinate to Congress alone. Justice White pointed out that it could actually be easier to impeach the comptroller general in the sense that only a simple majority would be required to bring charges in the House, whereas it would take two-thirds in each house to override a presidential veto of a joint resolution of dismissal. However, the Constitution limits impeachment to "Treason, Bribery, or other high Crimes and Misdemeanors" (Article II, section 4).

4. Constituency Time: Casework, Public Works, and Incumbency

1. To enhance readability, the term "district service" is used throughout this chapter as a substitute for "district-oriented public works." "Pork barrel" and "pork" are used to connote wasteful or inefficient public works projects

intended mainly to bring federal funds to a representative or senator's constituency, generally with the expectation that it will promote his or her incumbency. Ferejohn (1974, 43–46) reviews some of the conceptual and analytic difficulties faced in determining whether a project is clearly inefficient in terms of cost-benefit analysis.

2. The Legislative Reorganization Act of 1946 provided for increases in congressional pay, which several members thought would raise public ire (U.S. Congress 1946c, 10096–10101). However, much of the press was favorable to the overall reform (see U.S. Congress 1946c, 7958–7959, 9646).

3. According to Fiorina (1989, 116), Senate elections are typically more competitive than those for the House. They attract better challengers and are more ideological, issue-based, and visible.

4. Congressman Thomas Lane (D-MA) explained the problem as well as anyone: "The demands on [the member's] time are incessant and even oppressive, and . . . his sources of information and assistance inadequate: In the Seventy-seventh Congress a total of 10,793 bills were introduced and 541 joint resolutions. Out of this flood Congress passed 1,078 House bills and 476 Senate bills. Again in the second session of the Seventy-eighth Congress 953 bills and resolutions were passed, of which only 86 were subject to any real discussion. The other 867 were passed by voice vote or without objection. But it is not only in this flood of legislation that we are overwhelmed. I have mentioned the demands of committee work; yet we know too well that this is only part of the demand. The tremendous detail of office work, which we are unwilling to stint, the public appearances, the special investigations, the trips to or consultations with officers of the Federal agencies, meeting constituents, radio appearances, and so forth—the fact is, as we know well, that we are trying to do a great deal too many things which we regard as our responsibility without being able to do any of them as well as we would like or are able to do" (U.S. Congress 1946c, 10054).

5. Another loadshedding provision, originally Title VII, would have given "self-rule" to the District of Columbia. However, it was not enacted. See U.S. Congress 1946c, 6397, for the text, and Kefauver and Levin 1947, 122–125, for a brief discussion.

6. See chapter 8 of Rosenbloom and O'Leary 1997 for a discussion of constitutional torts.

7. 88 Stat. 50. See Warren 1996, 487–490, for a general discussion.

8. The House Committee on the Judiciary report on "Tort Claims Against the United States" (U.S. House of Representatives 1945, 2) does not include comprehensive or comparable data for each Congress. The Sixty-ninth and Seventy-first through Seventy-third Congresses are omitted altogether.

9. Many of these dealt with naturalization.

10. Fox and Hammond (1977, 20) explain that under previous laws, by 1946 an average of five personal staff were *authorized* for each representative and six for each senator.

11. In 1940 Representative Clare Hoffman (R-MI) claimed, "It is doubtful that there are more than a half-dozen Members of this House who have not become indignant at the treatment they have received [from administrators] when attempting to take up for some of their constituents some of the questions which they have brought here to Washington" (U.S. Congress 1940, 4541).

12. As a general rule of federal administrative law, individuals are required to exhaust their administrative remedies before seeking adjudication in an administrative or judicial forum. However, there are a number of exceptions. See Gellhorn and Levin 1997, 371–376. In order to counteract delay, sometimes statutes or administrative procedures authorize appeals after a specific number of days have elapsed from the time the individual initiated his or her request or complaint.

13. The 1998 reforms also grew out of whistle-blowing by IRS employees. See Roth and Nixon 1999; Farrell 1999.

14. The House bill did not require the Senate's consent. An amendment to require it was defeated 48 in favor to 58 opposed, largely on the basis that the president should not be hampered in selecting these "close advisers." It was also argued that they would be on a par with the director of the Bureau of the Budget, who at the time was not subject to Senate confirmation (U.S. Congress 1945a, 12074–12075). The act's final text is that of the conference committee.

15. As discussed in Chapter 3, the 1974 Congressional Budget and Impoundment Control Act improved legislative budgeting. However, by then monetary policy implemented by the Federal Reserve System had eclipsed budgeting as the major tool for stimulating growth and regulating inflation.

16. Another possibility is to impose an external control, as Congress tried to do with the Line Item Veto Act of 1996. However the act was ruled unconstitutional in *Clinton v. City of New York* (1998).

17. Representative Randolph agreed that "a hit-and-miss policy has not given the type of well-rounded public-works program which the people of this country desire" and also favored "funneling projects, as it were, through one channel and from that funneling we shall have ready as a backlog what the country will need in the way of public works" (U.S. Congress 1945a, 12015).

18. The highway is pursuant to a twenty-year-old treaty in which Canada provides a right-of-way that connects parts of Alaska. Davidson and Oleszek (1996, 329) suggest that some members are now holding federal projects up to a stricter standard, primarily because of environmental concerns and a desire to

balance the budget. Orvedahl (1995, chap. 5) documents a mixed picture in which there are both instances of successful resistance to spending and substantial public works appropriations.

19. Hibbing's conclusion pertains specifically to the House. Parker (1989, chap. 5) deals with career paths in both houses. See also Bullock 1972; Loomis 1984.

20. This needs to be emphasized. Fiorina's 1977 work on congressional incumbency was misread as "conspiratorial speculation" despite its clear statement that no "sinister motivation" was involved. See Fiorina 1989, 110–111.

21. Planning, Programming, Budgeting System (President Lyndon B. Johnson); Management by Objectives (President Richard M. Nixon); Zero Based Budgeting (President Jimmy Carter), Civil Service Reform Act of 1978, Total Quality Management (late 1980s and early 1990s), downsizing (especially Presidents Ronald Reagan and Bill Clinton), "reinventing" (Vice President Al Gore's National Performance Review/National Partnership for Reinventing Government initiative). See Rosenbloom (1998b) for a review of each.

5. Legislative-Centered Public Administration: Administrative Theory, Practice, and Reform

1. For examples regarding public administration see Dotson 1955 and Baker 1990. Such doctrines can enhance judicial power over the administrative state, just as legislative-centered public administration strengthens Congress's role in federal administration (see Rosenbloom and O'Leary 1997).

2. Meriam's work at Brookings was influential in Congress's defeat of the effort by the President's Committee on Administrative Management in 1937 to reorganize the executive branch thoroughly under the presidency (see Karl 1963, 31–41). George Galloway (1946, 230–231), staff director of the Joint Committee on the Organization of Congress, which proposed the Legislative Reorganization Act of 1946, quotes Willoughby's 1934 volume approvingly with regard to the appropriate congressional role in federal administration.

3. James Q. Wilson (1980) explains the politics of regulation in terms of the extent to which benefits and burdens are concentrated or dispersed.

4. Independently of the APA, since the 1950s the federal courts have developed broad judicial review of the constitutionality of administrative action involving individual rights (see Rosenbloom and O'Leary 1997). Administrative law has also been developed substantially by the courts (see Gellhorn and Levin 1997, chaps. 3 and 10; Warren 1996, chaps. 9 and 10).

5. In 1947, Louis Brownlow (1949, 116–117) described Congress's consti-

tutional function regarding ongoing administration in the following terms: "What the Congress should retain, what the Congress must retain, what the Congress cannot abdicate, is the power of the purse. To the extent that laws enacted in pursuance of the Constitution require appropriations, these funds must be voted by the Congress or they cannot be withdrawn from the Treasury. The Congress annually, therefore, has the opportunity to review, when it passes upon the President's budget, the whole vast machinery of the government."

6. By contrast, *Youngstown Sheet and Tube Co. v. Sawyer* (1952) provides important constitutional support to legislative-centered public administration in holding that the president has no inherent or implied power to place steel mills under federal management even during a national emergency.

7. To the extent that incumbency itself is a problem, more drastic measures might be necessary. Term limits are one proposed solution. Compulsory voting, as is practiced in Australia and some European democracies, is another approach, though one seldom advocated in the United States. It would presumably enlarge turnouts and thereby make congressional elections more competitive.

8. Meriam's (1939) work regarding Congress and federal administration has already been mentioned. Wyman (1903), Goodnow (1905), and Hart (1940) had written books on administrative law.

9. Writing about the immigrants, Woodrow Wilson claimed, "We are unquestionably facing an ever-increasing difficulty of self-command with ever-deteriorating materials, possibly with degenerating fibre" (Rohr 1986, 72).

10. In addition to Willoughby's legislative-centered view, there was an incipient Human Relations movement. See Rosenbloom 1998b, 151–153.

11. The New Public Administration of the late 1960s and early 1970s was the most ambitious. See Marini 1971.

12. Now that there is a New Public Management, post-orthodox public administration might be called "conventional" or "traditional" public administration.

13. As in the case of rulemaking, the APA establishes minimum requirements. The number of hearing examiners increased from 196 in 1947 to 1,185 in the early 1990s as the number of agencies using them expanded from 18 to 32 (Lubbers 1994, 287–288, 291; Dullea 1973, 43). In 1972 the Civil Service Commission changed their title to "administrative law judge" (see Dullea 1973).

14. The 1996 act permits binding arbitration in some circumstances and shields some information yielded in ADR from release under the Freedom of Information Act.

15. The literature dealing with the impact of the courts on public adminis-

tration is too vast to cite here. Much of it is reviewed in Rosenbloom and O'Leary 1997, chapter 9. For studies dealing with specific federal programs and agencies see Melnick 1983, 1994; O'Leary 1993.

16. Riggs (1991, 1994) observes that in other separation-of-powers systems presidents are prone to disbanding or ignoring legislatures, and military coups are used to depose presidents.

References

Aberbach, Joel. 1990. *Keeping a Watchful Eye.* Washington, DC: Brookings Institution.

American Bar Association. 1934. "Report of the Special Committee on Administrative Law." In U.S. Congress, Senate, Committee on the Judiciary, Subcommittee on Separation of Powers (1970). *Separation of Powers and the Independent Agencies: Cases and Selected Readings.* 91st Cong., 1st sess. Document 91-49, pp. 214–239. Washington, DC: U.S. Government Printing Office.

American Bar Association Journal. 1939. "House of Delegates—First Session: Report on Administrative Law." 25:93–97.

———. 1946. "The Federal Administrative Procedure Act Becomes Law." 32:377.

American Trucking Associations, Inc. v. U.S. Environmental Protection Agency. 1999. No. 97-1440 (U.S. Court of Appeals for the District of Columbia Circuit).

Appleby, Paul. 1945. *Big Democracy.* New York: Knopf.

———. 1949. *Policy and Administration.* University: University of Alabama Press.

Arnold, Peri. 1986. *Making the Managerial Presidency.* Princeton, NJ: Princeton University Press.

Arnold, R. Douglas. 1979. *Congress and the Bureaucracy.* New Haven, CT: Yale University Press.

Bailey, Stephen. 1950. *Congress Makes a Law: The Story behind the Employment Act of 1946.* New York: Columbia University Press.

Baker, Lynn. 1990. "The Prices of Rights." *Cornell University Law Review* 75 (September): 1185–1257.

Barnett, Vincent, Jr. 1948. "Judicialization of the Administrative Process." *Public Administration Review* 8 (Spring): 126–141.

Barr, Stephen. 1997a. "Congress Pushes Agencies on Results Act Deadline." *Washington Post,* June 5, p. A19.

———. 1997b. "Congress Seeks Seat at the Table." *Washington Post,* March 7, p. A19.

———. 1998. "GOP Sees No Results in Results Act." *Washington Post,* June 9, p. A4.

Beard, Charles. 1913. *An Economic Interpretation of the Constitution of the United States.* New York: Macmillan.

Bernstein, Marver. 1958. *The Job of the Federal Executive.* Washington, DC: Brookings Institution.

Bowsher, Charles. 1992. "Meeting the New American Management Challenge in a Federal Agency: Lessons from the General Accounting Office." *Public Administration Review* 52 (January/February): 3–7.

Bowsher v. Synar. 1986. 478 U.S. 714.

Brazier, James. 1993. *Who Controls the Administrative State? Congress and the President Adopt the Administrative Procedure Act of 1946.* Ann Arbor, MI: UMI.

Brownlow, Louis. 1949. *The President and the Presidency.* Chicago: Public Administration Service.

Buckley v. Valeo. 1976. 424 U.S. 1.

Bullock, Charles. 1972. "House Careerists: Changing Patterns of Longevity and Attrition." *American Political Science Review* 66 (December): 1295–1300.

Burkhead, Jesse. 1948. "Federal Budgetary Developments: 1947–48." *Public Administration Review* 8 (Autumn): 267–274.

Burnham, David. 1989. *A Law Unto Itself.* New York: Random House.

Burns, James. 1956. *Roosevelt: The Lion and the Fox.* New York: Harcourt, Brace & World.

Bush, George. 1990. "Statement by President George Bush Upon Signing S. 303." *Weekly Compilation of Presidential Documents* 26 (November 29): 1945.

Caiden, Gerald. 1991. *Administrative Reform Comes of Age.* New York: Walter de Gruyter.

Cain, Bruce, John Ferejohn, and Morris Fiorina. 1987. *The Personal Vote.* Cambridge: Harvard University Press.

Calvert, Randall, Mathew McCubbins, and Barry Weingast. 1989. "A Theory of Political Control and Agency Discretion." *American Journal of Political Science* 33 (August): 588–611.

Carter v. Carter Coal Co. 1936. 298 U.S. 238.

Chevron v. Natural Resources Defense Council. 1984. 467 U.S. 837.

Clinton v. City of New York. 1998. 118 S.Ct. 2091.

Coglianese, Cary. 1997. "Assessing Consensus: The Promise and Performance of Negotiated Rulemaking." *Duke Law Journal* 46:1255–1349.

Cohen, Daniel, and Peter Strauss. 1997. "Congressional Review of Agency Regulations." *Administrative Law Review* 49:95–110.

Cooper, Kenneth. 1993. "The House Freshmen's First Choice." *Washington Post,* January 5, p. A13.

Coyle, Marcia. 1995. "Agencies Ask for Less Sunshine." *National Law Journal,* September 25, p. A12.

Davidson, Roger, and Walter Oleszek. 1985. *Congress and Its Members.* 2nd ed. Washington, DC: CQ Press.

———. 1996. *Congress and Its Members.* 6th ed. Washington, DC: CQ Press.

Davis, Kenneth Culp. 1953. "Some Reflections of a Law Professor about Instruction and Research in Public Administration." *American Political Science Review* 47 (September): 728–752.

Dodd, Lawrence, and Bruce Oppenheimer. 1997. "Revolution in the House: Testing the Limits of Party Government." In *Congress Reconsidered,* ed. Lawrence Dodd and Bruce Oppenheimer, 29–60. 6th ed. Washington, DC: CQ Press.

Dodd, Lawrence, and Richard Schott. 1979. *Congress and the Administrative State.* New York: Wiley.

Dotson, Arch. 1955. "The Emerging Doctrine of Privilege in Public Employment." *Public Administration Review* 15 (Spring): 77–88.

Dullea, Charles. 1973. "Development of the Personnel Program for Administrative Law Judges." *Administrative Law Review* 25, no. 1:41–47.

Dye, Thomas, and Harmon Zeigler. 1975. *The Irony of Democracy.* 3rd ed. North Scituate, MA: Duxbury Press.

Evans, C. Lawrence, and Walter Oleszek. 1997. "Congressional Tsunami? The Politics of Committee Reform." In *Congress Reconsidered,* ed. Lawrence Dodd and Bruce Oppenheimer, 193–211. 6th ed. Washington, DC: CQ Press.

Fainsod, Merle. 1951. "The Presidency and Congress." *Public Administration Review* 11 (Spring): 119–124.

Farley, James. 1948. *Jim Farley's Story.* New York: McGraw-Hill.

Farrell, Gina. 1999. "Investigation Fails to Back IRS Whistleblower Claims." *Federal Times,* July 5, p. 4.

Federal Trade Commission v. Ruberoid. 1952. 343 U.S. 470.

Fenno, Richard. 1978. *Home Style: House Members in Their Districts.* Boston: Little, Brown.

Ferejohn, John. 1974. *Pork Barrel Politics: Rivers and Harbors Legislation, 1947–1968.* Stanford, CA: Stanford University Press.

Ferejohn, John, and Charles Shipan. 1990. "Congressional Influence on Bureaucracy." *Journal of Law, Economics and Organization* 6:1–20.

Fiorina, Morris. 1977. *Congress: Keystone of the Washington Establishment.* New Haven, CT: Yale University Press.

———. 1989. *Congress: Keystone of the Washington Establishment.* 2nd ed. New Haven, CT: Yale University Press.

Fiorina, Morris, and David Rohde. 1989. *Home Style and Washington Work.* Ann Arbor: University of Michigan Press.

Fitzgerald, Randall, and Gerald Lipson. 1984. *Porkbarrel.* Washington, DC: Cato Institute.

Fox, Harrison, and Susan Hammond. 1977. *Congressional Staffs: The Invisible Force in American Lawmaking.* New York: Free Press.

Friedly, Jock. 1998. "Pork: Highways in Canada, N.Y." *The Hill,* June 3, p. 4.

Galloway, George. 1946. *Congress at the Crossroads.* New York: Thomas Y. Crowell.

Gaus, John. 1950. "Trends in the Theory of Public Administration." *Public Administration Review* 10 (Summer): 161–168.

Gellhorn, Ernest, and Ronald Levin. 1997. *Administrative Law and Process.* 4th ed. St. Paul, MN: West.

Gellhorn, Walter. 1966. *When Americans Complain.* Cambridge: Harvard University Press.

Gill, Jeff. 1995. "Formal Models of Legislative/Administrative Interaction: A Survey of the Subfield." *Public Administration Review* 55 (January/February): 99–106.

Gitelson, Alan, Robert Dudley, and Melvin Dubnick. 1988. *American Government.* Boston: Houghton Mifflin.

Goodnow, Frank. 1905. *The Principles of the Administrative Law of the United States.* New York: Putnam.

Gore, Al. 1993. *From Red Tape to Results: Creating a Government That Works Better & Costs Less.* Washington, DC: U.S. Government Printing Office.

———. 1995. *Common Sense Government Works Better & Costs Less.* Washington, DC: U.S. Government Printing Office.

Gugliotta, Guy. 1997. "It's Only a Paper Moan." *Washington Post,* July 29, p. A13.

Gulick, Luther. 1937. "Notes on the Theory of Organization." In *Classics of Public Administration,* ed. Jay Shafritz and Albert Hyde, 80–89. 3rd ed. Pacific Grove, CA: Brooks/Cole, 1992.

Gunther, Gerald. 1975. *Cases and Materials on Constitutional Law.* 9th ed. Mineola, NY: Foundation Press.

Hall, Richard, and Gary McKissick. 1997. "Institutional Change and Behavioral Choice in House Committees." In *Congress Reconsidered,* ed. Lawrence Dodd and Bruce Oppenheimer, 212–228. 6th ed. Washington, DC: CQ Press.

Hamilton, Alexander. 1788. "Federalist No. 70." In *The Federalist Papers,* ed. C. Rossiter, 423–431. New York: New American Library, 1961.

Harris, Christy. 1997. "Agency Goals Score an F." *Federal Times,* September 8, p. 5.

Hart, James. 1940. *An Introduction to Administrative Law with Selected Cases.* New York: F. S. Crofts.

Hatry, Harry, and Harold Finger. 1998. *Effective Implementation of the Government*

Performance and Results Act. Washington, DC: National Academy of Public Administration.

Heidenheimer, Arnold. 1989. "Perspectives on the Perception of Corruption." In *Political Corruption,* ed. Arnold Heidenheimer, Michael Johnson, and Victor LeVine, 149–163. New Brunswick, NJ: Transaction Publishers.

Herring, E. Pendleton. 1936. *Public Administration and the Public Interest.* New York: McGraw-Hill.

Hibbing, John. 1991. *Congressional Careers.* Chapel Hill: University of North Carolina Press.

Hummel, Ralph. 1977. *The Bureaucratic Experience.* New York: St. Martin's Press.

Humphrey's Executor v. United States. 1935. 295 U.S. 602.

Hyneman, Charles. 1950. *Bureaucracy in a Democracy.* New York: Harper & Brothers.

Immigration and Naturalization Service v. Chadha. 1983. 462 U.S. 919.

Industrial Union Department, AFL-CIO v. American Petroleum Institute. 1980. 448 U.S. 607.

In re Neagle. 1890. 135 U.S. 1.

Jackson, Robert. 1941. *The Struggle for Judicial Supremacy.* New York: Knopf.

Johnson, John. 1981. *American Legal Culture, 1908–1940.* Westport, CT: Greenwood.

Joyce, Philip. 1993. "The Reiterative Nature of Budget Reform: Is There Anything New in Federal Budgeting?" *Public Budgeting and Finance* 13 (Fall): 36–48.

———. 1996. "Jesse Burkhead and the Multiple Uses of Federal Budgets." *Public Budgeting and Finance* 16 (Summer): 59–75.

J. W. Hampton, Jr. and Co. v. United States. 1928. 276 U.S. 394.

Kamen, Michael. 1987. *A Machine That Would Go of Itself.* New York: Knopf.

Kammerer, Gladys. 1949. "The Administration of Congress." *Public Administration Review* 9 (Summer): 175–181.

Karl, Barry. 1963. *Executive Reorganization and Reform in the New Deal: The Genesis of Administrative Management, 1900–1939.* Cambridge: Harvard University Press.

Katzmann, Robert. 1994. "Explaining Agency Decision-Making: The Federal Trade Commission and Antitrust Policy in the Reagan Era." In *Handbook of Regulation and Administrative Law,* ed. D. Rosenbloom and R. Schwartz, 325–341. New York: Marcel Dekker.

Kaufman, Herbert. 1956. "Emerging Conflicts in the Doctrines of Public Administration." *American Political Science Review* 50 (December): 1057–1073.

———. 1977. *Red Tape.* Washington, DC: Brookings Institution.

———. 1981. *The Administrative Behavior of Federal Bureau Chiefs.* Washington, DC: Brookings Institution.

Kefauver, Estes, and Jack Levin. 1947. *A Twentieth-Century Congress.* New York: Essential Books.

Kendall v. United States. 1838. 37 U.S. 524.

Kerwin, Cornelius. 1994. "The Elements of Rulemaking." In *Handbook of Regulation and Administrative Law,* ed. D. Rosenbloom and R. Schwartz, 345–381. New York: Marcel Dekker.

———. 1999. *Rulemaking.* 2nd ed. Washington, DC: CQ Press.

Keynes, John Maynard. 1936. *The General Theory of Employment, Interest, and Money.* New York: Harcourt, Brace, and World.

Kirst, Michael. 1969. *Government Without Passing Laws.* Chapel Hill: University of North Carolina Press.

Knott, Jack, and Gary Miller. 1987. *Reforming Bureaucracy.* Englewood Cliffs, NJ: Prentice Hall.

Kofmehl, Kenneth. 1977. *Professional Staffs of Congress.* West Lafayette, IN: Purdue University Press.

Krislov, Samuel. 1994. "The New Separation and Delegation of Powers Doctrine." In *Handbook of Regulation and Administrative Law,* ed. David Rosenbloom and Richard Schwartz, 37–69. New York: Marcel Dekker.

La Follette, Robert, Jr. 1943. "A Senator Looks at Congress." *Atlantic Monthly,* July, 91–96.

———. 1946. "Congress Wins A Victory Over Congress." *New York Times Magazine,* August 4, pp. 11ff.

———. 1947. "Systematizing Congressional Control." *American Political Science Review* 41 (February): 58–68.

Lewis, Carol. 1989. "The Field of Public Budgeting and Financial Management, 1789–1985." In *Handbook of Public Administration,* ed. Jack Rabin, W. Bartley Hildreth, and Gerald Miller, 129–192. New York: Marcel Dekker.

Light, Paul. 1993. *Monitoring Government: Inspectors General and the Search for Accountability.* Washington, DC: Brookings Institution.

———. 1997. *The Tides of Reform.* New Haven, CT: Yale University Press.

Lipsky, Michael. 1980. *Street-Level Bureaucracy.* New York: Russell Sage Foundation.

Local 2677, the American Federation of Government Employees v. Phillips. 1973. 358 F. Supp. 60.

Long, Norton. 1949. "Power and Administration." *Public Administration Review* 9 (Autumn): 257–264.

Loomis, Burdett. 1984. "Congressional Careers and Party Leadership in the

Contemporary House of Representatives." *American Journal of Political Science* 28 (February): 180–202.

——. 1996. *The Contemporary Congress.* New York: St. Martin's Press.

Lowi, Theodore. 1969. *The End of Liberalism.* New York: Norton.

Lubbers, Jeffrey. 1994. "Management of Federal Agency Adjudication." In *Handbook of Regulation and Administrative Law,* ed. D. Rosenbloom and R. Schwartz, 287–323. New York: Marcel Dekker.

——. 1997. "Paperwork Redux: The (Stronger) Paperwork Reduction Act of 1995." *Administrative Law Review* 49:111–121.

Lynn, Laurence, Jr. 1996. *Public Management as Art, Science, and Profession.* Chatham, NJ: Chatham House.

Madison, James. 1788. "Federalist No. 51." In *The Federalist Papers,* ed. C. Rossiter, 320–325. New York: New American Library, 1961.

Malbin, Michael. 1977. "Congressional Committee Staffs: Who's in Charge Here?" *The Public Interest* 47 (Spring): 16–40.

Mann, Thomas. 1978. *Unsafe at Any Margin.* Washington, DC: American Enterprise Institute.

Marini, Frank, ed. 1971. *Toward a New Public Administration.* Scranton, PA: Chandler.

Masser, Kai. 1998. "Public Sector Administrative Reforms." In *The International Encyclopedia of Public Policy and Administration,* ed. J. Shafritz, 1851–1862. Boulder, CO: Westview.

May, Randolph. 1997. "Reforming the Sunshine Act: Report and Recommendation by the Special Committee to Review the Government in the Sunshine Act." *Administrative Law Review* 49:415–428.

Mayhew, David. 1974. "Congressional Elections: The Case of the Vanishing Marginals." *Polity* 6 (Spring): 295–317.

McCarran, Pat. 1946. "Improving 'Administrative Justice': Hearings and Evidence; Scope of Judicial Review." *American Bar Association Journal* 32: 827ff.

McCubbins, Mathew, Roger Noll, and Barry Weingast. 1989. "Structure and Process; Politics and Policy: Administrative Arrangements and the Political Control of Agencies." *Virginia Law Review* 75:431–482.

McCubbins, Mathew, and Thomas Schwartz. 1984. "Congressional Oversight Overlooked: Police Patrols and Fire Alarms." *American Journal of Political Science* 28 (February): 165–179.

McMurtry, Virginia. 1991. "Chief Financial Officers Act of 1990." *CRS Report for Congress.* Washington, DC: Congressional Research Service. February 19.

Melnick, R. Shep. 1983. *Regulation and the Courts: The Case of the Clean Air Act.* Washington, DC: Brookings Institution.

———. 1994. *Between the Lines.* Washington, DC: Brookings Institution.

Meriam, Lewis. 1939. *Reorganization of the National Government: Part I: An Analysis of the Problem.* Washington, DC: Brookings Institution.

Millett, John. 1959. "The Constitution and Public Administration." In *Public Administration,* ed. R. Golembiewski, F. Gibson, and G. Cornog, 425–441. 3rd ed. Chicago: Rand McNally.

Monroney, A. S., Thomas Hargrave, Thurman Arnold, Arthur Sutherland, Jr., Don Price, and Edgar Mowrer. 1949. *The Strengthening of American Political Institutions.* Port Washington, NY: Kennikat Press.

Moore, Mark, and Margaret Gates. 1986. *The Inspectors-General: Junkyard Dogs or Man's Best Friend?* New York: Russell Sage Foundation.

Moreno, Angel. 1994. "Presidential Coordination of the Independent Regulatory Process." *Administrative Law Journal* 8:461–516.

Morrison v. Olson. 1988. 487 U.S. 654.

Mosher, Frederick. 1968. *Democracy and the Public Service.* New York: Oxford University Press.

———. 1984. *A Tale of Two Agencies.* Baton Rouge: Louisiana State University Press.

Murray, James. 1946. "A Program to Prevent 'Boom or Bust.'" *New York Times Magazine,* December 29, pp. 17ff.

Myers v. United States. 1926. 272 U.S. 52.

Nivola, Pietro. 1997. "Sweet and Sour Pork: Or Why Regulating Is More Succulent Than Spending." Paper delivered at the annual meeting of the American Political Science Association, Washington, DC, August 28–31.

Ogul, Morris. 1976. *Congress Oversees the Bureaucracy.* Pittsburgh: University of Pittsburgh Press.

O'Leary, Rosemary. 1993. *Environmental Change: Federal Courts and the EPA.* Philadelphia: Temple University Press.

Oppenheimer, Bruce. 1997. "Abdicating Congressional Power: The Paradox of Republican Control." In *Congress Reconsidered,* ed. Lawrence Dodd and Bruce Oppenheimer, 371–389. 6th ed. Washington, DC: CQ Press.

Ornstein, Norman, Thomas Mann, and Michael Malbin. 1996. *Vital Statistics on Congress, 1995–1996.* Washington, DC: Congressional Quarterly.

Orvedahl, Jerry, ed. 1995. *The Congressional Yearbook: 1994.* Washington, DC: CQ Press.

Orwell, George. 1977. *1984.* San Diego: Harcourt Brace Jovanovich (originally published in 1949).

Osborne, David, and Gaebler, Ted. 1992. *Reinventing Government.* Reading, MA: Addison-Wesley.

Panama Refining Co. v. Ryan. 1935. 293 U.S. 388.

Parker, Glenn. 1989. *Characteristics of Congress.* Englewood Cliffs, NJ: Prentice Hall.

Polenberg, Richard. 1966. *Reorganizing Roosevelt's Government: The Controversy Over Executive Reorganization, 1936–1939.* Cambridge: Harvard University Press.

Polsby, Nelson. 1968. "The Institutionalization of the U.S. House of Representatives." *American Political Science Review* 62 (March): 144–168.

Pritchett, C. Herman. 1948. *The Roosevelt Court.* New York: Macmillan.

Redford, Emmette. 1954. "Administrative Regulation: Protection of the Public Interest." *American Political Science Review* 48 (December): 1103–1113.

Reischauer, Robert. 1990. *A Profile of the Congressional Budget Office.* Washington, DC: U.S. Congressional Budget Office.

Rhode, William. 1959. *Committee Clearance of Administrative Decisions.* East Lansing: Bureau of Social and Political Research, Michigan State University.

Rieselbach, Leroy. 1986. *Congressional Reform.* Washington, DC: CQ Press.

Riggs, Fred. 1991. "Public Administration: A Comparativist Framework." *Public Administration Review* 51 (November/December): 473–477.

———. 1994. "Bureacracy and the Constitution." *Public Administration Review* 54 (January/February): 65–72.

Ripley, Randall. 1975. *Congress and Public Policy.* New York: Norton.

Rivers, Douglas, and Morris Fiorina. 1989. "Constituency Service, Reputation, and the Incumbency Advantage." In *Home Style and Washington Work,* ed. Morris Fiorina and David Rohde, 17–45. Ann Arbor: University of Michigan Press.

Rohr, John. 1986. *To Run a Constitution.* Lawrence, KS: University Press of Kansas.

Rosenbloom, David. 1971. *Federal Service and the Constitution.* Ithaca, NY: Cornell University Press.

———. 1983. "Public Administrative Theory and the Separation of Powers." *Public Administration Review* 43 (May/June): 219–227.

———. 1995. "The Use of Case Studies in Public Administrative Education in the USA." *Journal of Management History* 1, no. 1:33–46.

———. 1998a. "Administrative Law and Regulation." In *Handbook of Public Administration,* ed. J. Rabin, W. Hildreth, and G. Miller, 595–661. 2nd ed. New York: Marcel Dekker.

———. 1998b. *Public Administration: Understanding Management, Politics, and Law in the Public Sector.* 4th ed. New York: McGraw-Hill.

Rosenbloom, David, and Rosemary O'Leary. 1997. *Public Administration and Law.* 2nd ed. New York: Marcel Dekker.

Roth, William, Jr., and William Nixon. 1999. *The Power to Destroy.* New York: Atlantic Monthly Press.

Rourke, Francis. 1993. "Whose Bureaucracy Is This, Anyway? Congress, the President, and Public Administration." *PS: Political Science and Politics* 26 (December): 687–692.

Sargentich, Thomas. 1997. "The Small Business Regulatory Enforcement Fairness Act." *Administrative Law Review* 49:123–137.

Schechter Poultry Corp. v. United States. 1935. 295 U.S. 495.

Schick, Allen. 1980. *Congress and Money.* Washington, DC: Urban Institute.

———. 1995. *The Federal Budget.* Washington, DC: Brookings Institution.

Seidman, Harold. 1970. *Politics, Position, and Power.* New York: Oxford University Press.

Shafritz, Jay, Norma Riccucci, David Rosenbloom, and Albert Hyde. 1992. *Personnel Management in Government.* 4th ed. New York: Marcel Dekker.

Shannon, David. 1963. *Twentieth Century America.* Chicago: Rand McNally.

Shepsle, Kenneth. 1978. *The Giant Jigsaw Puzzle.* Chicago: University of Chicago Press.

Sherwood, Foster. 1947. "The Federal Administrative Procedure Act." *American Political Science Review* 41 (April): 271–281.

Simon, Herbert. 1946. "The Proverbs of Administration." *Public Administration Review* 6 (Winter): 53–67.

Sinclair, Barbara. 1997. "Party Leaders in the New Legislative Process." In *Congress Reconsidered,* ed. Lawrence Dodd and Bruce Oppenheimer, 229–245. 6th ed. Washington, DC: CQ Press.

Skowronek, Stephen. 1982. *Building a New American State.* New York: Cambridge University Press.

Skrzycki, Cindy. 1998a. "Congress: Fewer Forms or Budgets Will Suffer." *Washington Post,* August 14, pp. G1ff.

———. 1998b. "Will Congress Wake Up to Its Rule-Blocking Weapon?" *Washington Post,* February 13, pp. G1ff.

Smith, Steven, and Eric Lawrence. 1997. "Party Control of Committees in the Republican Congress." In *Congress Reconsidered,* ed. Lawrence Dodd and Bruce Oppenheimer, 163–192. 6th ed. Washington, DC: CQ Press.

Storing, Herbert. 1981. *The Complete Anti-Federalist.* Vol. 1: *What the Anti-Federalists Were For.* Chicago: University of Chicago Press.

Strauss, Peter, Todd Rakoff, Roy Schotland, and Cynthia Farina. 1995. *Gellhorn and Byse's Administrative Law: Cases and Commentary.* 9th ed. Westbury, NY: Foundation Press.

Thomas, Elbert. 1949. "How Congress Functions under Its Reorganization Plan." *American Political Science Review* 43 (December): 1179–1189.

Thompson, Victor. 1961. *Modern Organization.* New York: Knopf.

Thurber, James. 1997. "Centralization, Devolution, and Turf Protection in the Congressional Budget Process." In *Congress Reconsidered,* ed. Lawrence Dodd and Bruce Oppenheimer, 325–346. 6th ed. Washington, DC: CQ Press.

Truman, David. 1971. *The Governmental Process.* Rev. ed. New York: Knopf.

Truman, Harry S. 1956. *Memoirs.* Vol. 2, *Years of Trial and Hope.* Garden City, NY: Doubleday.

United States v. Lopez. 1995. 514 U.S. 549.

U.S. Attorney General's Committee on Administrative Procedure. 1941. *Final Report.* Washington, DC: U.S. Government Printing Office.

U.S. Bureau of the Census and Social Science Research Council. 1965. *Statistical History of the United States from Colonial Times to the Present.* Stamford, CT: Fairfield Publishers.

U.S. Commission on Organization of the Executive Branch of the Government. 1949. *Report.* Washington, DC: U.S. Government Printing Office.

———. 1955. *Report on Personnel and Civil Service.* Washington, DC: U.S. Government Printing Office.

U.S. Congress. 1938. *Congressional Record.* Vol. 83, 75th Cong., 3rd sess. Washington, DC: U.S. Government Printing Office.

———. 1939. *Congressional Record.* Vol. 84, 76th Cong., 1st sess. Washington, DC: U.S. Government Printing Office.

———. 1940. *Congressional Record.* Vol. 86, 76th Cong., 3rd sess. Washington, DC: U.S. Government Printing Office.

———. 1941. *Hearings on S. 674, S. 675, S. 918.* Senate, Subcommittee of the Committee on the Judiciary, 77th Cong. 1st. sess. (April 2–29). (No document number or publisher shown.)

———. 1945a. *Congressional Record.* Vol. 91, 79th Cong., 1st sess. Washington, DC: U.S. Government Printing Office.

———. 1945b. *First Intermediate Report: Organization of the Congress.* Joint Committee on the Organization of Congress, 79th Cong., 1st sess., April 2. (Senate Document 79-36). Washington, DC: U.S. Government Printing Office.

———. 1946a. *Administrative Procedure Act: Legislative History.* Senate Committee on the Judiciary. Washington, DC: U.S. Government Printing Office.

———. 1946b. *Congressional Directory.* Washington, DC: U.S. Government Printing Office.

———. 1946c. *Congressional Record.* Vol. 92, 79th Cong., 2nd sess. Washington, DC: U.S. Government Printing Office.

———. 1973. *Congressional Record.* Vol. 119, 93rd Cong., 1st sess. Washington, DC: U.S. Government Printing Office.

————. 1974. *Congressional Record.* Vol. 120, 93rd Cong., 2nd sess. Washington, DC: U.S. Government Printing Office.

————. 1976a. *Government in the Sunshine Act—S. 5 (PL 94-409): Source Book: Legislative History, Texts, and Other Documents.* Senate Committee on Government Operations and House Committee on Government Operations (Joint Committee Report), 94th Cong., 2nd sess. Washington, DC: U.S. Government Printing Office. (No document number shown.)

————. 1976b. *Legislative History of the Privacy Act of 1974: S. 3418 (Public Law 93-579): Source Book on Privacy.* Senate Committee on Government Operations and House Committee on Government Operations, Subcommittee on Government Information and Individual Rights, 94th Cong., 2nd sess. Washington, DC: U.S. Government Printing Office.

U.S. Department of Defense v. Federal Labor Relations Authority. 1994. 510 U.S. 487.

U.S. General Accounting Office. 1997a. *Managing for Results: Using the Results Act to Address Mission Fragmentation and Program Overlap.* Washington, DC: U.S. General Accounting Office.

————. 1997b. *Personnel Practices: Career Appointments of Former Political and Congressional Employees.* Washington, DC: U.S. General Accounting Office.

————. 1998a. *Federal Advisory Committee Act.* Washington, DC: U.S. General Accounting Office.

————. 1998b. *Federal Downsizing.* Washington, DC: U.S. General Accounting Office.

————. 1998c. *Federal Rulemaking: Agencies Often Published Final Actions without Proposed Rules.* Washington, DC: U.S. General Accounting Office.

————. 1998d. *Managing for Results.* Washington, DC: U.S. General Accounting Office.

————. 1998e. *Regulatory Management: Implementation of Selected OMB Responsibilities under the Paperwork Reduction Act.* Washington, DC: U.S. General Accounting Office.

————. 1998f. *The Results Act.* Washington, DC: U.S. General Accounting Office.

The U.S. Government Manual. 1995/1996. Washington, DC: Office of the Federal Register and National Archives and Records Administration.

U.S. House of Representatives. 1939. *Bills to Provide for the More Expeditious Settlement of Disputes with the United States and Other Purposes: Hearings on H.R. 4236, 6198, 6324.* Subcommittee No. 4 of the Committee on the Judiciary, 76th Cong., 1st sess. March 17 and April 5. Washington, DC: U.S. Government Printing Office. (No document number shown.)

————. 1945. *Tort Claims Against the United States.* Committee on the Judiciary,

79th Cong., 1st sess., Report 1287. November 26. Washington, DC: U.S. Government Printing Office.

———. 1970. *Legislative Reorganization Act of 1970.* Rules Committee (H.R. 17654). Report No. 91-1215. 91st Cong., 2nd sess. Washington, DC: U.S. Government Printing Office.

———. 1979. *Congressional Budget and Impoundment Control Act of 1974.* Committee on the Budget (H.R. 7130—S 1541). Report No. 93-658. 93rd Cong., 1st sess. Washington, DC: U.S. Government Printing Office.

———. 1990. *Chief Financial Officer Act of 1990.* Committee on Government Operations. Report No. 101-818. 101st Cong., 2nd sess. (H.R. 5687). Washington, DC: Government Printing Office.

———. 1995. *The Paperwork Reduction Act.* Committee on Government Reform and Oversight. 104th Cong., 1st sess. Report 104-37 for H.R. 830. Washington, DC: U.S. Government Printing Office.

U.S. Office of Management and Budget. 1985. *The United States Budget in Brief, Fiscal Year 1986.* Washington, DC: U.S. Office of Management and Budget.

U.S. President's Committee on Administrative Management. 1937. *Report of the Committee.* Washington, DC: U.S. Government Printing Office.

U.S. Senate. 1941. *Administrative Procedure: Hearings on S. 674, S. 675. and S. 918.* A Subcommittee of the Committee on the Judiciary. 77th Cong., 1st sess. Washington, DC: U.S. Government Printing Office. (No document number shown.)

———. 1946. *Administrative Procedure Act: Legislative History.* Committee on the Judiciary, 79th Cong., 2nd sess. (Doc. No. 248). Washington, DC: U.S. Government Printing Office.

———. 1967. *Legislative Reorganization Act of 1967.* Special Committee on the Organization of the Congress (S. 355). Report 1, 90th Cong., 1st sess. Washington, DC: U.S. Government Printing Office.

———. 1970. *Separation of Powers and the Independent Agencies: Cases and Selected Readings.* Committee on the Judiciary, Subcommittee on Separation of Powers. 91st Cong., 1st sess. Document 91-49. Washington, DC: U.S. Government Printing Office.

———. 1974. *Freedom of Information Act Source Book: Legislative Materials, Cases, Articles.* Committee on the Judiciary, Subcommittee on Administrative Practice and Procedure. 93rd Cong., 2nd sess. Washington, DC: U.S. Government Printing Office. (No document number shown.)

———. 1978. *Federal Advisory Committee Act (Public Law 92-463): Source Book: Legislative History, Texts, and Other Documents.* Committee on Governmental Affairs, Subcommittee on Energy, Nuclear Proliferation, and Federal Services. 95th Cong., 2nd sess. Washington, DC: U.S. Government Printing Office.

———. 1989. *Negotiated Rulemaking Act of 1989: Report.* Committee on Governmental Affairs, 101st Cong., 1st sess. Report 101-97 August 1. Washington, DC: U.S. Government Printing Office.

———. 1993. *Government Performance and Results Act of 1993.* Committee on Government Affairs (S. 20). 103rd Cong., 1st sess. Washington, DC: U.S. Government Printing Office.

Van Riper, Paul. 1958. *History of the United States Civil Service.* Evanston, IL: Row, Peterson.

Vaughn, Robert. 1994. "Federal Information Policy and Administrative Law." In *Handbook of Regulation and Administrative Law,* ed. D. Rosenbloom and R. Schwartz, 467–484. New York: Marcel Dekker.

Vermont Yankee Nuclear Power Corp. v. Natural Resources Defense Council. 1978. 435 U.S. 519.

Vogler, David. 1988. *The Politics of Congress.* 5th ed. Boston: Allyn and Bacon.

———. 1993. *The Politics of Congress.* 6th ed. Madison, WI: Brown & Benchmark.

Waldo, Dwight. 1948. *The Administrative State.* New York: Ronald Press.

———. 1984. *The Administrative State.* 2nd ed. New York: Holmes and Meier.

Walker, Wallace. 1986. *Changing Organizational Culture: Strategy, Structure, and Professionalism in the U.S. General Accounting Office.* Knoxville: University of Tennessee Press.

Warren, Kenneth. 1982. *Administrative Law in the American Political System.* St. Paul, MN: West.

———. 1988. *Administrative Law in the American Political System.* 2nd ed. St. Paul, MN: West.

———. 1996. *Administrative Law in the American Political System.* 3rd ed. Upper Saddle River, NJ: Prentice Hall.

Weingast, Barry, and Mark Moran. 1983. "Bureaucratic Discretion or Congressional Control? Regulatory Policymaking by the Federal Trade Commission." *Journal of Political Economy* 91 (October): 765–800.

White, Leonard. 1926. "Introduction to the Study of Public Administration." In *Classics of Public Administration,* ed. J. Shafritz and A. Hyde, 57–65. 3rd ed. Pacific Grove, CA: Brooks Cole, 1992.

———. 1945. "Legislative Responsibility for the Public Service." In *New Horizons in Public Administration: A Symposium,* 1–20. University: University of Alabama Press.

———. 1965a. *The Federalists.* New York: Free Press.

———. 1965b. *The Jacksonians.* New York: Free Press.

———. 1965c. *The Jeffersonians.* New York: Free Press.

———. 1965d. *The Republican Era.* New York: Free Press.

Wiener v. United States. 1958. 357 U.S. 349.

Wildavsky, Aaron. 1961. "Political Implications of Budgetary Reform." *Public Administration Review* 21 (Autumn): 183–190.

Willoughby, W. F. 1927. *Principles of Public Administration.* Washington, DC: Brookings Institution.

———. 1934. *Principles of Legislative Organization and Administration.* Washington, DC: Brookings Institution.

Wilson, James Q. 1967. "The Bureaucracy Problem." *The Public Interest* 6 (Winter): 3–9.

———. 1980. "The Politics of Regulation." In *The Politics of Regulation,* ed. James Q. Wilson, 357–394. New York: Basic Books.

Wilson, Woodrow. 1885. *Congressional Government.* Boston: Houghton Mifflin (republished by Johns Hopkins University Press in 1981).

———. 1887. "The Study of Administration." In *Classics of Public Administration,* ed. J. Shafritz and A. Hyde, 11–24. 3rd ed. Pacific Grove, CA: Brooks Cole, 1992.

Woll, Peter. 1963. *Administrative Law.* Berkeley: University of California.

Wood, B. Dan, and Richard Waterman. 1994. *Bureaucratic Dynamics.* Boulder, CO: Westview.

Wyman, Bruce. 1903. *The Principles of the Administrative Law Governing the Relations of Public Officers.* St. Paul, MN: Keefe-Davidson.

Young, Roland. 1948. "Legislative Reform." *Public Administration Review* 8 (Spring): 141–146.

Youngstown Sheet and Tube Co. v. Sawyer. 1952. 343 U.S. 579.

Index

New Public Administration, 171 (n. 11)
New Public Management, 57, 140, 171
    (n. 12)
Nivola, Pietro, 124
Nixon, Richard, 44, 86, 88, 170 (n. 21)
Nixon, William, 120, 169 (n. 13)
Noll, Roger, 165 (n. 29)
nondelegation doctrine, 27, 29, 59, 162
    (nn. 7, 9)

Occupational Safety and Health Act, 29
Occupational Safety and Health Ad-
    ministration, 29, 162 (n. 8)
O'Connor, Sandra Day, 99, 167 (n. 17)
Office of Economic Opportunity, 25
Office of Federal Administrative Proce-
    dure, 164 (n. 27)
Office of Management and Budget, 43–
    44, 54, 55, 56, 82, 84, 90, 91, 137,
    149
Office of Information and Regulatory
    Affairs, 55, 165 (n. 28)
Ogul, Morris, 165 (n. 4)
O'Leary, Rosemary, 20, 57, 168 (n. 6),
    170 (nn. 1, 4), 172 (n. 15)
Olezek, Walter, 75, 76, 77, 78, 117, 125,
    129, 169 (n. 18)
O'Mahoney, Joseph, 11, 122, 123
Oppenheimer, Bruce, 77, 78
order making, 2. *See also* adjudication
Ornstein, Norman, 107, 110, 115, 117,
    118, 127, 129
Orvedahl, Jerry, 170 (n. 18)
Orwell, George, 52
Osborne, David, 57

Panama Refining Company v. Ryan, 162
    (n. 6)
Paperwork Reduction Act (1980), 3, 23,
    53–56, 58, 132, 137, 159 (n. 3)
Paperwork Reduction Act (1995), 3, 23,
    53–56, 58, 132, 137, 159 (n. 3)
Paperwork Reduction Reauthorization
    Act, 55
Parker, Glenn, 129, 130, 170 (n. 19)
Patman, Wright, 11, 123, 161 (n. 10)
Pennsylvania Railroad System, 9

Pepper, Claude, 64, 72, 73, 161 (n. 10)
Percy, Charles, 86
Perkins, Frances, 5
Phillips, Howard, 150
Polenberg, Richard, 6, 10, 12, 18, 19, 21, 91
political machines, 143
Polsby, Nelson, 127
pork barrel, 3, 4, 108, 122, 123, 124, 141,
    154, 167 (n. 1)
Post Office, 125
Powell, Adam Clayton, 161 (n. 10)
Powell, Lewis, 99, 167 (n. 17)
PPBS (planning, programming, budget-
    ing system), 130, 170 (n. 21)
president, 6, 25, 31, 37, 50, 55, 77, 94, 98,
    129, 142, 149, 150, 152, 160 (nn.
    5, 7, 9), 162 (n. 4), 164 (n. 27),
    169 (n. 14)
    base closings, 126
    budgeting, 86, 88, 89, 171 (n. 5)
    Economic Report, 74, 121, 123
    executive powers, 27, 88, 134, 154,
        161–62 (n. 3), 171 (n.6)
    line item veto, 141, 166 (n. 14). *See
        also* Line Item Veto Act
    opposition to Federal Advisory Com-
        mittee Act, 44
    removal power, 26
    report on advisory committees, 43
    role in administration, 14, 16–22, 57–
        58, 63, 137–39, 144, 155
Price, Melvin, 161 (n. 10), 166 (n. 12)
principal-agent model, 134, 136
Pritchett, C. Herman, 28
Privacy Act, 3, 23, 49, 52, 53, 58, 77, 132,
    138
Progressives, 20, 143, 160 (n. 10)
Public Administration Review, 144, 145, 146
Public Building and Purchase Contract
    Act, 125
public works, 2, 3, 4, 5, 11, 103, 104, 105,
    108–9, 110, 120, 122–27, 128, 137,
    141, 167 (n. 1), 169 (n. 17)

Ramspeck, Robert, 32, 108
Ramspeck Act, 162 (n. 5)
Randolph, Jennings, 107, 169 (n. 17)

About the Author

David H. Rosenbloom is Distinguished Professor of Public Administration in the School of Public Affairs at American University in Washington, DC. He earned his Ph.D. in Political Science from the University of Chicago (1969) and holds an Honorary Doctor of Laws degree from Marietta College (1994). Before moving to American University, he taught at Syracuse University's Maxwell School of Citizenship and Public Affairs (1978–1990), the University of Vermont (1973–1978), Tel Aviv University (1971–1973), and the University of Kansas (1969–1970). In 1970–1971 he was an American Society for Public Administration (ASPA) Fellow in the Office of Federal Equal Employment Opportunity at the U.S. Civil Service Commission.

He served as editor in chief of *Public Administration Review* (1991–1996) and coeditor in chief of the *Policy Studies Journal* (1985–1990), both in partnership with Melvin Dubnick. In 1999, Rosenbloom received ASPA's Dwight Waldo Award for Outstanding Contributions to the Literature and Leadership of Public Administration Through an Extended Career. Other awards include the following: Outstanding Service Award, School of Public Affairs, American University (1999); Thomas Dye Award for Outstanding Service to the Policy Studies Organization (1996); Outstanding Scholar Award, School of Public Affairs, American University (1994); Charles Levine Memorial Award for Excellence in Public Administration, ASPA–National Association of Schools of Public Affairs and Administration (NASPAA) (1993); Distinguished Research Award, ASPA-NASPAA (1992); and the Syracuse University Chancellor's Citation for Academic Excellence (1986). Rosenbloom was elected to the National Academy of Public Administration in 1986. In 1992 he was appointed to the Clinton-Gore Presidential Transition Team for the U.S. Office of Personnel Management.

Rosenbloom writes extensively about public administration and democratic-constitutionalism. Major authored or coauthored titles include *Public Administration: Understanding Management, Politics, and Law in the Public Sector; Public Administration and Law; Representative Bureaucracy and the American Political System; Bureaucratic Government, USA; Federal Equal Employment Opportunity;* and *Federal Service and the Constitution.*

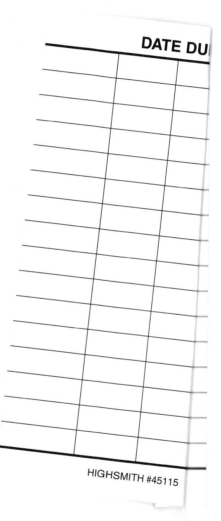

DATE DU

HIGHSMITH #45115